INSPIRE / PLAN / DISCOVER / EXPERIENCE

CUBA

CUBA

CONTENTS

DISCOVER 6

Welcome to Cuba 8

Reasons to Love Cuba 10

Explore Cuba 14

Getting to Know Cuba 16

Cuba Itineraries 20

Cuba Your Way 26

A Year in Cuba 48

A Brief History 50

EXPERIENCE HAVANA 56

La Habana Vieja 62

Centro Habana and Prado 84

Vedado and Plaza 112

Beyond the Centre 126

EXPERIENCE CUBA 140

Western Cuba 142

Central Cuba – West 166

Central Cuba – East 194

Eastern Cuba 226

NEED TO KNOW 266

Before You Go 268

Getting Around 270

Practical Information 274

Index 276

Phrase Book 284

Acknowledgments 287

Left: Men playing dominoes in Santiago de Cuba
Previous page: Panorama of Valle de Viñales

DISCOVER

The beguiling colonial city of Trinidad

Welcome to Cuba 8

Reasons to Love Cuba 10

Explore Cuba 14

Getting to Know Cuba 16

Cuba Itineraries 20

Cuba Your Way 26

A Year in Cuba 48

A Brief History 50

WELCOME TO
CUBA

With its bottle-green mountains, diamond-dust beaches and perfectly preserved colonial cities, Cuba is enchantingly picturesque. It also boasts a fascinating history, enthralling museums and a lively culture of music and dance. Whatever your dream trip to Cuba includes, this DK Eyewitness Travel Guide is the perfect companion.

1 A mural featuring Che Guevara in Baracoa.

2 The Saltón falls of the Manantiales river at Soroa.

3 Daiquiri cocktails, made with flavourful Cuban rum.

4 Cruising along the Malecón in Havana.

The largest of the Caribbean islands, Cuba's diverse landscape spans the pristine coral reefs at Jardines de la Reina to cloud-draped mountains in the Sierra Maestra, and everything in between. Dive in tropical seas, cycle through the Valle de Viñales or look for birds in the Parque Nacional Ciénaga de Zapata. Postcard-pretty villages throughout the island still resound to the crowing of roosters and clip-clop of hooves, made even more romantic by a lack of commercialism.

Island-wide, it is possible to trace the footsteps of conquistadors or follow the revolutionary trail, from Che Guevara's visage in Havana to Fidel Castro's grave in Santiago de Cuba. Indeed, Cuba's homegrown brand of Caribbean Communism is as colourful as its pastel buildings and vintage American cars.

Havana is one of the most exciting cities in the Americas, offering superb art galleries, a rising foodie scene, and a nightlife that encompasses ballet and moody hole-in-the-wall bars. To the west, with a vibrant art scene and bustling nightclubs, Trinidad is more than just its colonial façade, while Santiago de Cuba moves to the beat of Afro-Cuban culture.

With so many different things to discover and experience, Cuba can seem overwhelming. We've broken the island down into easily navigable chapters, with detailed itineraries, expert local knowledge and colourful maps to help you plan the perfect visit. Whether you're staying for a weekend, a week or longer, this Eyewitness guide will ensure that you see the very best that Cuba has to offer. Enjoy the book, and enjoy Cuba.

REASONS TO
LOVE CUBA

The scenery is spectacular. It has a profound history. Its vibrant energy is contagious. Ask any Cuban and you'll hear a different reason why they love their country. Here, we pick some of our favourites.

1 HISTORIC HAVANA

From colourful colonial mansions and beautifully restored cobbled plazas to raucous 1950s-style cabarets, the past is everywhere you look in Havana *(p56)*.

STAYING IN A CASA PARTICULAR 2

Rent a room in a private B&B and become an adopted member of a Cuban family. It's a great way to learn the local lifestyle and the food is always deliciously authentic.

3 SNORKELING IN THE CARIBBEAN SEA

The crystal-clear turquoise waters off Cuba's Caribbean shore teem with tropical fish. Head to Playa Larga *(p175)* and Playa Girón *(p176)* for the best snorkeling spots.

TRADITIONAL TRINIDAD *4*

Few colonial cities in the Americas can rival this enchanting hillside settlement for its authenticity and near-perfect state of preservation *(p200)*.

SENSATIONAL BEACHES *5*

Cuba's pure white beaches, shaded by lofty palms, are perfect for recharging. Some of the best stretches of sand are found on the cays of the Jardines del Rey *(p218)*.

SIPPING COCKTAILS *6*

Renowned for its rum, you're spoilt for choice when it comes to bars on this island. Historic favourites in Havana include La Bodeguita del Medio *(p70)* and Sloppy Joe's *(p108)*.

REVOLUTIONARY HISTORY 7

Traces of Cuba's quest for independence can be found throughout the nation, while key figures such as Fidel Castro and Che Guevara are honoured in every city.

VALLE DE VIÑALES 8

With its verdant tobacco fields and towering royal palms dwarfed by limestone cliffs, the Viñales Valley is home to Cuba's most quintessential and awe-inspiring scenery (p150).

9 CAPTIVATING LIVE MUSIC

Wherever you go on the island, you'll be greeted by the irresistible sounds of live music - from traditional *son* to sensual salsa (p34). No one stays seated when the music starts.

10 CLASSIC AMERICAN CARS

About 60,000 *yanqui* motors rumble down Cuba's highways, forming a rainbow parade of 1950s American iron. Relive Motown's glory years by hiring a convertible for a ride *(p99)*.

COPPELIA ICE CREAM 11

Every city has an outlet of this state-subsidized ice cream parlour, where Cubans indulge in delicious *helado*. It's a sweet tribute to the country's iconic revolutionary idealism *(p120)*.

SANTIAGO DE CUBA 12

Cuba's second largest city has a rich culture infused with Haitian and French influences and, as the birthplace of the revolution, it is full of fascinating sites to explore *(p232)*.

EXPLORE
CUBA

This guide divides Cuba into five colour-coded sightseeing areas, as shown on the map below. Find out more about each area on the following pages.

FLORIDA (USA)

Fort Lauderdale
Fort Myers
Miami
The Everglades

Florida Keys

Key West

Gulf of Mexico

HAVANA
p56

Mariel
Havana

Varadero
Matanzas

Archipiélago de Sabana

Sagua la Grande

WESTERN CUBA
p142

Batabanó

Golfo de Batabanó

CENTRAL CUBA – WEST
p166

Jagüey Grande

Cienfuegos

Santa Clara

Pinar del Río

Playa Larga

Isabel Rubio

Nueva Gerona

María La Gorda

Trinidad

Archipiélago de los Canarreos

Isla de la Juventud

Caribbean Sea

AROUND THE CARIBBEAN

USA

Atlantic Ocean

Gulf of Mexico

Havana

THE BAHAMAS

DOMINICAN REPUBLIC

CUBA

HAITI

JAMAICA

MEXICO

HONDURAS

GUATEMALA

NICARAGUA

COLOMBIA

VENEZUELA

COSTA RICA

PANAMA

GETTING TO KNOW
CUBA

Cuba is a land of incredible beauty and amazing contrasts, from white-sand beaches and azure seas to lush valleys and cloud-draped mountains. The country's urban centres are beautifully preserved slices of the past, adorned with exquisite colonial buildings and colourful vintage cars.

HAVANA

PAGE 56

Cuba's animated capital city lives up to its international reputation as a captivating time warp. While much of La Habana Vieja – the enchanting colonial quarter – has been restored to elegant grandeur, the rest of Havana's evocative urban centre has changed little since the 1950s. Classic American cars rumble past stunning buildings in a mesmerizing amalgamation of styles, from Art Nouveau to Art Deco. The city is also the epicentre of Cuba's exciting gastro-revolution, topped off by a vibrant nightlife that includes colonial-style drinking holes, opulent rooftop bars and sizzling nightclubs. As well as all of this, Havana boasts superb museums, innovative art galleries and grand theatres.

Best for
Exciting gastronomy

Home to
Palacio de los Capitanes Generales, Capitolio, Paseo del Prado, Museo de la Revolución, Museo Nacional de Bellas Artes, Necrópolis de Colón, Memorial José Martí

Experience
A drive down the Malecón in a 1950s convertible

WESTERN CUBA

West of Havana, in the provinces of Artemisa and
Pinar del Río, the landscape becomes increasingly
dramatic, reaching its zenith in the Valle de Viñales.
Visitors flock here for hiking, horseback riding and
other ecotourism activities. Don't miss the artistic
mountain community of Las Terrazas and the village
of Viñales, which is nestled in the valley surrounded
by tobacco fields and soaring *mogotes*. At the
western extreme of the island, the Península de
Guanahacabibes combines superb bird-watching with
scuba diving at María la Gorda, while the white sands
of Cayo Levisa, off the north coast, are perfect for
a reclusive escape.

Best for
Fantastic scenery

Home to
*Las Terrazas, Valle de Viñales,
Isla de la Juventud*

Experience
*A horseback ride to a tobacco
farm to discover how cigars
are made*

→

PAGE 166

CENTRAL CUBA – WEST

This diverse region is home to both captivating cities and stunning beaches with teeming offshore reefs. Here, you'll find Varadero, Cuba's largest and most developed resort. Fewer than 50 km (30 miles) away is the contrasting city of Matanzas, permeated with Afro-Cuban traditions and music. The Península de Zapata, meanwhile, offers both fantastic fishing and a superb museum at the site of the 1961 Bay of Pigs invasion. Cuba's revolutionary history is also keenly felt in the university city of Santa Clara, which is home to the Che Guevara monument, whereas Cienfuegos' gentle charms and musical heritage entice many a casual visitor to linger.

Best for
Encountering wildlife

Home to
Mantanzas, Varadero, Península de Zapata, Cienfuegos, Santa Clara, Jardín Botánico Soledad

Experience
A scuba dive among coral reefs and shipwrecks off Punta Francés on the Isla de la Juventud

PAGE 194

CENTRAL CUBA – EAST

Comprising the geographic heart of Cuba, this zone showcases sensational stretches of sand on the cays of the Jardines del Rey and sublime diving and fishing off Jardines de la Reina on the south coast. Enchanting Trinidad – the jewel in the crown of colonial cities – is justifiably one of Cuba's most popular sites, outshining even historic Camagüey. For those in search of wilderness, head to the verdant Valle de los Ingenios or Cayo Coco, where crocodiles and flamingoes are easily seen.

Best for
Colonial cities

Home to
Trinidad, Sancti Spíritus, Cayo Coco, Camagüey

Experience
A hike up the Sierra del Escambray, which surrounds the Valle de los Ingenios

PAGE 226

EASTERN CUBA

From the Moncada Barracks to Fidel's mountain rebel headquarters, the eastern side of the island marks the centre of Cuba's revolutionary history. The region's natural landscape is also noteworthy – Cuba's oldest city Baracoa enjoys a striking setting beneath the rainforest-clad Sierra Cristal, while the rugged Sierra Maestra offers the ultimate high with a trek up Pico Turquino. In Santiago de Cuba, the island's second largest city, history complements a colourful Afro-Cuban culture, vivacious nightlife and the country's liveliest carnival.

Best for
Revolutionary history

Home to
Holguín, Santiago de Cuba, Castillo del Morro, Parque Baconao, Baracoa

Experience
A trek to La Comandancia de la Plata – Fidel's guerrilla headquarters – in the Gran Parque Nacional Sierra Maestra

←

 Havana's Malecón.

2 Colourful sculptures in Fusterlandia, Havana.

3 Music in the streets of Havana.

4 El Nicho waterfall.

Cuba is a cornucopia of urban and rural beauty, and its relatively compact size means that the entire island is easily navigated. This itinerary will inspire you to make the most of your visit.

2 WEEKS

Day 1

Begin in Havana. Rent a chauffeured 1950s convertible on Parque Central *(p99)* and enjoy a wind-in-your-hair sightseeing tour of the city, taking in the Malecón *(p109)*, Hotel Nacional *(p123)*, Monumento a las Víctimas del *Maine (p120)*, Hotel Riviera *(p27)* and Plaza de la Revolución *(p119)*. Don't miss Fusterlandia *(p129)*, an enclave of surreal community art. After lunch at Italian Corte del Principe *(p137)*, stop by the Museo Ernest Hemingway *(p135)* and the coastal fishing village of Cojímar *(p133)*, before exploring Castillo El Morro *(p244)*. Dine at Mama Inés *(p69)* and close the evening with cocktails atop Gran Hotel Manzana Kempinski *(p98)*.

Day 2

After a leisurely breakfast at Dulcería Bianchini *(p81)*, drive east out of the city to the Península de Zapata *(p174)*, then turn south for Playa Larga. Lunch beside the bay at Restaurante Tiki *((54) 715 922)* and spend the afternoon relaxing on the beach or kitesurfing, with time perhaps for scuba diving, bird-watching or a guided nature excursion in search of crocodiles. End the day relaxing at Hostal Enrique *(p176)*, a *casa particular* in Playa Larga.

Day 3

Follow the coast road to Playa Girón, the key site in the Bay of Pigs invasion. Visit the museum before continuing inland to Cienfuegos *(p178)*, arriving in time for lunch at Finca del Mar *(p191)*. Focus your afternoon walking tour on Parque Martí *(p178)* before joining the locals for sunset on the Malecón (waterfront). Cienfuegos has plenty of nightlife options; look out for music events or catch a baseball game.

Day 4

Head east to the El Nicho waterfall *(p191)*, then follow the road through the Sierra Escambray for a stunning mountain drive. Your destination is Topes de Collantes *(p224)*, where *criolla* lunches are served at Restaurante Gran Nena *(Carretera Principal; (41) 540 338)*. There'll be time for a hike in the pine forests before descending to the lovely colonial city of Trinidad *(p200)*. Enjoy an open-air buffet dinner at Vista Gourmet *(p203)*, before checking out the lively evening entertainment.

Day 5

Spend the day exploring Trinidad. Start at the Plaza Mayor and take in the beautiful colonial houses; don't miss the 19th-century Palacio Cantero and the elegant Iglesia y Convento de San Francisco *(p205)*. After lunch at Restaurante Plaza Mayor *(p203)*, walk to the Cabildo de los Congos Reales de San Antonio *(p205)*. In the evening, make a beeline for the Casa de la Trova *(p204)*, where live bands always ensure a riotous evening.

Day 6

Journey through the Valle de los Ingenios *(p214)*, stopping at Hacienda Manaca Iznaga and Sitio Histórico Guaimiro to admire the restored plantation homes. The scenery is spectacular as you continue to Sancti Spíritus *(p206)*, where the colonial core is worth exploring on foot. Taberna Yayabo is the perfect place for a riverside lunch *(p207)*. Continue along the Carretera Central via Ciego de Ávila *(p216)*, before arriving in the city of Camagüey *(p210)* in the late afternoon. Savour the city's romance with an alfresco dinner at Restaurante 1800 *(p216)*.

→

Day 7

Begin your exploration of Camagüey on the main plaza, Parque Ignacio Agramonte (p210). Set aside half a day to wander the cobblestone streets, including the Plaza del Carmén and Plaza de los Trabajadores. After lunch – try Meson del Principe (Calle Astilleros No 7, e/ San Ramón y Lugareño; (32) 274 210) – travel southeast through rural villages to enjoy horseback riding and eco-activities at Finca La Belén, in the Sierra del Chorrillo (p219). You can stay overnight at the finca.

Day 8

Rise early for a guided bird-watching walk in the forest – it's well worth it. After, drive northeast to return to the Carretera Central, continuing via Las Tunas to Holguín (p242). Restaurante Los Almendros (p243) is known for its lobster and its farmstead-like decor is hard to beat. For a sensational panoramic vista over town, climb the 450-plus staircase to the top of Loma de la Cruz. Holguín's atmospheric Casa de la Trova (p243) is a good place to savour the nightlife.

Day 9

Head east into the heartland of sugar-cane production, stopping at the Museo Conjunto Histórico Birán (p252). Follow the road south to Palma Soriana, where the scenic Carretera Central leads past the Basílica del Cobre (p259), Cuba's most important Catholic shrine. Have a late lunch on the rooftop at Roy's Terrace Inn in Santiago de Cuba (p237). After learning about the Cuban quest for independence at Museo de La Lucha Clandestina (p235), walk to the waterfront for live music at Cervecería Puerto del Rey (p234).

Day 10

With just one full day to explore Santiago de Cuba, concentrate on the highlights: Parque Céspedes (p240), the Moncada Barracks (p238), San Juan Hill (p239) and Cementerio Santa Ifigenia (p234). For lunch, Paladar La Canasta (p237) serves up sea-food dishes in a beautiful garden. Head out to Castillo del Morro (p244) to enjoy the cañonazo (cannon-firing) ceremony at sunset before ending your day absorbing the music at the Casa de la Trova (p234).

1 Street in Holguín.
2 View of Guantánamo city.
3 Dining in Santiago de Cuba.
4 Cowboys in Finca La Belén.
5 Basilica del Cobre.
6 Museo del Carnaval,
Santiago de Cuba.

Day 11

Today begins with a winding drive through sugar cane country to Guantánamo city (p260), with its quirky Museo Zoológica Piedra ("Stone Zoo") in the mountains beyond town. Break for lunch at Mirador La Gobernadora (p260), with a view over Guantánamo bay. Today's highlight, however, is the scenic coastal drive along the Caribbean, before a snaking climb on the La Farola highway that ascends the Sierra Cristal and sweeps down to Baracoa (p248). Sample the local cuisine with dinner at Restaurante Calalú (p251).

Day 12

Baracoa's stunning setting entices visitors to immerse themselves in the natural world. Take a guided excursion that combines an early morning hike to the summit of El Yunque (p257) with a visit to a cacao farm, where lunch is served. Spend the afternoon walking through the historic core of Cuba's oldest city, then close the day by enjoying traditional regional music in the tiny yet ever-lively Casa de la Trova (p255).

Day 13

From Baracoa, follow the coastal road east beyond the Río Yumurí towards Punta Maisí (p263), pausing to enjoy the views of the Caribbean from the top of the lighthouse at Cuba's easternmost point. Then drive into coffee country following the beautiful narrow road through a semi-arid region studded with cacti. Continue through Guantánamo and turn north to Mayarí Arriba (p253) for a lesson in revolutionary history at the impressive Conjunto Histórico de Museos del Segundo Frente. Returning to Santiago de Cuba, enjoy a final night on the town.

Day 14

Spend your morning exploring Santiago de Cuba's Tivolí district and Calle Heredia, which house a plethora of quirky sights and museums. Not-to-be-missed highlights include the fascinating Museo Emilio Bacardi (p234) and the colourful Museo del Carnaval (p235). Enjoy lunch at St. Pauli (p237) before departing Cuba's second city for home.

Central Cuba has something for everyone, from mountains and beaches to colonial cities and revolutionary sites. This itinerary focuses on the best of Central Cuba.

7 DAYS

In Central Cuba

Day 1

Morning Start your road trip by following the scenic north coast road from Havana to Matanzas *(p170)*, which is famed for its rich Afro-Cuban heritage. Explore the Cuevas de Bellamar *(p189)*, with their fantastical dripstone formations, and have lunch at stylish Paladar La Mallorca *(p191)*.

Afternoon Continue to Varadero *(p172)*, Cuba's top resort, which has a dazzling beach unfurling along the 12-km- (7-mile-) long peninsula. There are lots of inclusive hotels, but it's far more intimate to stay in a *casa particular* in the village itself.

Evening Dine at retro Varadero 60 or the luxurious Restaurante Kike-Kcho *(p173)*.

Day 2

Morning Drive to Santa Clara via Cárdenas *(p188)*, which is worth a stop to visit the quirky Museo Oscar María de Rojas. Next, head south to San Miguel de los Baños *(p189)*, a former spa town teeming with tumbledown mansions, and a good stop for a coffee. Then, follow the Carretera Central through a series of dusty country towns to reach Santa Clara *(p182)*.

Afternoon After lunch at Restaurante Santa Rosalia *(p183)*, you'll have plenty of time to visit the Complejo Escultórico Comandante Ernesto Che Guevara *(p184)*, the Tren Blindado Monument *(p183)* and Parque Leoncio Vidal *(p182)*.

Evening For dinner head to Don Quijote *(p183)*, then check out the fun nightlife at El Mejunje *(Calle Marta Abreu 12)*.

Day 3

Morning Take a short drive northeast through the scenic tobacco country of Vuelto Arriba to Remedios *(p192)*, a beautifully preserved colonial city. Check out the church and pause at El Louvre café. Suitably refreshed, you can learn about sugar cane production at the Museo de Agroindustria Azucarera in Caibarién *(p193)*.

Afternoon Enjoy the sensational drive along the 50-km- (30-mile-) long causeway to the Jardines del Rey *(p218)*. Spend the rest of the day lazing on the sand on one of these enchanting islands.

Evening Spend the night in one of the many all-inclusive resorts.

1 Varadero's idyllic beach.

2 Picturesque Remedios.

3 A military plane at the Museo Girón, Playa Girón

4 A beach at Cayo Coco.

5 The stunning view over Topes de Collantes.

Day 4

Morning Return to the mainland and follow the north coastal road via Yaguajay (p216) and its monument to Rebel Army commander Camilo Cienfuegos.

Afternoon Lunch at Restaurante Maité de Qaba (p216) in Morón, before continuing north to the beaches of Cayo Coco (p208).

Evening Stay at either Pullman Cayo Coco or Iberostar Playa Pilar (p209).

Day 5

Morning Drive back to Morón, turning west at Ciego de Ávila to follow the Carretera Central into Sancti Spíritus (p206). You'll reach the city in time for lunch overlooking the river at Taberna Yayabo (p207).

Afternoon It's a picturesque journey via the gorgeous Alturas de Banao and Valle de los Ingenios (p214) to Trinidad (p200). Once there, start at the iconic Iglesia y Convento de San Francisco (p205) and wander through the city's cobbled streets.

Evening Dine alfresco atop the roof at Vista Gourmet (p203), before heading to Casa de la Trova for live music (p204).

Day 6

Morning Learn about Trinidad's beautiful buildings at the Museo de Arquitectura Colonial (p202), then check out Lázaro Niebla's unique carved portraits (p201).

Afternoon Following lunch at Sol Ananda (p203), head into the mountains to Topes de Collantes (p224). After admiring the natural beauty here, drive via Manicuragua to Cienfuegos (p178).

Evening Treat yourself to dinner at Finca del Mar, which overlooks the bay (p191).

Day 7

Morning Spend an hour or two exploring downtown Cienfuegos, before setting off for Playa Girón (p176), with its superb museum dedicated to the Bay of Pigs invasion. Continue along the shoreline for a seafood lunch at open-air Restaurante Tiki ((54) 715 922) on Playa Larga (p176).

Afternoon Take the Autopista back to Havana, arriving with enough time to visit the Museo Ernest Hemingway (p135).

Evening Enjoy extravagant Italian fare at Corte del Principe (p137).

Set in Stone

The delicate caryatids, marble adornments, and organ pipe-inspired balconies and window grills on the Gran Teatro de La Habana Alicia Alonso *(p98)*, built in 1915, are an eclectic Cuban version of Baroque. To fully appreciate the building, take a guided tour of the show-stopping interior, which has been the set for many performances over the years.

←

The dramatically curving staircases of the Gran Teatro de La Habana

CUBA FOR
ARCHITECTURE

Cuba's astonishing architecture spans five centuries in an eclectic amalgam of styles, with the colourful streetscape mixing classical aristocractic mansions, 1950s Modernist ice-cream parlours, Art Deco office buildings and more.

TOP 5 COLONIAL BUILDING FEATURES

Alfarje
Moorish ceiling with heavy, star-patterned crossbeams.

Entresuelo
The lower mezzanine level of a home. It used to be where domestic servants slept.

Reja
Eighteenth-century decorative metal window grill.

Mampara
A half-length double swing door for rooms.

Zaguán
Entrance hallway large enough for carriages to pass through.

Mudéjar Marvel

The Moorish influence on early colonial architecture can be seen in Cuba's oldest building, the Casa de Diego Velázquez *(p233)*. Take a guided tour of this building, which was built in 1530, to see its exquisite details up close.

→

The Moorish exterior of the Casa de Diego Velázquez

Astounding Art Deco

Appearing to be assembled using Lego® bricks, Havana's towering Edificio Bacardí *(p80)* was built in 1930 as the headquarters of the famous rum corporation. It is one of Cuba's most striking Art Deco edifices, and it's seen as an icon of the city – particularly its bell tower, which you can ascend (for a fee) to look over the capital.

→

The brick exterior of the Art Deco Edificio Bacardí

INSIDER TIP
A Bacardí Bar

Although Edificio Bacardí is not officially open to the public, head to its wood-panelled mezzanine bar for a tipple and a peek inside.

Modernist Masterpiece

Built by mobster Meyer Lansky in 1957, Havana's Hotel Riviera *(p125)* is a fabulous example of mid-century Modernism with its perfectly preserved lobby. You don't have to stay here to see inside; simply visit one of the bars. Don't miss the coffin-shaped pool.

←

The jazzy blue exterior of the Hotel Riviera

Colonial Grandeur

The capital's grandiose Palacio de los Capitanes Generales in La Habana Vieja *(p66)* was built in 1791. Its sturdy coral-stone exterior is an example of the colonial Baroque style. Inspired by classical aesthetics, it's fronted by a broad loggia, providing shade.

→

The Palacio de los Capitanes Generales' classical loggia

A photographic work by Enrique Rottenberg on display in Fábrica de Arte ↑

CUBA FOR
ART LOVERS

Heavily influenced by both early Classicism and innovative European movements, Cuba's rich artistic heritage also draws on Afro-Cuban spiritualism and a yearning for a *criollo* identity. More recently, avant-garde artists have blossomed under state sponsorship, and local street artists have responded to the boom in tourism.

Instituto Superior de Arte

Since the revolution, the state-run Instituto Superior de Arte *(p128)* has trained contemporary artists. The stormy post-revolutionary decades are reflected in shifting moods of hope and despair in graduates' artworks, from Servando Cabrera Moreno's buoyant *Peasant militia* to Antonia Eiriz's grotesque statements on the anguish of censorship. A new generation of artists are stretching the boundaries of both eroticism and political statement. Head to Fábrica de Arte *(p121)* to see some of these works.

→

The original, controversial, campus of the Instituto Superior de Arte

Vanguardia Movement

Inspired by independence and a search for a genuine Cuban identity, early 20th-century art reflected the nation's new cosmopolitanism, as many artists returned from study abroad. The Vanguardia movement valued Modernist experimentation above academic training. Carlos Enriquez's *The Abduction of the Mulattas* is perhaps the most quintessential work from this era. The Museo Nacional de Bellas Artes *(p94)* displays pieces by Vanguardia artists including Wilfredo Lam and Amelia Peláez.

← The avant-garde *The Balcony* by Amelia Peláez

TOP 3 OFFBEAT ART VENUES

Fábrica de Arte
Specializes in changing galleries of provocative avant-garde art *(p121)*.

Fusterlandia
An entire area adorned with whimsical ceramics *(p129)*.

Callejón de Hamel
Fantastical street art inspired by the Santería religion *(p108)*.

💬 INSIDER TIP
Unknown Galleries

Visitors can join tours of off-beat galleries, such as Galería Continua and René Peña's gallery, with Cuba Art Tours *(www.cubartours.com)*.

↑ *Paisaje cubano* by Esteban Chartrand

Stylistic Classicism

The San Alejandro Fine Arts Academy, founded in 1818 under the direction of French artiste Juan Bautiste Vermay, trained virtually every notable 19th-century Cuban artist. Echoing classical European styles of the era, the school focused on an idealized version of Cuba with romanticized rural scenes, such as Esteban Chartrand's works titled *Paisaje cubano* (Cuban landscape). The Palacio de Bellas Artes, which is part of Havana's Museo Nacional de Bellas Artes *(p94)*, displays hundreds of pieces by Cuban artists painted during colonial rule, including many heavily stylized works.

▷ Fascinating Caves

Over millions of years, Cuba's bedrock of mainly porous limestone was lifted from beneath the sea by tectonic forces. As a result of this process, the isle is now riddled with caverns. The Gran Caverna de Santo Tomás *(p151)* in the Valle de Viñales is the largest system, with some 45 km (28 miles) of labyrinthine galleries. Take a guided tour to appreciate the caves' architecture.

◁ Vibrant Wetlands

Parque Nacional Ciénaga de Zapata *(p176)* protects the largest wetlands in the Caribbean, formed of coastal mangroves, marsh and semi-deciduous forest. On a guided boat or kayak trip you can see crocodiles, manatees and myriad birds, including the Cuban parrot.

CUBA FOR
NATURAL
WONDERS

This island's remarkable array of natural wonders is one of its greatest attractions. From underground caverns to forest-clad mountains, there are endless scenes to explore, both on land and beneath the sea.

◁ Fabulous Formations

Rising up from the plains, is it any wonder that the Spanish were mystified by Cuba's *mogotes?* Although a few other regions are studded with these flat-topped limestone formations, the Valle de Viñales *(p150)* has the greatest concentration and they dramatically frame the verdant valley.

△ Soaring Mountains

The densely forested Sierra Maestra *(p258)* forms a rugged spine along Cuba's southeast shore. Guided overnight hikes ascend to the cloud-draped summit - Pico Turquino - where you can have your picture taken with a bronze bust of José Martí.

◁ Wonderful Waterfalls

Only a few of Cuba's many falls are easily accessible. Fortunately, a well-maintained trail leads to perhaps the most beautiful cascade on the island. Sitting at the base of the Sierra de Escambray mountain range, shower-like El Nicho *(p191)* will take your breath away. Visit in late summer when it's at its most dramatic and take swimwear to bathe in the jade-coloured pool.

▷ Gorgeous Reefs

Don scuba gear to marvel at the abundant marine life off Cuba's southern shore. At Punta Francés, on the Isla de la Juventud *(p154),* a reef wall populated by vibrant fish plunges into the inky depths. Here, you'll see the world's tallest coral column - the "Caribbean Cathedral".

▷ How to Tackle It

One of the reasons that Ernest Hemingway fell in love with Cuba was because of its fishing. The country offers superb, well-regulated fly-fishing opportunities; the Península de Zapata *(p174)* and Jardines de la Reina *(p222)* are top sites.

▷ Diving High

Cuba is fringed by some of the most pristine coral reefs in the northern hemisphere, although you'll also find Spanish galleons, sunken Soviet warships and even aircraft just a few fathoms down at many dive sites. Punta Francés, off Isla de la Juventud *(p154)*, is considered the best spot.

CUBA FOR
OUTDOOR ACTIVITIES

This island nation is tailor-made for active adventures. With its green mountains, immaculate reefs and country lifestyle, you can experience everything from cycling across the island to diving into the deep tropical sea.

◁ Life on Two Wheels

Although few Cubans in Havana and Santiago de Cuba ride bikes, other Cuban cities resemble Amsterdam without the canals – bikes are everywhere! Bring your own bike or take a guided excursion with Bike Rental & Tours Havana *(www.bikerentalhavana.com)*. You can also take a multi-day tour with Cubania *(www.cubaniatravel.com)*.

▷ **Foaling Around**
Horseback excursions for all abilities are available throughout the island. It's a great way to experience off-the-beaten-track Cuba and to learn about the traditional country lifestyle. "Horse whisperer" Julio Muñoz offers guided tours (www.trinidadphoto.com).

◁ **Feathered Friends**
Cuba has 374 bird species, with 25 species found nowhere else in the world. Twenty-one of these, including the zunzuncito (the world's smallest bird), can be seen at Parque Nacional Ciénaga de Zapata (p176), the country's best site for keen twitchers. Cuba's national bird, the tocororó or Cuban trogon, is easily spotted in mountain zones.

 INSIDER TIP
Save Energy
Hire an energy-efficient electric bicycle for a guided tour of Havana with Cuba Private Travel (www.cuba privatetravel.com).

▷ **Walk This Way**
Cuba's mountains are laced with trails, but most of these routes require that visitors travel with a guide. Some of the finest hiking in Cuba is in the Sierra Escambray (p191) and Gran Parque Nacional Sierra Maestra (p258); the overnight trek to Pico Turquino is a popular route.

▷ Delightful Danzón

This slow, formal 19th-century dance form is kept alive by elder Cubans. A Caribbean and Creole adaptation of European country dancing, *danzón* is marked by elegant set footwork and long pauses. You can see couples swaying daily in Santa Clara's Casa de la Cultura, off Parque Leoncio Vidal *(p182)*, and during the Danzón Habana Festival, which is held every June.

◁ Simply Son Cubano

The precursor to salsa, *son* was born in Eastern Cuba and evolved to become the national music form. It was adopted by big bands and spawned the cha-cha-cha and mambo. Check it out at the Casa de la Trova *(p234)* in Santiago de Cuba.

CUBA'S
RHYTHM

Cuba's musical heritage spans a spectrum of sensual sounds and fuels a dizzying panorama of dance forms. The entire island sways to tropical rhythms, while classical genres thrive thanks to the state-sponsored promotion of the arts.

▷ On Pointe

The Ballet Nacional de Cuba and Ballet de Camagüey are among the world's top companies. The country's leading venue for ballet is Havana's Gran Teatro de La Habana Alicia Alonso *(p98)*, named for Cuba's prima ballerina.

◁ Learn to Dance Salsa

Salsa is the sensual dance of choice in Cuba and almost every nightclub features sizzling salsa sounds. Why not learn some moves before giving it a go? Book classes with La Casa del Son *(www.bailarencuba. com)* or Club Salseando Chévere *(www. salseandochevere.com)*.

◁ Classical Cuba

Cubans adore choral and classical music, which is kept alive by choirs and ensembles nationwide, who sometimes play music by home-grown composers, such as Guido López Gavilán. In the capital, Teatro Nacional *(www.teatronacional.cu)* and Basílica de San Francisco *(p78)* offer year-round programs, while Santa Clara's Teatro la Caridad *(p182)* also stages opera and other classical music.

TOP 5 CUBAN MUSICIANS

Los Van Van
Cuba's premier big-band salsa ensemble.

Chucho Váldez
Jazz pianist, composer and bandleader.

Silvio Rodríguez
The foremost modern folk musician.

X-Alfonso
An Afro-rock fusion and hip-hop star.

Buena Fé
Top Latin pop music duo.

△ Enjoy a Traditional Rumba

Working-class parties keep alive Afro-Cuban folkloric music and dance forms, such as *yambú*, *columbia* and the salacious *guanguancó*. Together, these different traditions make up the rumba genre. A great place to dance rumba is Havana's El Patio de EGREM *(410 San Rafael)*.

¡Viva la Revolución!

Billboards and murals nationwide capture the spirit of the Cuban revolution, with Che Guevara as the most popular subject. One of the most famous images of this iconic revolutionary adorns the concrete façade of the Hotel Habana Libre *(p123)* in Vedado. Use a slow shutter speed to punctuate your photo with a passing classic American car.

A vintage American car driving past the Hotel Habana Libre

CUBA FOR
PHOTOGRAPHY

It's hard to imagine a more photogenic destination than vibrant, trapped-in-time Cuba. Here are some iconic shots that capture the best of Cuba's fabulous architecture, stunning landscapes and colourful culture.

PHOTO TOURS

To learn how to perfect your photography skills, sign up for a tour led by a professional photographer and Cuba expert. Jim Cline Photo Tours *(www.jimcline phototours.com)* specializes in Cuba and features hidden venues and unique local spots.

Valley Vista

For the most beautiful scenery in Cuba, shoot the Valle de Viñales *(p150)* from the hilltop Hotel Los Jazmines *(p163)*. The valley is framed by the distinctive towering *mogotes* (steep, round hills) and the scene is studded with thatched *bohíos* (farmsteads). Palms rising over rust-red tobacco fields complete the scene.

Street Life

Don't leave your camera in your hotel - Cuba's streetscapes are made for photography. The *calles* (streets) of La Habana Vieja and Centro Habana are stand-out subjects. Look for the details – locals chatting on steps, or businesses tucked inside tenement stairwells.

INSIDER TIP
Working with Tropical Light

To avoid Cuba's intense sunlight, try to shoot photos during the "golden hour"– the hour following sunrise and before sunset. At midday, shoot in shadow to avoid extreme contrast.

↑ A local street scene in Centro Habana, looking towards the Capitolio

Classic Americana

Havana's Malecón *(p109)* is the perfect place to photograph pre-revolutionary American cars as they rev their way along the seafront. To capture them in motion, stand on the ocean side and follow a car's movement as you click the shutter, or use a telephoto lens to capture the whole boulevard with Vedado behind.

← Classic car driving next to the ocean in Havana's Malecón

Cuban Pastoral

With its ox-drawn ploughs, thatched *bohios* (farmsteads) and weathered farmhands, Cuba's countryside transports visitors back in time. Don't be shy! For the most impactful images, engage the farmers and ask if you can take their photos. Get up close. If you're lucky, they'll be wearing a well-worn straw hat and holding a half-smoked cigar.

↑ The distinctive palm trees and *mogotes* of Valle de Viñales

→ A farmhand working in a tobacco field in Cuba's countryside

A scene from *Our Man in Havana*, starring Alec Guinness →

CUBA
ON PAGE,
ON SCREEN

This inspiring island has been immortalized in novels, poems and films from Cold War intrigues to tales of love in the city. Follow the trail of your favourites to see the sights behind the set and pen.

Buena Vista Social Club

This 1999 movie brought together a bunch of aged and forgotten musicians, and launched Cuba-mania. It was largely filmed on the streets of La Habana Vieja and Centro Habana; roaming the *calles* (streets), you'll often hear songs by the ensemble drifting down the cobbles.

→

Members of the Buena Vista Social Club performing

Dirty Havana Trilogy

Set in the grim days of the "Special Period" *(p55)*, Pedro Juan Gutiérrez's gritty, unsentimental and salacious 2002 novel is located amid the crowded tenements of Centro Habana. Gutiérrez's novel pulsates with sex, drugs, alcohol, music and the picturesque streets of Havana. The novel is banned in Cuba.

↑ The streets of Centro Habana, immortalized in the grimy, gripping *Dirty Havana Trilogy*

Our Man in Havana

The movie of Graham Greene's *Our Man in Havana (p90)*, which is set in pre-revolutionary Cuba, was filmed in the city. Wormold, the hapless protagonist who feeds fabricated information to MI6, lives on Calle Lamparilla, taking his daughter to Tropicana *(p128)* for her birthday and famously frequenting Sloppy Joe's *(p108)*.

Strawberry and Chocolate at Coppelia

Cuba's only Oscar-nominated movie, *Strawberry and Chocolate* (1993) tells the story of David, a student who agrees to spy on Diego, a homosexual artist seen as an enemy of the Communist regime. The film opens at Coppelia ice cream parlour in Vedado *(p120)*; the flavours are loaded with sexual meaning: strawberry for gay; chocolate for straight.

←

Strawberry and Chocolate's famous duo

The Old Man and the Sea

Ernest Hemingway used his real-life experiences with the fishermen of Cojímar *(p133)* – where he berthed his boat, *Pilar* – as the basis for his 1952 Pulitzer Prize-winning novel. A bust of the author looks over the bay, while the paintings above the bar at La Terraza de Cojímar honour both the writer and the story.

↑ A bust of Hemingway looking out over Cojímar

Bewitching Beaches

The Cayos de Villa Clara *(p218)* – comprising Cayo Ensenachos, Cayo Las Brujas (Witches Cay), and Cayo Santa María – are a sunseeker's paradise. Swim in the warm, shallow waters or fish for bonefish and tarpon here.

→

A bridge to the beach on Cayo Ensenachos

CUBA FOR
BREATHTAKING BEACHES

A nation of beach-lovers, Cubans are spoilt for choice when it comes to sensational stretches of sand. Sugary sand awaits you wherever you go on the island, with each beach offering something different.

Naked Beauty

Cuba's strict laws against public nudity don't apply on Cayo Largo *(p165)*, but you don't have to strip off. Whether you're staying here for a week or taking a two-day excursion from Havana, you will be greeted with sands as soft as talcum powder. Our pick of the island's beaches is Playa Sirena.

←

Palm trees on the white sands of Playa Sirena on Cayo Largo

Escape the Crowds

Unspoiled Cayo Sabinal (p218) has no large-scale hotels, despite the miles of superlative sand found on its shores. The highlight of the island is the mesmerizingly beautiful Playa Los Pinos, which is sheltered by a barrier reef. It has minimal facilities but makes the perfect day-trip excursion from Santa Lucía if all you're craving is some peace and quiet.

→

The stark white Faro Colón lighthouse on Cayo Sabinal

Get Sporty

Varadero (p172), Cuba's main beach resort, has more than 60 large all-inclusive resorts along 12 km (7 miles) of unbroken white-sand beaches on the Atlantic shore of the Hicacos Peninsula. As well as a nature reserve, the resort also boasts all manner of watersports. Try your hand at kitesurfing above the sparkling waters, jet-ski through the mangroves or go scuba diving with Marlin Náutica (www.nauticamarlin.com).

←

A woman kitesurfing over Cuba's waters

TOP 5 CITY BEACH ESCAPES

Playas del Este
These sands are packed with Habaneros on weekends (p134).

Cayo Levisa
This tiny beach-fringed isle is a short distance from Viñales (p163).

Playa Ancón
Popular picnic spot near Trinidad (p214).

Playa Siboney
Parque Baconao's beach (p246) is close to Santiago de Cuba.

Guardalavaca
Eastern Cuba's most developed resort (p251).

Family Fun

Protected by an offshore reef, Maguana beach in the Parque Nacional Alejandro de Humboldt (p262) is the perfect place to paddle and play. Alternatively, kids will love looking for flamingos and white ibis at Cayo Coco (p208), or playing on the snow-white sand as soft as icing sugar.

↑ A Cuban family on Maguana beach

Explore the Museo de la Revolución

Havana's most important museum *(p92)* is housed in Batista's former presidential palace and gives visitors a good overview of the revolution's origins, events and outcomes. To the rear, the *Granma* Memorial displays the yacht Granma (encased in glass), which brought Fidel and 81 other revolutionaries from Mexico in 1956.

←

A painting in the Museo de la Revolución

CUBA FOR
REVOLUTION
SITES

From funky street murals to the reverence shown to key personalities, you can't escape *la revolución* in Cuba. Here, we've picked the unmissable revolution sites that will tell Cuba's story.

TOP 5 FORMIDABLE FEMALES

Haydee Santamaría
A key figure in Castro's government.

Celia Sánchez
This fomer guerilla fighter became Fidel Castro's secretary.

Vilma Espín
Raúl Castro's wife founded the Cuban Women's Federation.

Melba Hernández
A significant Cuban diplomat who fought with the rebel army.

Aleida March
The fighter became Che Guevara's wife.

Visit Moncada Barracks

The revolution was launched with an audacious attack on these army barracks in Santiago de Cuba by Fidel's revolutionaries on 26 July 1953 *(p238)*. It is now a school, but there is a superb museum inside dedicated to the infamous assault on site.

→

The striking exterior of Moncada Barracks

INSIDER TIP
Take a Tour

Follow in the footsteps of revolutionaries on a guided tour with The Nation (*www.the nation.com*).

Relive History at Playa Girón

The site of the main battle during the 1961 Bay of Pigs invasion *(p177)* is now home to a superb museum, with extensive maps, photographs and gory mementos. You can also see early 20th-century Soviet and US tanks here.

→

Fighter plane on display at Playa Girón

Learn about Che Guevara

The Complejo Escultórico Memorial Comandante Ernesto Che Guevara *(p184)* in Santa Clara features a massive statue of Cuba's adopted hero. It is surrounded by murals showing the life of the Argentine Marxist's exploits. Beneath the relaxed silhouette of Guevara, a mausoleum contains Che's remains. Don't miss the fabulous museum, which displays many of his personal artifacts.

←

A statue of Che Guevara, Santa Clara

Pay Your Respects at Fidel's Grave

A steady stream of visitors bring roses to lay at Fidel Castro's simple grave every day. Appropriately, the burial place of Cuba's first Communist leader is marked by an unassuming boulder bearing a bronze plaque that simply says "Fidel". It is not insignificant that he was laid to rest next to the mausoleum of national hero José Martí in the Cementerio Santa Ifigenia *(p237)*.

→

A man laying flowers in front of Fidel Castro's grave

CUBA
AFTER DARK

Salsa may be the first thing you think of when contemplating Cuba by night, but it is only one of the many rhythms that flow through the nation's bloodstream. The island sizzles with cabarets, raves and everything in between.

Cuba Live

There's no shortage of opportunities to hear live music in Cuba. The country, which famously banned The Beatles in the 1960s and 70s, even hosted the Rolling Stones in Havana in 2016. Every town has a Casa de la Trova for traditional *son (p34)*, but Santiago de Cuba's is the stand-out venue on the island *(p234)*. The best selection of music and dance can be found in the capital, however, with Havana's night scene buzzing with cutting-edge sounds at venues like Jazz Café *(Galerías de Paseo, Calle 1 y Paseo; 7838 3302)*.

→ The Casa de la Trova in Baracoa Guantánamo

Catch a Cabaret

Flamboyant, fantastical and fun, retro-themed cabarets are as quintessentially Cuban as cigars and rum. Every city has at least one glitzy cabaret *espectáculo*, but the largest and most flamboyant is Havana's open-air Tropicana *(p128)*, which first opened on New Year's Eve in 1939. With swirling showgirls in sensational costumes, gravity-defying acrobats and talented crooners, they are a riot for the senses.

←

Colour and cabaret at the open-air Tropicana

TOP 3 LGBT VENUES

mYXto
A disco bar in Havana, with drag shows *(Jovellar No. 3 e/ Oquendo y Marina)*.

Bar Karabalí
Vibrant twice-weekly parties are held on Havana's La Rampa *(Avenida 23 y Avenida Paseo)*.

Cabaret Las Vegas
This Havana dive bar is popular for its kitschy drag shows *(Infanta 104, e/ Calles 25 y 27)*.

Club Life

Havana's dance-crazy club scene spans a spectrum of sounds from rap to salsa. Many venues are no-frills affairs, such as Havana's Casa de la Música *(p131)*, but they come to life with sizzling music. Go to Fábrica de Arte *(p121)* for a hedonistic night out or dance the night away underground at "Disco Las Cuevas" in Trinidad's Disco Áyala *(Calle Pólvora)*.

→

The musicians at Fábrica de Arte pulsate the dance floor *(inset)*

Cuban Classics

There's no more quintessential Cuban dish than *ropa vieja*. Ignore its unappealing name ("old clothes") and savour strips of braised beef or lamb, simmered with sweet peppers and onions, and served with rice, black beans and fried plantains. You'll also find plenty of seafood on the Cuban menu. Lobster and shrimp are usually prepared with a garlic and tomato sauce *(enchilada)*. To finish, Cubans nourish their sweet tooth with such desserts as flan, *natilla* (chocolate custard) and *tres leches* (a sponge cake made with three milks).

→

People buying fruit and vegetables at a lively market in Havana

CUBA FOR
FOODIES

From *moros y cristianos* (rice and beans) to garlicky grilled lobster tails, the Cuban menu is full of tasty treats. Gastronomic innovation is sweeping Havana, while regional restaurants have upped their game thanks to an enterprising crop of *paladares* (private eateries). Don't miss these must-eats.

Havana's Blossoming Food Scene

Forget the antiquated tales you may have heard about the capital's unappetising food scene. Talented chefs – many returning to their homeland after stints abroad – serve up inventive menus that fuse Cuban field-to-fork ingredients with global cuisine. Our pick of these fine-dining restaurants is La Guarida, which boasts a sensational setting *(p105)*.

> 💬 INSIDER TIP
> **Hit the Culinary Trail**
>
> For a fascinating inside-the-kitchen insight into Cuba's foodie scene, sign up for an eight-day culinary tour with Access Culinary Trips *(www.accesstrips.com)*.

TOP 5 **CUBAN TIPPLES**

Mojito
Savour this Cuban classic at La Bodeguita del Medio (p70).

Daiquirí
El Floridita (p73) serves Hemingway's preferred drink, the "papa doble".

Cerveza
Sample craft beer at La Factoria Plaza Vieja (p75).

Batidos
Cool down with an iced fruit shake from one of the street stalls found throughout the island.

Añejo Rum
Compare aged rums at the Museo del Ron (p79).

← A plate of *ropa vieja*, one of Cuba's traditional dishes

↑ A waiter serving customers at an eatery in Havana

↑ Tucking into a bowl of ice cream at Coppelia in Havana

Ice Cream Fanatics

Every city has a branch of Coppelia, the state-run *heladería* (ice cream store) created following the revolution to guarantee an egalitarian indulgence. The iconic Coppelia parlour in Havana's Vedado (p120) serves up to 30,000 customers every day and is nicknamed La Catedral de Helado (The Cathedral of Ice Cream). Don't sit in the tourist section - dine with the locals instead.

A YEAR IN
CUBA

JANUARY

Triunfa de la Revolución *(1 Jan)*. Cities nationwide celebrate the "triumph of the revolution".

Festival de la Trova Longina *(mid-Jan)*. Santa Clara is enlivened by *trova* music during this fiesta.

△ **Festival Internacional de Jazz** *(late Jan)*. Cuban and international jazz maestros perform at venues throughout Havana.

FEBRUARY

△ **Fería Internacional de los Libros** *(early Feb)*. This book fair starts in Havana before moving to other cities.

Habanos Festival *(late Feb)*. Cuba's premier cigar festival takes place in the capital.

JUNE

△ **Festival Internacional de Boleros de Oro** *(third week)*. A week of concerts celebrating romantic *bolero* ballads at various Havana venues.

Carnaval San Juan Camagüeyano *(late Jun)*. Floats and street parties populate Camagüey.

Festival Internacional de Coros *(last week)*. A nationwide celebration of choral music.

MAY

△ **Día de los Trabajadores** *(1 May)*. Half-a-million people parade through Havana's Plaza de la Revolución for Labour Day.

Romerías de Mayo *(first week)*. Cultural activities and a religious pilgrimage take place in Holguín.

OCTOBER

△ **Festival Internacional de Ballet** *(late Oct; held in even-numbered years)*. A biennial ballet event hosted by Havana's Gran Teatro.

Festival Iberoamericana de la Cultura *(late Oct)*. Holguín's week-long cultural festival.

Festival de La Habana de Música Contemporaneo *(last week)*. Chamber, classical and instrumental music in Havana.

SEPTEMBER

△ **Día de la Caridad del Cobre** *(8 Sep)*. Pilgrimage to Basílica del Cobre to honour Cuba's patron saint and her avatar, Ochún.

Haban'Arte *(mid-Sep)*. Havana hosts this multicultural arts festival.

MARCH

Festival del Tambor *(mid-Mar)*. The sound of drums playing myriad genres of music can be heard at venues throughout Havana.

△ **Festival Internacional de Trova Pepe Sánchez** *(mid-Mar)*. Traditional *trova* and *son* are celebrated at Santiago de Cuba's Casa de la Trova.

APRIL

Festival Piña Colada *(first week)*. Ciego de Ávila's music festival spans everything from hip-hop to *trova*.

△ **Festival de Semana Santa** *(Good Friday)*. Join in the solemn Easter processions through the streets of Trinidad.

Bienal de la Habana *(late Apr; held in odd-numbered years)*. Taking place every two years, Havana showcases contemporary art in its Biennial.

JULY

Festival Internacional del Cine de Gibara *(first week)*. Off-the-beaten-track Gibara hosts this International Film Festival.

Fiesta del Caribe *(early Jul)*. Week-long commemoration of Caribbean culture in Santiago de Cuba.

△ **26 de Julio** *(26 Jul)*. Cities across the country celebrate the launch of the revolution in 1953.

Carnaval de Santiago de Cuba *(late Jul)*. A cacophony of colourful revelry can be expected from Cuba's top carnival.

AUGUST

△ **Carnaval de la Habana** *(early Aug)*. Havana's sensual carnival spans two weekends.

Festival Internacional de Rumba Cubana *(all month)*. Watch talented dancers perform Afro-Cuban rumbas in Havana, Camagüey and other cities.

DECEMBER

Festival de Música Popular Benny Moré *(mid-Dec)*. Cienfuegos moves to the sounds of Benny Moré.

Procesión de los Milagros *(17 Dec)*. Devotees make a pilgrimage to the Santuario de San Lázaro in Rincón.

△ **Parrandas de Remedios** *(Christmas week)*. Remedios explodes with awesome firework displays during this carnival-like party.

NOVEMBER

△ **Marahabana** *(third Sunday)*. The Havana marathon is Cuba's premier running event.

Festival del Nuevo Cine Latinoamericano *(last week)*. Long lines form at Havana's cinemas for this week-long film festival.

A BRIEF
HISTORY

Cuba has had a tumultuous history owing to its strategic location as the "Key to the New World". The island's colourful colonial past is shadowed by slavery and a passionate quest for independence, but following the revolution Cuba became a world leader in literacy, health care and music.

Pre-Columbian Cuba

Until as recently as 5,500 years ago, the island of Cuba appears to have been uninhabited. The first settlers, the Guanahatabeys, were hunter-gatherers who lived in caves. They were followed by the Siboneys, another pre-ceramic tribe that may have arrived from the North American mainland. Around 1,500 years ago, the Taíno arrived from the Orinoco basin in South America. They developed a more advanced culture, living in tribal units under *caciques* (chiefs) and becoming skilled farmers, potters and weavers, as well as evolving basic astronomical charts.

Did You Know?

The British returned Havana to the Spanish in 1763 in exchange for Florida and Georgia.

Timeline of events

3500 BC
First inhabitants settle on the island of Cuba.

500 AD
Taíno arrive from South America and displace the Siboneys.

1492
Christopher Columbus "discovers" Cuba.

1511
The Spanish begin to settle the island, led by Diego Velázquez de Cuéllar.

1515
Foundation of Santiago de Cuba and Santa María del Puerto del Príncipe (Camagüey).

Spanish Conquest and the Heyday of Sugar

The peaceful Taíno culture was swiftly decimated following the landing of Christopher Columbus on the shores of Cuba on 27 October 1492. The first settler expedition followed in 1511. Those Taíno not put to the sword for resisting Spanish subjugation succumbed to European diseases, and within a century the native population had perished.

In 1553, Havana was named Cuba's capital. Vast treasure fleets passed through the city's harbour on their way to Spain, resulting in regular attacks by pirates and privateers. Castles and fortresses were built in Cuban cities for protection, while forests were felled for precious timber and to raise cattle for hides bound for Europe. A significant slave trade also evolved at this time.

Spain's monopolistic treatment of Cuba inspired several revolts. In 1762, a British fleet captured Havana and lifted Spain's trade restrictions. Although the conquest was brief, this change caused a surge in trade with North America and a rapid expansion of sugar plantations and, in consequence, the slave trade. By the mid-1800s, Cuba had become the world's largest supplier of sugar and Havana was more sophisticated than Madrid.

1 A historical print of Havana.

2 Models at a modern reproduction of a traditional Taíno village.

3 An engraving showing Taíno chief Hatuey being burned to death by Spanish soldiers.

4 A scene at a Cuban sugar plantation.

1553
Havana becomes the island's capital.

1740
Spain creates the Real Compañía, with a monopoly on Cuban trade.

1762
The British seize Havana and establish free trade.

1519
Havana is founded beside a bay at the mouth of the Gulf of Mexico, at the site of a natural deepwater port.

1662
Welsh privateer Henry Morgan and his pirates sack Havana.

Quest for Independence

By 1826, all of Spain's Latin American colonies, apart from Puerto Rico and Cuba, had gained independence. Spain ruled Cuba to its own benefit with indifference to *criollo* (local) sentiment. On 10 October 1868, planter Carlos Manuel de Céspedes freed his slaves and launched a war of independence – the Ten Years' War – in which white and black *criollos* fought side by side. Although generals Máximo Gómez and Antonio Maceo liberated much of Cuba, the uprising was brutally suppressed and one-fifth of the population were killed. In 1895 a second war was launched and by 1898 the independence fighters were close to victory, when a US warship exploded in Havana's harbour. The US had long coveted Cuba and, blaming Spain, declared war. Spain was vanquished and the US military administered Cuba until independence was granted in 1902.

The Quasi-Republic

US entities came to own more than 50 per cent of the Cuban economy and Washington, DC tolerated a series of corrupt presidents as long as they supported US economic interests.

1 A monument to General Antonio Maceo. ↑

2 The destruction of the USS *Maine* in 1898.

3 Fulgencio Batista *(centre left)* in 1933.

4 Fidel Castro addressing crowds in Santa Clara.

Did You Know?

Ernesto Guevara was nicknamed "Che" for his use of the interjection, meaning "Hey!" or "mate".

Timeline of events

1808
US attempts to purchase Cuba from Spain.

1895
Independence fighter José Martí is martyred.

1898
US declares war on Spain and seizes Cuba.

1868
Carlos Manuel de Céspedes launches the ill-fated Ten Years' War for independence.

1886
Slavery abolished in Cuba.

1902
US grants Cuba formal independence.

In 1933, Fulgencio Batista seized power in the Sergeants' Revolt. At first, he enacted progressive reforms and was elected president. After retiring to Florida, he seized power again in 1952, granted the Mafia free rein and imposed a brutal dictatorship to which the US turned a blind eye. Popular opposition to Batista's rule was marked by assassinations and bombings.

Cuban Revolution

Fidel Castro, a 26-year-old lawyer, launched the revolution to topple Batista with an attack on the Moncada Barracks in Santiago de Cuba on 26 July 1953. It failed miserably, but Batista caved in to popular support and granted Fidel and his brother Raúl amnesty. This proved to be a fateful error as the Castros left for Mexico to organize a Rebel Army. On 2 December 1956, Fidel Castro and 81 others, including Che Guevara, landed in Cuba. Only 16 survived an ambush and made it to the safety of the Sierra Maestra. As volunteers swelled their ranks, the Rebel Army consolidated control of the mountains. On 31 December 1958, after Che Guevara's guerrilla force captured the city of Santa Clara, Batista fled Cuba.

↑ The *New York Daily News* report of Castro's revolutionary triumph

1933
Fulgencio Batista seizes power following the Sergeants' Revolt.

1952
Batista returns from retirement and seizes power in a second coup.

1953
Fidel Castro attacks the Moncada Barracks.

1956
The *Granma* brings Fidel Castro's Rebel Army ashore.

1959
Batista flees and the revolution triumphs.

Five Decades of Fidel

Fidel Castro and leaders of several other revolutionary groups had agreed on a civil government, led by President Manuel Urrutia. But Fidel usurped Urrutia, seized power and, embracing Communism, enacted radical reforms to rid Cuba of racism, poverty, illiteracy and unequal health care. He negotiated the support of the Soviet Union and manipulated a break with the US. In retaliation, President Dwight D Eisenhower imposed the US embargo on Cuba in 1960.

The US also sponsored an invasion by Cuban-American exiles on 17 April 1961 at the Bay of Pigs (p177). Following this failed coup, the US launched Operation Mongoose, with the aim to rid Cuba of Castro once and for all. Stalemate was the result, however, as Castro asked the Soviet Union to install nuclear missiles on the island as a deterrent. The Cuban Missile Crisis of 1962 was only resolved when President Kennedy promised not to invade Cuba.

Fidel Castro was now free to pursue his dreams. The Great Literacy Campaign eradicated illiteracy, and education and health care were extended to the entire country. But, as every

THE US EMBARGO

Initiated by President Eisenhower in 1960, the US trade embargo with Cuba was made permanent in 1996. Condemned by the United Nations, it cannot be lifted until Cuba renounces communism, holds "free and fair elections", and becomes a multi-party democracy.

Timeline of events

1961
US launches a CIA-sponsored invasion at the Bay of Pigs.

1962
Soviets install nuclear missiles in Cuba, triggering the Missile Crisis.

1980
125,000 Cubans emigrate from the small harbour at Mariel.

1991
Collapse of Soviet Union plunges Cuba into a period of severe economic crisis.

1998
Pope John Paul II's visit to Cuba (21–25 January) is a significant turning point.

4

business was nationalized, the economy tanked and Cuba became entirely dependent on the Soviet Union for its supplies. When the Soviet bloc collapsed in 1991, Cuba entered the "Special Period" of extreme economic crisis and turned to tourism to save the day.

Cuba Today

In 2006, Fidel Castro fell gravely ill and handed power to his younger brother Raúl, who in 2011 initiated far-reaching economic reforms to stimulate private enterprise. That same year, President Barack Obama expanded travel opportunities by lifting restrictions against US citizens visiting Cuba. In 2015 the two countries formally re-established diplomatic relations and, in March 2016, President Obama became the first president since Calvin Coolidge in 1928 to visit Cuba. Fidel died on 25 November 2016, two weeks after Donald Trump was elected president. In 2017, Trump reinstated many restrictions on Cuba. In April 2018, almost 60 years of Castro rule came to an end when Raúl stepped down as Cuban president. He was replaced by a civilian, Miguel Díaz-Canel.

① An illustration of the US landing at the Bay of Pigs.

② A US patrol plane during the Missile Crisis.

③ A literacy campaign.

④ President Obama's historic visit.

Did You Know?

Cuba is the only country in the Americas ranked 100 per cent literate by UNESCO.

2000
1,774,000 tourists visit Cuba in one year.

2016
President Obama visits Cuba; Fidel Castro dies.

2018
Miguel Díaz-Canel becomes president.

2006
Fidel Castro is taken seriously ill and hands power to his brother Raúl .

2011
President Obama authorizes travel to Cuba for all US citizens.

EXPERIENCE
HAVANA

People milling around Plaza Vieja

2 Days in Havana 60

La Habana Vieja 62

Centro Habana and Prado 84

Vedado and Plaza 112

Beyond the Centre 126

EXPLORE
HAVANA

This section divides Havana into three
sightseeing areas, as shown on this
map, plus an area beyond the city.
Find out more about each on the
following pages.

MALECÓN

Parque Martí

Parque de los
Suspiros

MALECÓN

MALECÓN

LINE A

Hotel
Nacional

AVENIDA 23

Parque de
la Juventud

CALZADA DE INFANTA

LINE A

Parque
El Quijote

AVENIDA DE LOS PRESIDENTES (CALLE 6)

Museo de Artes
Decorativas

Parque
Víctor Hugo

VEDADO AND PLAZA
p112

AVENIDA 23

Museo
Napoleónico

AVENIDA PASEO

MALECÓN

Jardín
Botánico

LINE A

AVENIDA SALVADOR
ALLENDE (CARLOS III)

EL VEDADO

AVENIDA 23

CALZADA   ZAPATA

Río Almendares

AVENIDA PASEO

Teatro
Nacional

National
Library

Cementerio
Colón

PASEO

AVENIDA 23

Memorial
José Martí

CALLE 25

Palacio
de la
Revolución

AVENIDA 26

Cementerio
Hebreo

NUEVO VEDADO

LA CEIBA

0 metres   500
0 yards   500

N

Caleta de San Lorenzo

CASABLANCA

Castillo de
San Salvador
de la Punta

MALECÓN

Canal de Entrada

AVE CARLOS M DE CÉSPEDES

MALECÓN

Museo de la
Revolución

COLÓN

Catedral de
La Habana

Parque Antonio
Maceo

Edificio
Solimar

Museo Nacional de
Bellas Artes

LA HABANA VIEJA
p62

CENTRO HABANA AND PRADO
p84

Parque
Central

PLAZA DE
SAN FRANCISCO

Parque
de Trillo

Capitolio

PLAZA
VIEJA

CENTRO
HABANA

BARRIO
CHINO

Parque
El Curita

HABANA
VIEJA

AVENIDA SIMÓN BOLÍVAR (REINA)

MÁXIMO

Museo José
Martí

Parque
Jose M.
Perez

Bahía de la
Habana

CALZADA DE INFANTA

AVENIDA ARROYO (MANGLAR)

AVENIDA DEL PUERTO

AVENIDA DE MÉXICO

Castillo de
Atarés

CUBA

Estadio
Latinoamericano

EL CERRO

SANTOS SUÁREZ

←

1 The Baroque façade of Havana's cathedral.

2 Museo de la Revolución.

3 A classic mojito.

4 A picturesque street in La Habana Vieja.

2 DAYS

In Havana

Day 1

Morning The best place to begin your exploration of Havana is at its foundation site – El Templete – which sits in La Habana Vieja's cobbled Plaza de Armas *(p71)*. Explore the Museo de la Ciudad and Castillo de la Real Fuerza *(p70)* before strolling to Plaza de la Catedral *(p82)*, with its remarkable Baroque cathedral. Pause for a delicious cappuccino at Dulcería Bianchini *(p81)* before continuing down Calle Mercaderes to Plaza Vieja *(p75)*, which bustles with local life.

Afternoon Have lunch at La Factoria de Plaza Vieja *(San Ignacio & Muralla; 7866 4453)*, which serves hearty Cuban dishes – best enjoyed alfresco with a refreshing beer. After visiting Plaza Vieja's Cámara Oscura and Museo de Nipes, make your way along Calle Brasil to Plaza del Cristo *(p80)*. Here you'll find the astonishing Capitolio *(p88)*; venture inside and tread the sumptuous marble floors. Don't forget to admire the façade of the Baroque Gran Teatro de La Habana Alicia Alonso *(p98)* as you enter Parque Central *(p110)*.

Evening For the ultimate sunset venue, choose to sip cocktails at the Gran Hotel Manzana Kempinski *(p98)* before taking a ride along the Malecón *(p109)* in a classic convertible car. Ask your driver to take you to La Guarida *(p105)*, a real jaw-dropper of a dinner venue. Feast on fine Cuban fusion fare, then head up the decorative spiral staircase to the open-air rooftop bar for a nightcap.

Day 2

Morning Begin your day at Parque Central and walk down the Paseo de Martí. At Calle Trocadero, divert east past the Hotel Sevilla to see the astounding contemporary art collection in the Museo Nacional de Bellas Artes *(p94)*. Your cultural experience continues at the adjacent Museo de la Revolución *(p92)*, where you will learn all about the events of the Cuban revolution. Next, take a leisurely stroll along the Malecón *(p109)* and up La Rampa to admire Amelia Peláez's mural on the façade of the Hotel Habana Libre *(p123)*.

Afternoon The hotel's Café Habana Libre is the perfect place for lunch, topped off by an ice cream at the Coppelia *(p120)* nearby. Next, hop in a taxi to the Necrópolis de Colón *(p116)* and explore the marble mausoleums of the vast cemetery. Look out for the worshippers praying at La Milagrosa – the "miraculous" tomb that inspired a huge spiritual cult.

Evening For an atmospheric dinner, book a table at Café Laurent *(p119)* and order the delicious garlic shrimp, followed by the slow-roasted lamb with garlic, mint and cream reduction. Finally, amble two blocks northeast to the iconic Hotel Nacional *(p123)* to savour some flavoursome *añejo* rum on the garden patio overlooking the Malecón, accompanied by great music. End the day with a show at the hotel's sensational Cabaret Parisién.

LA HABANA VIEJA

The historic heart of Havana, which was declared part of the "cultural heritage of humanity" by UNESCO in 1982, is the largest colonial centre in Latin America. The city was founded here in 1514, as San Cristóbal de la Habana by the Spanish conquistador Diego Velázquez de Cuéllar, and it quickly became the chief dock for transporting treasure from the Americas to Spain. This affluence attracted pirates and in 1555 the French buccaneer Jacques de Sores sacked and burned this part of the city, triggering Spain to fortify the area. By 1863, Cuba's capital had grown beyond La Habana Vieja's walls due to the constant ebb and flow of precious cargo through the port.

In the early 20th century, however, the area had fallen into disrepair and it became an area where crime ran wild. By the end of the 1980s, the area had no working plumbing and electricity. After years of neglect, restoration work under the direction of Eusebio Leal Spengler, the *historiador de la ciudad* (Superintendent of Cultural Heritage), is reviving the former splendour of this district.

LA HABANA VIEJA

Must See

1 Palacio de los Capitanes Generales

Experience More

2 Palacio del Marqués de Arcos
3 Catedral de San Cristóbal
4 Museo de Arte Colonial
5 Castillo de la Real Fuerza
6 La Bodeguita del Medio
7 Centro Cultural Félix Varela
8 El Templete
9 Calle Oficios
10 Calle Obispo
11 Calle Mercaderes
12 Casa de la Obra Pía
13 Casa de África
14 Plaza Vieja
15 Iglesia de Nuestra Señora de la Merced
16 Iglesia del Espíritu Santo
17 Museo-Casa Natal de José Martí
18 Plaza de San Francisco
19 Museo del Ron
20 Catedral Ortodoxa Nuestra Señora de Kazán
21 Alameda de Paula
22 Edificio Bacardí
23 Iglesia de San Francisco de Paula
24 Iglesia del Ángel Custodio
25 Avenida del Bélgica

Eat

1 Mama Inés
2 Doña Eutimia
3 El del Frente
4 Azúcar

Drink

5 Bar Dos Hermanos
6 El Chanchullero
7 Dulcería Bianchini

Stay

8 Hotel Santa Isabela
9 Casa Vitrales
10 Loma del Ángel

Shop

11 Habana 1791
12 Centro Cultural Almacenes de San José
13 Museo de Chocolate

Castillo del
San Salvador
de la Punta

MALECÓN

CALLE SAN LÁZARO

PASEO DE MARTÍ (PRADO)

CALLE AGUILA

CALLE TROCADERO

CALLE INDUSTRIA

CALLE CONSULADO

CALLE

ANIMAS

CALLE

VIRTUDES

CALLE NEPTUNO

CENTRO HABANA AND PRADO p84

CALLE SAN MIGUEL

PASEO DE MARTÍ (PRADO)

AGRAMONTE (ZULUETA)

COLÓN

Gran
Teatro

CALLE

CALLE GALIANO

CALLE AMISTAD

CALLE AGUILA

Capitolio

DRAGONES

AVENIDA SIMÓN BOLÍVAR (REINA)

MÁXIMO GÓMEZ (MONTE)

ENRIQUE BARNET (ESTRELLA)

CALLE

CALLE CORRALES

CALLE FACTERÍA

CALLE MALOJA

CALLE GLORIA

CALLE MISIÓN

0 metres   250
0 yards   250

N

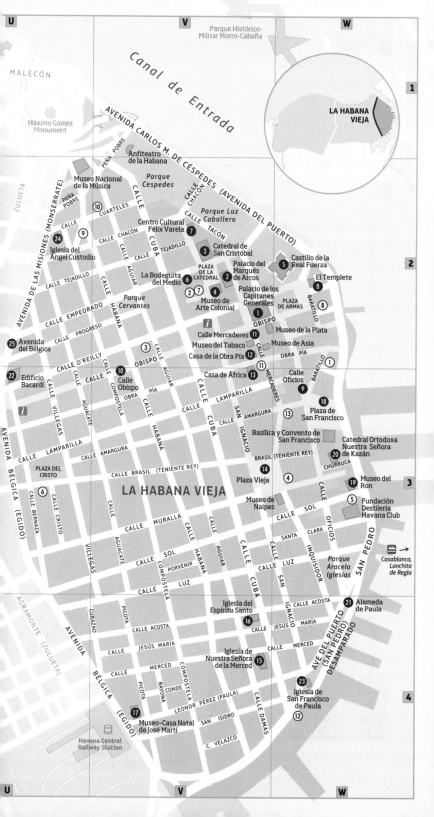

❶ ⌖ ⌖ 🗁

PALACIO DE LOS CAPITANES GENERALES

📍 V2 🏛 Plaza de Armas, Calle Tácon, e/ O'Reilly y Obispo
📞 7866 8980 🕙 9:30am–4pm Tue–Sun

This grand palace, which was once the seat of the Cuban government, offers an overview of the history of Havana, with exhibits reflecting both Cuba's grand colonial past and the island's struggle for independence.

Construction of the Palacio de los Capitanes Generales, a splendid example of Cuban Baroque, took place from 1776 to 1791. It was commissioned by the governor Felipe Fondesviela and designed by engineer Antonio Fernández de Trebejos y Zaldívar. The palace originally housed the Spanish governor's residence and a house of detention, which until 1834 occupied the west wing. The seat of the Cuban Republic from 1902, the building became the Museo de la Ciudad (City Museum) in 1967, but the original structure of the sumptuous residence and political centre has not been altered. Take a tour of the hallowed rooms and admire the artifacts on display, from 18th-century devotional objects to late-19th-century makeshift cannons.

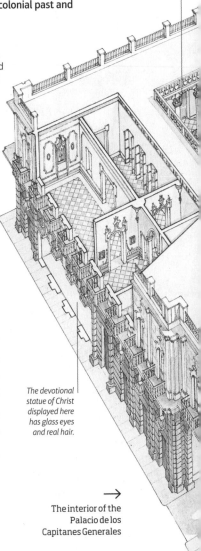

Hall of Flags

The devotional statue of Christ displayed here has glass eyes and real hair.

→ The interior of the Palacio de los Capitanes Generales

↑ The façade of the Palacio de los Capitanes Generales, with its shady arcade

① The Hall of Flags contains objects from the independence wars, including the flag of Carlos Manuel de Céspedes *(p52)*.

② A statue of Christopher Columbus sits in the centre of the internal courtyard, which is overlooked by the gallery.

③ In 1899, the end of Spanish rule was proclaimed in the light-filled Salón de los Espejos, and in 1902 the first president of the Republic took office here.

The gallery features a collection of busts by Luigi Pietrasanta.

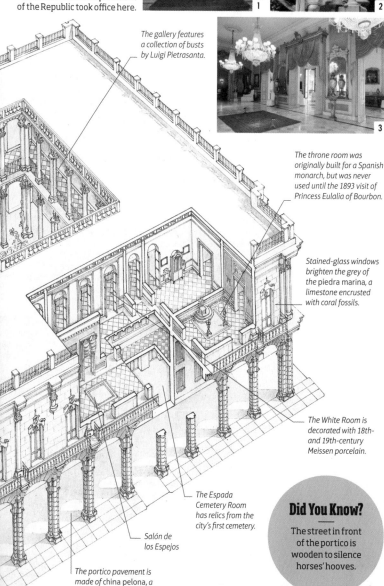

The throne room was originally built for a Spanish monarch, but was never used until the 1893 visit of Princess Eulalia of Bourbon.

Stained-glass windows brighten the grey of the piedra marina, a limestone encrusted with coral fossils.

The White Room is decorated with 18th- and 19th-century Meissen porcelain.

The Espada Cemetery Room has relics from the city's first cemetery.

Salón de los Espejos

The portico pavement is made of china pelona, a hard, shiny stone.

Did You Know?

The street in front of the portico is wooden to silence horses' hooves.

EXPERIENCE MORE

Palacio del Marqués de Arcos

📍V2 🏛Calle Mercaderes, 16 🕑9:30am-5pm Tue-Sun

Completed in 1741 for the royal treasurer Diego Peñalver y Angulo, this sombre Baroque mansion on the southeast corner of Plaza de la Catedral reopened in 2017 as a cultural centre following an extensive restoration. Check out the original cistern in the patio before climbing the staircase, which is painted with colonial-era motifs, to rooms displaying historical lithographs and exquisite *mediopunto* stained-glass windows.

A life-size bronze statue of Spanish flamenco dancer Antonio Gades (1936-2004) leans against a pillar facing the plaza. Although the building can be entered from this plaza, the main entrance – flanked by Doric pilasters – is on Calle Mercaderes. Here, you'll find a letter box in the form of a Greek tragic mask, recalling the building's illustrious past as both a post office and, later, the city's Artistic and Literary Lyceum. The name of the palace's café also reflects this erstwhile function.

Catedral de San Cristóbal

📍V2 🏛Calle Empedrado, 156 📞7861 7771 🕑9am-5pm Mon-Fri, 9am-noon Sat & Sun

Havana's cathedral had a tumultuous beginning. Construction of the Catedral de San Cristóbal (Cathedral of St Christopher) began in 1748 under the supervision of Jesuit priests. Expelled from Cuba following conflict with the Spanish crown, the Jesuits were replaced by Franciscans, who finished the church in 1777. It became a cathedral after the collapse of the old Parroquial Mayor (main parish church), which was caused by the explosion of a ship in the nearby port. With its newfound status, it required an additional bell tower.

In 1789, it was consecrated as Catedral de la Virgen María de la Inmaculada Concepción, but in 1796 it was given its current name because, according to popular belief, from that year until 1898 it housed the remains of Christopher

🔍 HIDDEN GEM
Mural Artístico-Histórico

Facing the Palacio del Marqués de Arcos, this mural features life-size representations of 67 leading 19th-century Cuban literary figures, including José Martí.

Did You Know?

The Catedral de San Cristóbal's bell towers are asymmetrical because of a lack of space.

Columbus. A plaque to the left of the pulpit tells the same story, though there is no official historical record.

The architecture, like other Jesuit churches throughout the world, is in a Latin cross layout, chapels on the sides and to the rear, the nave higher than the side aisles. The Cuban Baroque façade is grandiose, with its two large, bell towers and an abundance of niches and columns, which Cuban author Alejo Carpentier described as "music set in stone".

By comparison, the Neo-Classical interior is rather disappointing. Large piers separate the nave from the aisles, which have eight chapels. The largest is the Sagrario chapel, while the oldest was designed by Lorenzo Camacho in 1755 and is dedicated to the Madonna of Loreto. Inside, the quaint, tiny houses are used as *ex votos* (offerings to saints).

The three frescoes behind the high altar are by Giuseppe Perovani, while the wooden and plaster ceiling was the work of Frenchman Jean Baptiste Vermay, who founded the San Alejandro Fine Arts Academy *(p29)*. The high altar was created by Italian artist Giuseppe Bianchini in the 1800s. To the right is a huge wooden statue of St Christopher, carved by the Seville sculptor Martín de Andújar in 1636. The legs are out of proportion with the trunk, as they were cut in order to allow the statue to pass through the portal.

On 16 November, the saint's feast day, a solemn Mass is held here, during which the faithful file past the statue to silently ask for his blessing, which is given as long as they do not utter a word until they have left the church.

The cobbled square in front of the Catedral de San Cristóbal

↑ The historic blue-and-yellow courtyard of the Museo de Arte Colonial

Museo de Arte Colonial

📍 V2 🏠 Calle San Ignacio, 61 📞 7801 7440 🕐 9:30am–5pm Tue–Sun

This 18th-century mansion, built by Don Luis Chacón, governor of Cuba, has since 1969 been the home of a museum dedicated to colonial art. Constructed around an elegant courtyard, the building is a fine example of a colonial home.

The 12 rooms on the ground floor and first floor contain furniture, chandeliers, porcelain and other decorative pieces from various 18th- to 19th-century middle-class and aristocratic houses in Havana, combining European, Creole and colonial traditions. Besides a remarkable collection of furniture made of tropical wood, the museum has an exceptional collection of stained-glass windows *(mediopunto)*, typical of Cuba's Creole artisans.

There is also a thirteenth room in which contemporary art and crafts exhibitions, inspired by colonial art, are held. During the week the museum conducts tours for the city's schoolchildren and offers various leisure activities for the elderly.

EAT

Mama Inés
Fidel's former private chef conjures up superb fusion dishes in a colonial mansion.

📍 W2 🏠 Calle de la Obra Pía, 60 📞 7862 2669 🕐 Sun

💲💲💲

Doña Eutimia
This intimate family-run restaurant serves *criolla* classics.

📍 V2 🏠 Callejón del Chorro, 60C 📞 7861 1332 🕐 Sun

💲💲💲

El del Frente
You can either enjoy tapas and mojitos on the roof terrace or inside the 1950s-inspired interior at this *paladar*.

📍 V2 🏠 Calle O'Reilly, 303 📞 7863 0206

💲💲💲

Azúcar
Overlooking Plaza Vieja, Azúcar provides light meals and live music.

📍 W3 🏠 Calle Mercaderes, 315 📞 7801 1563

💲💲💲

5

Castillo de la Real Fuerza

W2 **O'Reilly e/Tacón y Avenida del Puerto** **7801 7490** **9:30am–5pm Tue-Sun**

This fortress (castillo) was built in 1558–77 to protect the city from pirate attacks, following a raid by the French buccaneer Jacques de Sores in 1555, in which the original fort was destroyed and Havana devastated. Despite its moat and thick walls, the castle soon proved to be quite inadequate as a defensive bulwark because of its poor strategic position, too far inside the bay. Consequently, the castle became the residence of governors, military commanders and leading figures, as well as a safe place to store treasures brought from America and en route to Spain.

In 1634, a weathervane known as La Giraldilla was placed on the lookout tower, which soon became the symbol of Havana. The original is on display in the entrance and a copy has been placed on the tower. In 1851, part of the fortress's façade was demolished to enable Calle O'Reilly to be extended to the waterfront. This street was named for Alejandro O'Reilly, an Irishman who

↑ The moat encicling the 16th-century Castillo de la Real Fuerza

became a Spanish military commander in the 18th century and who advised King Carlos III of Spain on improving Havana's defences after the British invasion of 1762.

Today, the fortress houses a shipwreck museum with displays of artifacts, jewels and a large model of the naval ship Santísima Trinidad.

6

La Bodeguita del Medio

V2 **Calle Empedrado, 207** **7867 1374** **10:30am-11:30pm daily**

Standing exactly at the halfway point in a typical small street in old Havana, a few steps away from the cathedral, La Bodeguita del Medio (literally, "little shop in the middle") has become a big attraction.

The bodega was founded in 1942 as a place for the local population to trade rice, beans, sugar and other goods. A bar serving alcoholic drinks was added and the place became a haunt for intellectuals, artists and politicians. Today it is no longer a shop but a bustling bar at the front serves shots of rum and Cuban cocktails and a good restaurant hidden in the back offers typical Creole dishes. Take the time to admire the

↑ A traditional live music performance at La Bodequita del Medio

walls of the iconic bar, which are plastered with photographs, drawings, graffiti and visitors' autographs, including those of famous patrons such as the singer Nat King Cole, poets Pablo Neruda and Nicolás Guillén, and the writers Gabriel García Marquez, Alejo Carpentier and Ernest Hemingway, who was a regular here. You'll find a note on the wall, supposedly from the American author, proclaiming "My Mojito in La Bodeguita; My daiquiri in El Floridita". Unfortunately, it is a forgery and the slogan in fact originated as a marketing ploy dreamt up by the owners of La Bodeguita del Medio in the 1950s. Despite it's inauthenticity, the classic drink to order here is still the "Hemingway Mojito".

PICTURE PERFECT
Local Life

In Havana's plazas you will often see women in full-length traditional costumes carrying floral baskets. Licensed by the City Historian's Office, they will pose for photographs in exchange for tips.

7 **8**

Centro Cultural Félix Varela

V2 **Tacón e/Chacón y Mercaderes** **7862 6989** **8am-6pm Mon-Fri, 8am-noon Sat** **1 Jan, 26 Jul, 10 Oct, 25 Dec**

This building was erected by the Jesuits in the mid-18th century to house a seminary first founded in 1689. Famous Cuban intellectuals and patriots studied here, including Padre Félix Varela (1788–1853), who laid down the theoretical bases for the Cuban war of independence *(p52)*. The Catholic cultural centre that now occupies the building takes its name from this Cuban hero.

The large central courtyard is the only one of its kind in Cuba: it has galleries on three levels, the first with simple columns, the second with double columns and the third with plain wooden piers.

The ornate inner stairway leading to the first floor has trapezoidal motifs instead of the more common arch, and fine black mahogany banisters.

El Templete

W2 **Plaza de Armas, Calle Baratillo y O'Reilly** **9am-5pm Tue-Sun** **1 Jan, 1 May**

Small and austere, this Neo-Classical building, resembling a temple, stands on the spot where, legend has it, the city was founded in 1599. Here, under a leafy ceiba – a tropical tree considered sacred by all natives of Central America – the first meeting of the local government and the first Mass reputedly took place. A ceiba still stands in front of El Templete, although it is not the original. Next to it is the Columna de Cacigal, named after the governor who had it built in 1754.

El Templete, completed in 1828, was modelled after a monument in the town of Guernica in northern Spain. Inside are three huge canvases by Jean-Baptiste Vermay, depicting scenes from the history of Havana.

STAY

Hotel Santa Isabela
A palatial hotel in an unbeatable location.

W2 **Calle Baratillo, 9** **gaviotahotels.com**

$ $ $

Casa Vitrales
You'll find eclectic furnishings and a superb rooftop breakfast here.

U2 **Calle Habana, 106** **cvitrales.com**

$ $ $

Loma del Ángel
This chic *casa particular* has two suites.

V2 **Calle Cuarteles, 104** **lomadel angel.com**

$ $ $

↑ The unassuming Neo-Classical exterior of El Templete

Did You Know?

The Mezquita Abdallah (*Calle Oficios, 18*) is the only mosque in Cuba. Only Muslims may enter it.

⑨

Calle Oficios

⊘ W3

One of the capital's oldest streets, Calle Oficios is among only four in existence from the end of the 16th century. It was originally a link between the military centre of Plaza de Armas and Plaza de San Francisco (*p78*), the city's commercial hub. Together with Calle Obispo, this is one of the most atmospheric streets in Old Havana and most of the façades date from the 18th and 19th centuries.

The street is bisected by the Plaza de San Francisco. At the intersection you will find a bronze statue of El Caballero de París (The Gentleman of Paris), who roamed Havana's streets in the 1950s engaging passersby in discussions about philosophy and politics. North of the plaza is the 18th-century **Casa de los Arabes**. It displays 18th- and 19th-century Hispanic-Arab bronzes, fabrics, rugs and furn- iture in three permanent and two temporary exhibitions rooms. This ethnographic display of Arab objects serves as

evidence of the presence of an old Lebanese, Syrian and Palestinian colony in Cuba.

South of Plaza de San Francisco is the **Coche Mambí**, a handsome green-and-white train coach dating from 1900. For several decades from 1912, it served as the official railway accommodation for presidents of Cuba. Visitors can board to look at the plush reception room, dining rooms and lounge, which all have dark wood panelling, and the neatly fitted bedroom and kitchen.

Casa de los Arabes

🅐 Calle Oficios, 16 📞 7801 1868 🕒 9:30am– 5pm Tue–Sat, 9:30am–1pm Sun

Coche Mambí

⊛ 🅐 Calles Oficios y Churruca 🕒 9:30am– 5:30pm Tue–Sat, 9:30am–1pm Sun

→ Life-size statue of El Caballero de París, by José Villa Soberón (2001), on Calle Oficios

↑ Tables in front of the Taquechel pharmacy on Calle Obispo

⑩

Calle Obispo

⊘ V3

The liveliest and most characteristic street in La Habana Vieja is like a long, narrow bridge linking the two architectural souls of the historic centre, the colonial and the Art Nouveau-eclectic. At one end is the Plaza de Armas, the Cuban Baroque heart of the old city, while at the other is Avenida Bélgica and the famous El Floridita restaurant, marking the start of the more modern district. The street name comes from the residence of the city bishop (*obispo*), on the corner of Calle Oficios.

Restoration work promoted by the Oficina del Historiador de la Ciudad has salvaged the best buildings, so Calle Obispo retains the elegance, vivacity and colours of the colonial period. There is plenty to see on an afternoon stroll here:

perfected the original recipe. The new-style cocktail, a blend of white rum, lemon, sugar and a few drops of maraschino and ice, was devised with the help of Ernest Hemingway, who was a regular. Today, in luxurious El Floridita, besides Constante's classic cocktails you can feast on lobster and other shellfish in the company of a bust of the great novelist, sculpted by Fernando Boada.

Casa del Agua la Tinaja
🏠 Calle Obispo, 111 🕐 10am-7pm daily

Taquechel
🏠 Calle Obispo, 155 🕐 9am-4:30pm daily

Hotel Ambus Mundos
🏠 Calle Obispo, 153
🌐 gaviotahotels.com

No 117–19 is the oldest house in Havana, and there's also the small **Casa del Agua la Tinaja**, which for centuries has been dispensing well water purified by very old but still efficient ceramic filters. Here, you'll find a plaque on the left-hand side of the Palacio de los Capitanes Generales, bearing quotations made by the great Cuban patriot José Martí concerning Garibaldi's stop at Havana.

Don't miss the fascinating **Taquechel**, an old pharmacy which sells cosmetics and natural and homeopathic products, all created and produced in Cuba. Quaint shelves hold a collection of pretty 17th- and 18th-century glass and Italian majolica jars, alembics and antique objects.

One of the major sights in the street is the restored **Hotel Ambos Mundos**. This eclectic hotel is rich in literary links. Hemingway stayed here for long periods from 1932 to 1939, and began writing *For Whom the Bell Tolls* in room 511.

El Floridita restaurant is known as "the cradle of the daiquiri". Here, in the 1930s, barman Constante (real name Constantino Ribalaigua)

El Floridita
🏠 Calle Obispo, 557
🌐 floridita-cuba.com

⓫
Calle Mercaderes
🗺️ V2

Curling north to south through the heart of the restored quarter between Plaza de la Catedral and Plaza Vieja, narrow Calle Mercaderes (Street of Merchants) is lined with little museums and shops. It is home to the Mural Artístico-Histórico *(p68)*, as well as the **Maqueta de Centro Histórico**, which houses a scale model of Habana Vieja, and the **Museo del Tabaco**.

On the next block, the **Armería 9 de Abril** museum recalls an assault by Fidel's revolutionaries on this former gun shop.

Maqueta de Centro Histórico
♿ 🏠 Calle Mercaderes, 116
🕐 9am-6pm daily

Museo del Tabaco
🏠 Calle Mercaderes, 120
🕐 10am-5pm Mon-Sat

Armería 9 de Abril
🏠 Calle Mercaderes, 157
🕐 1-5pm Mon, 9am-5pm Tue-Sat

SHOP

Habana 1791
This perfumery sells traditional fragrances.
🗺️ V2 🏠 Calle Mercaderes, 176
📞 7861 3525 🕐 Sun pm

Centro Cultural Almacenes de San José
Havana's largest artisan market.
🗺️ W4 🏠 Av de los Desamparados y Calle San Ignacio 📞 7864 7793

Museo de Chocolate
Artisan confectionary is for sale here.
🗺️ W3 🏠 Calle Mercaderes, 251
📞 7866 4431

→

Customers sampling fragrances at Habana 1791 on Calle Mercaderes

12

Casa de la Obra Pía

📍 V2 🏠 Calle Obra Pía, 158, esq Mercaderes ☎ 7861 3097 🕐 9:30am–5pm Tue-Sat, 9:30am–12:30pm Sun 🚫 1 Jan, 26 Jul, 10 Oct, 25 Dec

Calle Obra Pía (literally Charity Street) was named after this mansion, which earned its moniker from the pious actions of Martín Calvo de la Puerta y Arrieta. A wealthy Spanish nobleman, he lived here in the mid-17th century and gave an annual dowry to five orphan girls. A century later the residence became the home of Don Agustín de Cárdenas, who was elevated to marquis for taking Spain's side in 1762 during the British occupation (p51).

A jewel of Cuban Baroque architecture, its upper rooms have colonial furnishings and ornaments. The mansion also houses a museum of sewing machines and an art gallery.

At the corner of calles Obra Pía and Mercaderes is the **Casa de México**, a cultural centre reflecting the close links between Mexico and Cuba. It has a library and a museum with handmade glass, silver and other objects. Opposite is the **Casa de Guayasamín**, which displays works by the Ecuadorean painter Oswaldo Guayasamín (1919–99).

Casa de México

♻ 📍 V2 🏠 Calle Obra Pía, 116 ☎ 7861 8166 🕐 9am–2:30pm Tue-Sun

Casa de Guayasamín

📍 W2 🏠 Calle Obra Pía, 112 ☎ 7861 3843 🕐 9am–4:30pm Tue-Sun

↑ The yellow façade of Casa de la Obra Pía, with its turquoise windows

13

Casa de África

📍 V3 🏠 Calle Obra Pía, 157, e/ San Ignacio y Mercaderes ☎ 7861 5798 🕐 9:30am–5pm Tue-Sat, 9am–1pm Sun 🚫 1 Jan, 26 Jul, 10 Oct, 25 Dec

Opposite the Casa de la Obra Pía is a 17th-century building, rebuilt in 1887 to house a family of plantation owners

← Roberto Fabelo's *Viaje Fantástico* (2012) on Plaza Vieja, showing a woman riding a cockerel

→ A restaurant, shaded beneath one of the arcades on Plaza Vieja

on the upper floor and a tobacco factory, worked by slaves, below. The building is now a museum containing more than 2,000 objects linked to the history of sub-Saharan Africa and the various ethnic groups taken into slavery. Many items belonged to the ethnographer Fernando Ortíz, a specialist in the African roots of Cuban culture. The museum includes sections on Afro-Cuban religions and batá drums, as well as a library.

Plaza Vieja

📍 V3

Laid out in 1559, this square was originally called Plaza Nueva (New Square). In the 19th century, after further city development, it lost its role as the city's main square and was renamed, but has since been restored to its original look.

Plaza Vieja is surrounded by arcades and several historic buildings from four centuries. In the middle of the square, you'll find the surreal *Viaje Fantástico* statue, as well as a replica of a fountain dating from 1796.

Don't miss the **Casa de los Condes de Jaruco**. This mansion was once the home of the Countess de Merlin, a Cuban romantic novelist who also wrote a travel book about Cuba. The edifice of the building is a fusion of Baroque and Spanish Moorish styles. Today, it houses an art gallery.

On the corner of calles Muralla and Mercaderes is the eye-catching Art Nouveau Hotel Palacio Cueto, which was built in 1908. On the east side of the plaza, the **Planetario** has high-tech interactive exhibits, while **Fototeca de Cuba** holds photographic exhibitions.

> **Plaza Vieja is surrounded by arcades and several historic buildings from four centuries. In the middle of the square you'll find *Viaje Fantástico*.**

GREAT VIEW
Real-Life Movie

For a sweeping view of La Habana Vieja ascend to the rooftop of Edificio Gómez Villa on Plaza Vieja. Here, a Cámara Oscura (a revolving peep-hole camera) projects a real-time panorama onto a screen.

La Factoria Plaza Vieja, on the southwest corner, is a lively brewpub.

Casa de los Condes de Jaruco
📍 V3 📞 7862 2633 🕒 Daily

Planetario
🎟 📍 W3 📍 Calle Mercaderes, 311 e/Teniente Rey y Muralla 🕒 10am-3:30pm Wed-Sun

Fototeca de Cuba
📍 W3 📍 Mercaderes, 307 e/ Teniente Rey y Muralla 🕒 10am-5pm Tue-Sat

La Factoria Plaza Vieja
📍 V3 📍 San Ignacio y Muralla 🕒 11am-midnight daily

SANTERÍA

Different religions co-exist in Cuba as the result of its history. Both the Roman Catholicism of the Spanish conquerors and the practices of the African slaves have survived. The most widespread of the African faiths is Santería.

SANTERÍA'S BELIEFS

Also called Regla de Ocha, Santería (Way of the Saints) is based on the beliefs of Yoruba slaves, with some additional Christian elements. The main Santería god is Olofi, the creator divinity, similar to the God of Christianity but without contact with Earth. The gods who mediate between him and the faithful are the orishas, who listen to the latter's prayers.

↑ An offering during a Santería ritual taking place on a Cuban street

THE ORISHAS

Obatalá
A hermaphrodite god and the chief intermediary between Olofi and humankind.

Oshún
The goddess of love lives in rivers and corresponds to the Virgen del Cobre (p259).

Yemayá
The sea goddess and mother of orishas wears blue. She is capable of both great sweetness and great anger, and is linked with the Virgen de la Regla (p132).

Changó
The virile and sensual god of fire and war adores dancing and corresponds to St Barbara.

↑ A Santería altar with Christian, secular and personal offerings

 15

Iglesia de Nuestra Señora de la Merced

V4 ⌂ Calle Cuba, 806, esq Merced ☎ 7863 8873 ⏰ 8am–noon, 3–5pm Mon–Sat, 8am–1pm Sun

Construction of this church began in 1637 but ended only in the following century, while the lavish decoration of the interior dates from the 19th century. The church is popular among those who follow Santería, a local Afro-Cuban religion. According to their beliefs, Our Lady of the Merced corresponds to a Yoruba divinity, known as Obatalá, principal figure among the gods and the protector of mankind, who imparts wisdom and harmony.

 16

Iglesia del Espíritu Santo

V4 ⌂ Calle Cuba, esq Acosta ☎ 7862 3410 ⏰ 9:30am–noon Tue–Sun, 3–6pm Tue, Thu & Sat, 3–5pm Wed & Fri

The Church of the Holy Ghost (Espíritu Santo) is one of the oldest Roman Catholic churches in Havana. It was built in 1637 by freed African slaves. Thanks to a papal bull and a royal decree from Carlos III, in 1772 it acquired the exclusive right to grant asylum to all those persecuted by the authorities.

From an architectural standpoint, the building's most striking feature is the extremely tall tower. The church was radically rebuilt in the 19th century, and it retained the Hispanic-Arab look, which once defined the building, only in the characteristic double pitch roof.

→ Rich decoration in the nave of the Iglesia de Nuestra Señora de la Merced

 17

Museo-Casa Natal de José Martí

V4 ⌂ Calle Leonor Pérez, 314, e/ Egido y Picota ☎ 7861 3778 ⏰ 9:30am–4:30pm Tue–Sat, 9:30am–12:30pm Sun ⏰ 1 Jan, 1 May, 26 Jul, 10 Oct, 25 Dec

This modest 19th-century building in the Paula quarter became a national monument thanks to the importance attached to José Martí, the object of great patriotic veneration. The author and national hero, who died in combat on 19 May 1895 during the wars of independence against the Spanish, was born here in 1853. After his death his mother, Leonor Pérez, lived here and when she died it was rented to raise money to bring up her grandchildren. In 1901, it was bought by the municipality after city-wide fundraising, and became a museum in 1925.

The historic house has been beautifully restored and faithfully furnished, and contains paintings and first editions of the writer's works. Objects of great historic value include the inkpot and ivory pen used by Máximo Gómez and José Martí to sign the *Manifesto de Montecristi*, marking the beginning of the war against Spain. Everyday objects include the penknife Martí had in his pocket when he died, and the album with dedications and signatures from friends on his marriage to Carmen Zayas-Bazán.

→

Plaza de San Francisco, with its imposing basilica and ornate fountain

18

Plaza de San Francisco

📍 W3

Bordering the port, this picturesque square has an Andalusian character and evokes images of a distant age when galleons loaded with gold and other cargo set sail for Spain. In the middle of the square is the Fuente de los Leones, modelled on the famous fountain in the Alhambra in Granada. This work by the Italian sculptor Giuseppe Gaggini was donated in 1836 by the fiscal superintendent, Don Claudio Martínez de Pinillos, Count of

Did You Know?

The railway line along the harbourfront is only used by an antique steam train hauling tourists.

Villanueva, and for many years it supplied the ships docked here with drinking water.

The original commercial nature of the area can be seen in two buildings: the Aduana General de la República (the old customs house), built in 1914, and the Lonja del Comercio (the former stock exchange, 1908), with a dome crowned by a statue of Mercury, the Roman god of commerce. It houses the offices of some of the top foreign firms now operating in Cuba.

The most important building in the square by far, however, is the **Basílica Menor y Convento de San Francisco de Asís**, built in 1580–91 as the home of the Franciscan community and partly rebuilt in the 1700s. The three-aisle interior has a Latin cross layout and contains a wooden statue of St Francis. The

basilica also holds the remains of major Havana citizens, including the Marquis González, who died during the British siege of 1762.

Because of its exceptional acoustics, this church has been converted into a concert hall for choral and chamber music every Saturday at 6pm.

In the cloister and rooms of the adjacent monastery, which dates back to 1739, is a museum of holy art with

→

An enchanting statue in the courtyard of the Museo del Ron

visitors see exhibits that explain the fermentation, distillation, filtration, blending and bottling processes. The central hall has a fascinating model of an *ingenio* (sugar plantation), including a miniature steam train. Tours end in a bar where visitors can relax and sample three-year-old rum and cocktails made from younger bottles of rum. There's often live music here too.

 INSIDER TIP
Ferry Tale

Hop on the funky *lancha* (ferry) that runs between the Emboque de Luz terminus and Regla for a fabulous vista of the Havana waterfront. It costs a mere 20 centavos (you'll need *peso cubano*).

⑳ Catedral Ortodoxa Nuestra Señora de Kazán

 W3 Avenida del Puerto é Sol y Santa Clara 7802 2962 10am-3pm daily

Surrounded by Spanish colonial buildings, the Russian Orthodox Our Lady of Kazán Cathedral rises incongruously over the waterfront. Built to a classical Byzantine design, it features voluptuous cupolas capped in bronze and an interior adorned with gold-leaf-backed murals.

Completed in 2008, its construction was funded by the Soviet Embassy to symbolize Cuban-Russian friendship. It serves the Russian Orthodox offspring of Soviet personnel who once lived in Cuba.

㉑ Alameda de Paula

W4

This short waterfront promenade forms part of the rebirth of the Havana bayside area. With trees, benches and balustrades, the promenade is marked at its southern end by the small Iglesia de Paula, once the chapel of a 17th-century hospital. Today, it hosts classical music concerts. Across the road is Havana's largest craft market, the Antiguo Almacenes San José.

Nearby, the waterfront **Museo del Automóvil** has an eclectic selection of vehicles, including a Bel-Air Chevrolet once owned by Che Guevara.

Museo del Automóvil
 Avenida del Puerto 9:30am-4:30pm Tue-Sat, 9am-1pm Sun 1 Jan

18th- to 19th-century missals, votive objects and 16th- to 18th-century ceramics.

Basílica Menor y Convento de San Francisco de Asís
7801 2524 9:30am-4:30pm Tue-Sat 1 Jan, 1 May, 26 Jul, 10 Oct, 25 Dec

⑲ Museo del Ron

W3 Calle San Pedro, 262 Museum: 9am-5pm Mon-Thu, 9am-4pm Fri-Sun; bar: 9:30am-midnight havanaclubmuseum.com

The manufacture of Havana Club, the most famous brand of Cuban rum, is explored at this museum. Visuals and models explain the production process of the spirit described as the "cheerful child of sugar cane" by Cuban writer Fernando Campoamor.

The tours begin in the courtyard of the Havana Club Foundation. After watching a brief film about sugar cane,

↑ Gold-leaf murals in the Catedral Ortodoxa Nuestra Señora de Kazán

← The Art Deco interior of Edificio Bacardí, an iconic Havana landmark

 23

Iglesia de San Francisco de Paula

🅆W4 **🄰Alameda de Paula y Calle San Ignacio** **🕘9am-5pm daily**

This lovely little church occupies the Plazuela de Paula, at the southern end of the Alameda de Paula. Built in 1745, the church was originally in the shape of a Latin cross, with an octagonal cupola, and was attached to a women's hospital. The latter was demolished in 1907 by the Havana Railroad Company but the church, despite its grave disrepair, was saved from demolition by a popular public outcry.

The pre-Churrigueresque (late Spanish Baroque) façade is adorned with pilasters, with alcoves containing statues, and topped by a triple bell-cot. It also features beautiful *vitrales* (stained-glass windows) by prominent Cuban artists Nelson Domínguez and Rosa María de la Terga. The bright interior is also enhanced by a permanent collection of works of art by other significant contemporary artists.

The church, which has a fine 19th-century organ, is today Havana's premier venue for concerts of ancient and sacred music.

> 🔍 HIDDEN GEM
> **Plaza del Cristo**
>
> Long overlooked by visitors, this restored plaza is now an after-dark destination, with several cool cafés and bars, including El Chanchullero cocktail bar and the tiny El Dandy (*www.barel dandy.com*).

 22

Edificio Bacardí

🅀U3 **🄰Avenida de Bélgica, 261**

An astounding example of Art Deco architecture, the former headquarters of the Bacardi rum corporation is a classic Havana landmark and, on completion in 1930, was the city's tallest building.

Designed by Cuban architect Esteban Rodríguez, the stunning 12-storey edifice was constructed with two-tone pink Bavarian granite. The structure is further adorned with glazed terracotta motifs depicting naked nymphs by the American artist Maxfield Parrish, known for his Neo-Classical influences.

Inside, the lobby is clad entirely with triple-tone European marble, symbolizing Bacardí's white, gold and dark *añejo* rums, and features etched glass, gold leaf and ornamental brass in which bats – the Bacardi symbol – feature prominently. A giant bronze bat is perched on top of the Mesopotamian-inspired bell tower too.

Appearing as if made of Lego® bricks, the building, which was renovated in 2001 by the Office of the Historian of the City, currently houses various offices and is not open to the public except for the Café Barrita. This wood-panelled mezzanine bar overlooks the exuberant foyer and was frequented by socialites in the 1950s. Just don't expect to be able to buy a Bacardi rum here! As a leading supporter of the US embargo, the company is derided in Cuba.

A small tip to the staff in the lobby will grant you access to the rooftop, which offers amazing views over the cityscape of Havana.

Iglesia del Ángel Custodio

◉ U2 **⌂ Calle Compostela, 2, esq Cuarteles** **☎ 7861 0469** **⏱ 8:30am–6pm Mon–Fri, 8:30am–noon Sun**

Built in 1693 on the Peña Pobre or "Loma del Ángel" hill, first as a hermitage and then transformed into a church in 1788, the Neo-Gothic Ángel Custodio looks rather insipid and unreal as a result of vigorous "restoration".

In a key position between the former presidential palace, which is now home to the Museo de la Revolución (*p92*), and the old town, the church has literary connections. The 19th-century Cuban novelist Cirilo Villaverde used the Loma del Ángel hill as the setting for his story *Cecilia Valdés*, which told of the tragic love affair between a Creole woman and a rich white man.

The famed independence leaders Félix Varela and José Martí (*p101*) were both baptized in this church.

→ The historic Iglesia del Ángel Custodio

↑ A vintage steam train in a park on Avenida del Bélgica

Avenida del Bélgica

◉ U2

Known colloquially by its pre-revolutionary name – Monserrate – Avenida del Bélgica runs south from the Museo de la Revolución (*p92*) and follows the empty space that was left when the 9-m-(30-ft-) tall colonial city wall, the Cortina de la Habana, was removed in 1863. Remnants of the wall, which was built between 1671 and 1797, are still standing in front of the museum, most notably at the southern end of Bélgica. Here, a former

arsenal rises over the Parque de los Agrimensores, at Calle Arsenal. In this park, you'll find around a dozen antique steam trains, which once hauled sugar cane. The trains are displayed here because the park adjoins Havana's grandiose Estación Central de Ferrocarriles (Central Railway Station). With its two towers, the station is a melting pot of Spanish Revival and Italian Renaissance architecture.

Further to the south, the Puerta de la Tenaza is the only remaining example of the original nine city gates, built by the Spanish.

DRINK

Bar Dos Hermanos
This harbourfront bar was one of writer Ernest Hemingway's favourite drinking spots. The cocktails, still as good as they were in the writer's day, and live music make a visit worthwhile.

◉ W3 **⌂ Avenida del Puerto, 305** **☎ 7861 3514**

El Chanchullero
An immensely popular bohemian hole-in-the-wall on Plaza del Cristo, serving mouth-watering tapas dishes and killer cocktails.

◉ U3 **⌂ Calle Brasil** **🌐 el-chanchullero.cm**

Dulcería Bianchini
This tiny Swiss-run café makes excellent cappuccinos and other coffees, as well as cakes. There's another branch at Calle Sol 12.

◉ W3 **⌂ Callejón del Chorro** **☎ 7862 8477**

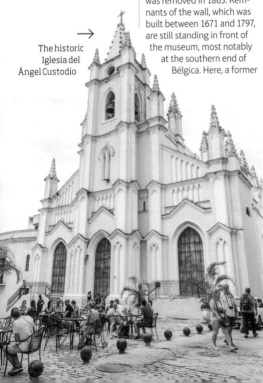

A SHORT WALK
PLAZA DE LA CATEDRAL

Distance 600 m (1,968 ft) **Time** 15 minutes
Nearest bus route P5

Dominated by the elegant profile of its church, Plaza de la Catedral is one of the symbols of La Habana Vieja. A 16th-century plaque in the square marks the spot where the Zanja Real, the city's first aqueduct (and the first Spanish aqueduct in the New World) was located. Reaching the square in 1592, it began at the Almendares river, 11 km (7 miles) away, and was built to provide water to ships docking in the harbour, as well as to local residents. The surrounding aristocratic buildings and present-day cathedral were built in the 18th century. An amble around Plaza de la Catedral is an essential activity for anyone visiting the historic centre. Women in colonial costume stroll under the arcades and read fortunes, and there are several bar-restaurants where you can relax in the shade and listen to music.

The modern entrance of the 18th-century **Seminario de San Carlos y San Ambrosio** echoes the Baroque decorative motifs of the cathedral.

Former entrance to the seminary

CALLE SAN IGNACIO

Centro Wifredo Lam, housed in an 18th-century palazzo, promotes contemporary art with exhibitions and lectures.

Casa de la Condesa de la Reunión, a 19th-century building surrounding a splendid courtyard, is the headquarters of the Alejo Carpentier Foundation.

START

CALLE EMPEDRADO

La Bodeguita del Medio (p70) is legendary thanks to Ernest Hemingway, who came here to drink mojitos.

The **Taller Experimental de Gráfica** holds theoretical and practical courses in graphic art for Cubans and foreigners, and houses a Gallery of Engravings.

← Ordering a mojito in the iconic La Bodeguita del Medio

↑ The atmospheric surroundings of the Plaza de la Catedral at twilight

Locator Map
For more detail see p64

LA HABANA VIEJA

The Baroque façade of **Catedral de San Cristóbal** *(p68), declared a national monument, is considered one of the most beautiful in the Americas.*

CALLE TACÓN

FINISH

Did You Know?

Palacio del Marqués de Arcos was once the main post office; the letter box is still visible on its wall.

CALLE EMPEDRADO

CALLE MERCADERES

Palacio del Conde Lombillo *is home to the Historiador de La Habana, which hosts temporary exhibitions of photographs, paintings and lithographs.*

PLAZA DE LA CATEDRAL

Palacio del Marqués de Arcos, *built in the 1700s, houses an art gallery where handicrafts and prints are on sale.*

Palacio de los Marqueses de Aguas Claras *was built in the second half of the 18th century. It is now a bar-restaurant, El Patio, with tables in the inner courtyard as well as in the picturesque square.*

CALLEJÓN DEL CHORRO

CALLE SAN IGNACIO

Dating from 1720, the **Museo de Arte Colonial** *(p69) is one of the city's finest examples of early colonial domestic architecture. It houses an exhibition of colonial furniture and objects.*

0 metres   40
0 yards   40

N ↑

CENTRO HABANA AND PRADO

Centro Habana has the air of an impoverished aristocrat – a noble creature whose threadbare clothes belie a splendid past full of treasures. This varied quarter developed beyond La Habana Vieja's city walls (which ran parallel to present-day Avenida Bélgica and Avenida de las Misiones) during the 1800s and was initially built to provide housing and greenery for the citizens. Most of the construction in the area took place after 1863, when the walls began to be demolished to make more land available. The work was finally completed in the 1920s and 30s, when French architect Jean-Claude Nicolas Forestier landscaped the area of the Paseo del Prado, the Parque Central, the Capitolio gardens and Parque de la Fraternidad.

The building of the Capitolio here shows the area's status in the early 20th century, but by the 1950s affluent families were evacuating the area for Miramar and Vedado. When the Cuban-Soviet partnership collapsed in the 1990s the buildings continued to deteriorate, but restoration work is gathering pace and luxurious new hotels are springing up in the area.

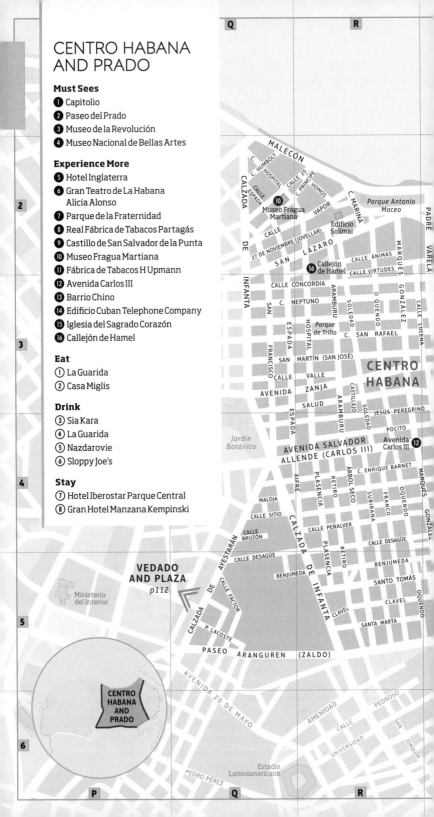

CENTRO HABANA AND PRADO

Must Sees
1. Capitolio
2. Paseo del Prado
3. Museo de la Revolución
4. Museo Nacional de Bellas Artes

Experience More
5. Hotel Inglaterra
6. Gran Teatro de La Habana Alicia Alonso
7. Parque de la Fraternidad
8. Real Fábrica de Tabacos Partagás
9. Castillo de San Salvador de la Punta
10. Museo Fragua Martiana
11. Fábrica de Tabacos H Upmann
12. Avenida Carlos III
13. Barrio Chino
14. Edificio Cuban Telephone Company
15. Iglesia del Sagrado Corazón
16. Callejón de Hamel

Eat
1. La Guarida
2. Casa Miglis

Drink
3. Sia Kara
4. La Guarida
5. Nazdarovie
6. Sloppy Joe's

Stay
7. Hotel Iberostar Parque Central
8. Gran Hotel Manzana Kempinski

VEDADO AND PLAZA p112

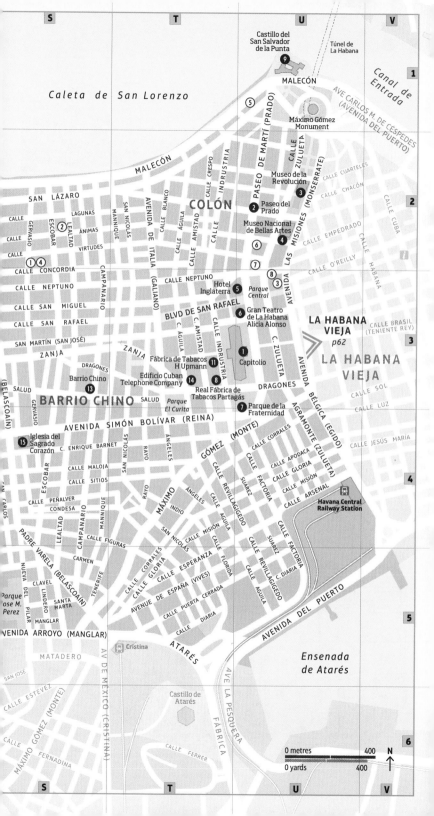

S

T

U

V

Castillo del
San Salvador
de la Punta
9

Túnel de
La Habana

1

MALECÓN

Canal de
Entrada

AVE CARLOS M. DE CÉSPEDES
(AVENIDA DEL PUERTO)

Caleta de San Lorenzo

⑤

Máximo Gómez
Monument

MALECÓN

PASEO DE MARTÍ (PRADO)

CALLE ZULUETA

CALLE CUARTELES

CALLE CHACÓN

Museo de la
Revolución
3

CALLE CRESPO

CALLE INDUSTRIA

LAS MISIONES (MONSERRATE)

CALLE CUBA

SAN LÁZARO

LAGUNAS

ÁNIMAS

VIRTUDES

SAN NICOLÁS

MANRIQUE

AVENIDA DE ITALIA (GALIANO)

CALLE BLANCO

AVENIDA DE

CALLE AGUILA

CALLE AMISTAD

CALLE

COLÓN

Paseo del
Prado
2

Museo Nacional
de Bellas Artes
⑥   **4**

CALLE EMPEDRADO

CALLE HABANA

2

CALLE
GERVASIO

ESCOBAR

LEALTAD

②

CALLE CONCORDIA

①④

CALLE NEPTUNO

CALLE SAN MIGUEL

CALLE SAN RAFAEL

SAN MARTÍN (SAN JOSÉ)

ZANJA

CAMPANARIO

CALLE NEPTUNO

BLVD DE SAN RAFAEL

ZANJA

C. AGUILA

C. AMISTAD

CALLE INDUSTRIA

Hotel
Inglaterra ⑤

Parque
Central

Gran Teatro
de La Habana
Alicia Alonso
6

⑦

⑧
③

AVENIDA

C. ZULUETA

CALLE O'REILLY

i

LA HABANA
VIEJA
p62

CALLE BRASIL
(TENIENTE REY)

3

LA HABANA
VIEJA

DRAGONES

Barrio Chino
13

BARRIO CHINO

Fábrica de Tabacos
H Upmann **11**

Edificio Cuban
Telephone Company **14**

SALUD

Parque
El Curita

Real Fábrica de
Tabacos Partagás
8

Capitolio
1

DRAGONES

Parque de la
Fraternidad
7

CALLE SOL

CALLE LUZ

AVENIDA BÉLGICA (EGIDO)

SALUD

GERVASIO

AVENIDA SIMÓN BOLÍVAR (REINA)

GÓMEZ (MONTE)

CALLE CORRALES

AGRAMONTE (ZULUETA)

CALLE JESÚS MARÍA

4

Iglesia del
Sagrado
Corazón **15**

ESCOBAR

C. ENRIQUE BARNET

CALLE MALOJA

CALLE SITIOS

CALLE PEÑALVER

CONDESA

RAYO

ANGELES

SAN NICOLÁS

MÁXIMO

GÓMEZ (MONTE)

INDIO

CALLE CORRALES

CALLE APODACA

CALLE GLORIA

CALLE MISIÓN

CALLE ARSENAL

SUAREZ

FACTORIA

Havana Central
Railway Station

CALLE FIGURAS

CAMPANARIO

MANRIQUE

LEALTAD

CARMEN

PADRE VARELA (BELASCOAÍN)

ANGELES

SAN NICOLÁS

CALLE MISIÓN

CALLE CORRALES

CALLE GLORIA

CALLE ESPERANZA

CALLE FLORIDA

AGUILA

CALLE REVILLAGIGEDO

SUAREZ

C. DIARIA

NUEVA DEL
PILAR

CLAVEL

SANTA
MARTA

MANGLAR

LINDERO

Parque
José M.
Perez

AVENIDA ARROYO (MANGLAR)

TENERIFE

AVENUE DE ESPAÑA (VIVES)

CALLE PUERTA CERRADA

CALLE DIARIA

CALLE FACTORIA

CALLE REVILLAGIGEDO

AGUILA

AVENIDA DEL PUERTO

5

MATADERO

SAN JOSÉ

Cristina

ATARÉS

AV DE MÉXICO (CRISTINA)

AV LA PESQUERA

Ensenada
de Atarés

CALLE ESTEVEZ

MÁXIMO GÓMEZ (MONTE)

CALLE

FERNADINA

Castillo de
Atarés

FÁBRICA

CALLE FERRER

0 metres   400

0 yards   400

N
↑

6

S

T

U

V

❶ ⊘ Ⓜ 🖐

CAPITOLIO

📍 U3 🏛 Paseo de Martí (Prado), esq San José
📞 7801 1535 🕐 10am–3pm Tue & Thu–Sat, 10am–
12pm Wed & Sun

A symbol of the city, the Capitol (Capitolio) combines the elegance of Neo-Classicism with Art Deco elements. After an extensive renovation, in 2018 it returned to its original role as the seat of Cuba's government.

↑ The iconic dome dominating the Captiolio's exterior

Standing in an area once occupied by a botanical garden and later by the capital's first railway station, the Capitol is a loose imitation of that in Washington, DC, but is even taller – the dome was the highest point in the city until the 1950s. During Machado's rule, the building witnessed many major historic events and, after the revolution it became the headquarters of the Ministry of Science, Technology and the Environment.

Did You Know?

The Salón de los Pasos Perdidos (Hall of Lost Steps) takes its name from its unusual acoustics.

The Statue of the Republic stands at 17 m (56 ft) high and weighs 49 tons. It is the world's third tallest statue.

National Library of Science and Technology

The Chamber of Deputies is decorated with bas-reliefs by Gianni Remuzzi.

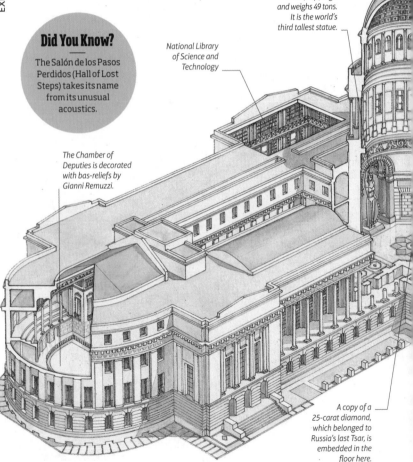

A copy of a 25-carat diamond, which belonged to Russia's last Tsar, is embedded in the floor here.

Timeline

1929
△ Gerardo Machado inaugurated the grand building.

1933
△ The police fired on a crowd gathered here during an anti-Machado demonstration.

1959
△ After the revolution, the government leaves the building.

2018
△ The National Assembly moves back to the building.

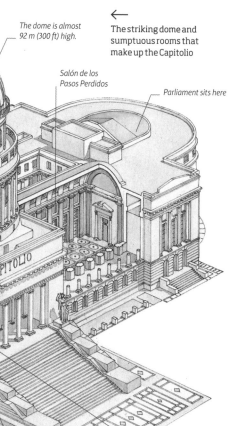

The dome is almost 92 m (300 ft) high.

Salón de los Pasos Perdidos

Parliament sits here

← The striking dome and sumptuous rooms that make up the Capitolio

PITOLIO

The bronze doors are ornamented with 30 bas-relief panels by Cuban sculptor Enrique García Cabrera.

Angelo Zanelliflank's 7-m- (20-ft-) high bronze sculptures represent work and virtue and each weigh 15 tonnes.

↑ The *Statue of the Republic*, covered in 22-carat gold leaf

↑ Salón de los Pasos Perdidos, with its marble floor

❷ 🍴 ☕ 🛍️

PASEO DEL PRADO

📍U2

The most picturesque boulevard in Havana is popular with locals at any time of the day – it's perfect for a gentle stroll and gossip in the shade of the trees, and at sunset, it becomes a lively haunt.

The Marquis de la Torre had the Paseo laid out in 1772 outside the city walls, and it rapidly became the favourite spot for city aristocrats to take their carriage rides. Bands were positioned in five spots along the boulevard to play for their enjoyment. The Paseo was used for military and carnival parades in the 19th century, when the paving was redone. In 1927 the French architect Jean-Claude Nicolas Forestier designed the Paseo as we see it today: it was widened and decorated with bronze lions and marble benches. Along this majestic promenade, you'll find some of Havana's grandest buildings, including historic hotels that inspired novels, as well as theatres and mansions. Although many of these are in a state of disrepair, they retain their charm.

↑ Strolling down the tree-shaded Paseo del Prado

Hotel Sevilla

Palacio de los Matrimonios

The building at the corner of Calle Virtudes, richly decorated and with mudéjar arches, shows many architectural influences and is typical of Havana.

GRAHAM GREENE IN HAVANA

The classic espionage thriller *Our Man in Havana* (1958), by the English author Graham Greene, is an excellent description of Havana at the eve of the revolution. In the book Greene narrates the adventures of a vacuum cleaner salesman who becomes a secret agent against his will. The novel is imbued with a dry sense of humour, and is set against an intriguing environment filled with casinos and roulette wheels, New York skyscrapers and decadent Art Nouveau villas, cabarets and prostitution. The Hotel Sevilla is a constant presence throughout.

Did You Know?

The street's official name is Paseo de Martí, but everyone calls it by its old name, "Prado".

Dr Carlos Finlay, who discovered that mosquitoes spread yellow fever, lived here.

Casa del Científico was the residence of José Miguel Gómez, second President of the Republic of Cuba.

Elegant wrought-iron street lamps and the multicoloured marble pavement were added in 1834.

The Art Deco Teatro Fausto was built in 1938 over the foundations of an old theatre of the same name.

The Escuela Nacional de Ballet (National School of Ballet) is housed in a three-story Renaissance-style palace.

↑ The different buildings lining the majestic Paseo del Prado

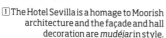

1 The Hotel Sevilla is a homage to Moorish architecture and the façade and hall decoration are *mudéjar* in style.

2 Civil weddings are celebrated under this ornate ceiling in the Palacio de los Matrimonios.

3 Eight imposing bronze lions, symbolizing Havana, were added to the boulevard in 1927.

3 🗓️ 🎥 💻 🛍️

MUSEO DE LA REVOLUCIÓN

📍U2 🏠 Calle Refugio, 1, e/ Avenida de las Misiones y Zulueta 📞 7801 5491 🕐 9:30am–5pm daily (last entry 4:15pm)

Once the presidential palace of the overthrown dictator Fulgencio Batista, it is symbolic that this building now houses the Museum of the Revolution.

Designed by the Cuban architect Rodolfo Maruri and the Belgian architect Paul Belau, the presidential palace was inaugurated in 1920 by Mario García Menocal, and it remained the residence for all subsequent presidents until 1965. The building has Neo-Classical elements, and was decorated by Tiffany of New York. It contains works by the leading Cuban decorators of the early 1900s and by sculptors such as Juan José Sicre, Esteban Betancourt and Fernando Boada. In stark contrast, the museum features documents, photographs and memorabilia presenting an overview of the Cubans' struggle for independence from the colonial period on, focusing in particular on the 1959 revolution – from the guerrilla war to the "Special Period" in the 1990s.

→
The former presidential palace's grand exterior and luxurious rooms

GRANMA MEMORIAL

The large glass-and-cement pavilion behind the museum contains the yacht *Granma* (named after its first owner's grandmother). In 1956, this boat brought Fidel Castro and some of his comrades from Mexico to Cuba to begin the struggle against Batista. The yacht is now immortalized in the museum to remind visitors of Castro's bravery and willpower.

The third floor contains photos and memorabilia from colonial times to 1959.

The side wing of the palace was home to Batista's office.

↑ A dome topping the Museo de la Revolución's exterior

1. The monumental staircase still bears bullet marks shot on 13 March 1957 by students on a mission to kill Batista. The dictator saved his life by escaping to the upper floors.

2. Lined with vast mirrors *(espejos)*, the Salón de los Espejos has frescoes by Cuban painters Armado Menocal and Antonio Rodríguez Morey.

3. The collection features many revolutionary paintings.

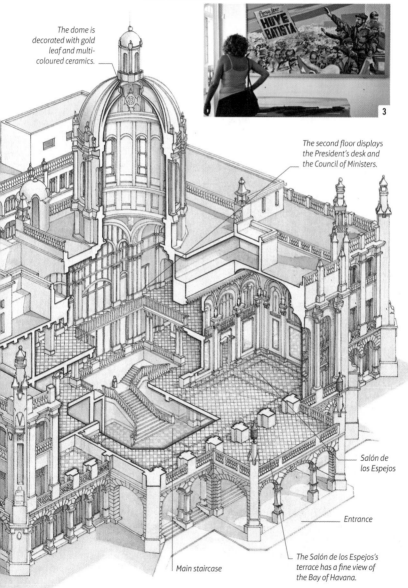

The dome is decorated with gold leaf and multi-coloured ceramics.

The second floor displays the President's desk and the Council of Ministers.

Salón de los Espejos

Entrance

The Salón de los Espejos's terrace has a fine view of the Bay of Havana.

Main staircase

↑ The striking exterior of the Palacio de Bellas Artes, housing Cuban art

MUSEO NACIONAL DE BELLAS ARTES

U2 **Palacio del Centro Asturiano: San Rafael, e/ Zulueta y Monserrate; Palacio de Bellas Artes: Calle Trocadero, e/ Zulueta y Monserrate** **9am-5pm Tue-Sat, 10am-2pm Sun** **1 Jan, 1 May, 26 Jul, 10 Oct, 25 Dec** **bellasartescuba.cult.cu**

The finest art gallery in the whole of Cuba, the Museo Nacional de Bellas Artes (National Fine Arts Museum) is housed in two distinct 20th-century buildings. The grand former Palacio de Bellas Artes is dedicated to Cuban art, while works from all around the world are displayed in the eclectic Palacio del Centro Asturiano.

The Museo Nacional de Bellas Artes was founded in 1913 thanks to the efforts of the architect Emilio Heredia, its first director. After frequent moves, the collections eventually found a definitive home in the block once occupied by the old Colón market. The original design was changed when the arcades of the building were demolished and in 1954 the new Palacio de Bellas Artes was inaugurated, a Rationalist building with purely geometric lines designed by the architect Rodríguez Pichardo. Once the collection expanded after the 1959 revolution, the Palacio del Centro Asturiano, which was designed in 1927 by architect Manuel del Busto and overlooks the Parque Central, was taken over by the museum and the collection was split geographically across the two sites.

Locator Map
For more detail see p86

1 European works, together with the collection of ancient art, are on display in the Palacio del Centro Asturiano.

2 A visitor admires a piece by a contemporary Cuban artist in the Palacio de Bellas Artes.

3 Cuban sculptor Rita Longa's marble *Form, Space and Light* (1953), at the entrance to the Palacio de Bellas Artes, is characterized by a fluid concept of volume.

PALACIO DEL CENTRO ASTURIANO (INTERNATIONAL)

The collection of international art comprises paintings and sculptures displayed in specific sections. These include ancient art, the Middle Ages, Italy, Germany, Flanders, the Netherlands, Great Britain, France and Spain. There are also works from various European schools, the United States and Latin America.

The Collection

Among the finest works in the collection are the 17th-century Flemish paintings and 19th-century Spanish pictures. In his *Entre Naranjos* (1903), Joaquín Sorolla depicts a banquet in the Spanish countryside, using the play of the figures, light and shadow to create an Impressionist-like atmosphere. The same can be said of the movement of the water and the garden in the background in *Clotilde en los Jardines de la Granja*, which is a portrait of the artist's wife. Other Spanish artists include Murillo and Zurbarán.

The Italian collection includes a group of landscape paintings, including one by Canaletto: *Chelsea College, Rotunda, Ranelagh House and the Thames* (1751), in which the painter brilliantly renders the atmosphere of London. Other Italian works are *St Christopher* by Jacopo Bassano (c 1515–92), *Alpine Landscape with Figures* by Alessandro Magnasco (1667–1748) and *The Spinstress* by Giovanni Battista Piazzetta.

The ancient art section exhibits Greek, Roman and Egyptian works, as well as Mesopotamian, Phoenician and Etruscan finds. The Fayoum portraits are especially interesting, but the *Panathenaean Amphora* is one of the most important pieces in the collection. This terracotta pot, in the black figure style, once belonged to the Count de Lagunillas.

 TOP 5 ARTISTS TO LOOK OUT FOR

Guillermo Collazo
His technical portraits represent Cuban art in the 19th century.

Joaquín Sorolla
A 20th-century Spanish painter, Sorolla is renowned for his use of light.

Augustín Cárdenas
This Cuban sculptor was influenced by the European avant-garde and African art.

Hans Memling
The *Virgin and Child* triptych exemplifies why this artist was one of the great masters of Flemish painting.

Wilfredo Lam
Mixing Cubism and Surrealism, this Cuban painter is shown in the Palacio de Bellas Artes.

Did You Know?

After Sorolla's death, his widow - Clotilde - left many of his paintings to the Spanish public.

DRINK

Café del Edificio de Arte Universal
Decorated with beautiful mosaics depicting a work by Spanish painter Diego Velázquez, this café is a great place for a coffee during the day or a drink in the evening.

⌂ Ground floor, Palacio del Centro Asturiano

Joaquín Sorolla's ↑ *Clotilde en los Jardines de la Granja* (1907)

↑ Contemporary Cuban art on display in the Palacio de Bellas Artes

PALACIO DE BELLAS ARTES (CUBAN ART)

The permanent exhibition of 18th–21st-century Cuban art offers a complete overview of works by individuals and schools, and highlights the leading trends in each period. The temporary exhibition of prints and drawings, as well as of paintings, adds variety and richness to the permanent collection.

The Collection

Two of the major figures on display are painter Wifredo Lam and sculptor Agustín Cárdenas. Don't miss Lam's *La Silla* (1943), which shows a Cubist chair with a vase on it set in the magical context of the jungle, or Cárdenas's *Figure* (1953). The free play of volumes in the wooden sculpture, less than 1 m (3 ft) high, expresses to the full the African-derived sensuality that informs Cárdenas's style.

Cuban art in the 19th century, characterized by its technical skill, is represented by the portraits of Guillermo Collazo and landscapes by the Chartrand brothers.

The intrepid pioneers of modern Cuban art are particularly interesting. One of these is Víctor Manuel García, an exceptional landscape painter who conveys peaceful atmospheres with silently flowing rivers and figures with sinuous movements. There are also several works by Amelia Peláez, who revived the still-life genre by merging Cubism and specifically Cuban motifs.

After the victory of the revolution in 1959, Cuban art embraced extremely varied styles. Servando Cabrera first took guerrillas as his subject and then made an erotic series.

Of the leading artists of the 1970s there are works by Ever Fonseca, Nelson Domínguez, and illustrator Roberto Fabelo, who has a unique style. Look out for *El Malecón* (1975) by Manuel Mendive, which depicts the city's famous promenade as if it were a sacred site.

Among the younger artists, Tomás Sánchez, with his archetypal landscapes, and José Bedia, with his bold installations, stand out.

 INSIDER TIP
Take a Tour

The Museo Nacional de Bellas Artes offers a variety of tours to visitors, ranging from specialized talks on French paintings to guides examining the depiction of women in paintings from around the world. There are also apps and games available for kids and tours geared especially towards teenagers.

> **Don't miss Lam's *La Silla* (1943), which shows a Cubist chair with a vase on it set in the magical context of the jungle, or Cárdenas's *Figure* (1953).**

EXPERIENCE MORE

Hotel Inglaterra

📍 T3 📍 Paseo de Martí (Prado), 416, esq San Rafael 🌐 hotelinglaterra-cuba.com

Although this hotel is built in the style of late 19th-century Havana Neo-Classical architecture, its soul is *mudéjar* (Moorish). The fine ochre, green and gold majolica tiles of the interior were imported from Seville, the foyer is decorated with Andalusian mosaics and the wooden ceilings are reminiscent of Moorish inlay. Plus, one of the columns in the *salón-café* bears a classical Arabic inscription: "Only Allah is the victor."

The Hotel Inglaterra dates from 1875, when a small hotel merged with the lively Le Louvre night spot and its adjacent ballroom. The pavement outside the hotel, known as the "Louvre sidewalk"', was an animated meeting point for Havana liberals. It was here that the young José Martí *(p101)* advocated the total separation of Cuba from Spain, as opposed to more moderate liberal demands for autonomy. It's historical importance continued as General Antonio Maceo, a hero of the wars of Cuban independence, prepared plans for the insurrection in this hotel.

Among the many illustrious guests who stayed here were the great French actress Sarah Bernhardt, star of Alexandre Dumas' *La Dame aux Camélias*, and the Russian ballet dancer Anna Pavlova, here to perform at the Gran Teatro de La Habana Alicia Alonso.

Gran Teatro de La Habana Alicia Alonso

📍 U3 📍 Paseo de Martí (Prado) y San Rafael 📞 7861 7391 🕐 9am–5pm Tue–Sun

One of the largest opera houses in the world, the Gran Teatro de La Habana Alicia Alonso is part of the monumental Palacio del Centro Gallego (1915). Designed by Belgian architect Paul

→

Traffic passing the Gran Teatro de La Habana Alicia Alonso

STAY

Hotel Iberostar Parque Central

On Parque Central, this hotel has spacious rooms and good service.

📍 U2 📍 Calle Neptuno e/ Prado y Zulueta 🌐 iberostar.com

$$$

Gran Hotel Manzana Kempinski

Cuba's first truly deluxe hotel has a rooftop bar, overlooking a luxurious infinity pool.

📍 U3 📍 Calle San Rafael e/ Monserrate y Zulueta 🌐 kempinski.com

$$$

Belau, the structure was built to host the social activities of Havana's large and affluent Spanish community.

The magnificent façade is decorated with four sculpture groups by the Italian sculptor Giuseppe Moretti, depicting

Charity, Education, Music and Theatre. The building was constructed over the foundations of the Teatro Nuevo or Tacón, and from 1837 to the early 20th century this was the venue for performances by world-famous artists, including the Austrian ballet dancer Fanny Essler, who made her debut here in 1841. In the mid-19th century Antonio Meucci, the inventor of the "talking telephone", worked here as a stagehand, and his invention was patented in the US, thanks to the support of the Gran Teatro's impresario.

The theatre was inaugurated on 22 April 1915 with a performance of Verdi's opera, *Aida*, and became a stage for great dramatic occasions. Sarah Bernhardt performed here in 1918, and the pianist Arthur Rubinstein the following year. Cuban composer Ernesto Lecuona and the great Spanish guitarist Andrés Segovia have also appeared.

In 1959 the Gran Teatro, though continuing its purpose as a concert hall and theatre, also became the "home" of Alicia Alonso, the great Cuban ballet dancer. She founded the dance company Ballet Nacional de Cuba, which is still based in the capital, and she was responsible for organizing the inaugral Festival Internacional de Ballet de La Habana (*p48*).

After a sensitive and meticulous renovation project, which lasted two years, the theatre reopened in 2016. The building now looks particularly magnificent at night when the exterior is majestically illuminated by golden light.

7 Parque de la Fraternidad

📍 U3

The spacious area of greenery behind the Capitol was called Campo di Marte (Parade Ground) during the 19th century, because it was close to the Paseo Militar, which was used frequently for army drill. In 1928 it became known as the Parque de la Fraternidad, and it commemorates Cuba's common roots with the other people of Latin and North America, with monuments to major historical figures such as the Mexican politician Benito Juárez, the Venezuelan Simón Bolívar and US president Abraham Lincoln.

In the middle of the park is a gate with a plaque which bears a heartfelt exhortation by José Martí: "It is time to gather and march together united, we must go forward as compact as the silver in the depths of the Andes. Peoples unite only through bonds of friendship, fraternity and love."

Beyond the gate is a monument to American friendship and solidarity: a large ceiba – a tree sacred to both the indigenous people and the slaves taken to the

↑ Benito Juárez bust, one of the memorials in the Parque de la Fraternidad

New World. It was planted here around 1920, symbolizing the long-standing bond between the peoples.

In front of the square is a white marble fountain, sculpted in 1831 by Giuseppe Gaggini. The fountain is known as the "Fuente de la India" or "La Noble Habana" – an allegorical representation of the city.

Nowadays the Parque de la Fraternidad is usually full of old American cars, most of which are operated as private taxis or used for guided tours.

CLASSIC AMERICAN CARS

From open-topped Ford Model Ts from the 1920s, to the stylish Ford Thunderbird, or "T-bird", of the 1950s, classic American cars add to Cuba's time-warped splendour. You'll find cars that are eight decades old on Cuba's roads, with nearly one in six predating the revolution. These four-wheeled survivors of a bygone era are kept running by their resourceful owners, despite decades of US embargoes. Many serve as taxis and some offer sightseeing tours.

Real Fábrica de Tabacos Partagás

♀ T3 🏠 San Carlos, 813
☏ 7879 1459

Cuba's largest cigar factory, with its Neo-Classical façade, is a good example of 19th-century industrial architecture. It was founded in 1845 by the ambitious Catalan business-man Jaime Partagás Ravelo, who never revealed the sources of his tobacco leaves or how they were processed. In fact, the only information that survives is that he was the first person to use wooden barrels to ferment the leaves in order to heighten the aroma.

With the profits made from his high-quality cigars, Partagás bought a plantation in the province of Pinar del Río. He wanted to oversee all aspects of the cigar-making process personally, from growing the plants to the placing of a wrapper leaf around the filler and binder leaves rolled by the *torcedor* (p103). However, Partagás was assassinated in mysterious circumstances and the project failed. His factory was then purchased by another shrewd businessman, Ramón Cifuentes Llano.

On the tour, you will see dozens of people at work in

Statue of Francisco de Miranda at the Castillo de San Salvador de la Punta

the aroma-filled interior. Nowadays, there is no longer someone reading aloud to alleviate the monotony of the work by entertaining and educating the workers, as was the case in the 19th century (Partagás himself introduced this custom to Cuba), but there is a loudspeaker that alternates reading passages with music and news on the radio. Connected to the factory is La Casa del Habano, an excellent shop with a back room that is used for sampling cigars.

Castillo de San Salvador de la Punta

♀ U1 🏠 Malecón y Paseo de Martí (Prado) ☏ 7860 3195
🕐 10am-6pm Wed-Sun

A modest fortified block on the west bank of the port entrance, this *castillo* (fortress) played a crucial role in the past as part of the defence system of the capital. Today, it is a modest three-room museum comprising naval-themed exhibits along with displays on the history of the fortress.

> 📷 PICTURE PERFECT
> **Panoramic Park**
> The Parque de la Punta sits in front of the fortress and is lined with benches. Come here at sunset for an awesome view of the fort. For the perfect picture, capture a brave local jumping into the sea in front of the fort.

Designed by Giovanni Bautista Antonelli, Juan de Tejeda and Cristóbal de Roda, and built in 1590–1630, it was part of the city's first line of defence, together with the much larger Castillo de los Tres Reyes del Morro on the other side of the bay. A large floating chain of wooden and bronze rings, an ingenious device added by the Italian engineer Antonelli in the late 16th century, connected the two fortresses. It was stret-ched tightly as soon as an enemy ship was sighted, to block access to the port. In the open space in front of the Castillo are the three cannons to which the chain was tied.

The adjacent open space across the road has several attractions that are more important historically than artistically. In the middle is

↑ The Neo-Classical façade of the historic Real Fábrica de Tabacos Partagás

the equestrian statue of Generalissimo Máximo Gómez, the hero of the wars of independence, by Italian sculptor Aldo Gamba (1935). Behind this, you'll see a dilapidated chapel. Surprisingly, this building is still in use and regularly hosts stamp exhibitions and history lectures. It originally belonged to the Real Cárcel prison, where José Martí was kept for 16 years for subversive activities against the Spanish crown. Some cells still stand, as does a section of the wall against which some medical students were executed on 27 November 1871 as punishment for rebelling against Spanish rule. A sombre cenotaph in their honour stands in the Necrópolis de Colón (p116).

Museo Fragua Martiana

Q2 **Calle Principe, 108, esq Hospital** **7870 7338** **8am-4pm Mon-Sat**

The Museo Fragua Martiana (Museum of Martí's Forging) preserves a portion of the former San Lázaro quarry where, in 1870, 16-year-old José Martí was forced to break rocks after being sentenced to hard labour for sedition. The small museum displays shackles and other miscellany related to Martí's servitude and the independence movement he later led. A corner of the limestone quarry has been turned into a garden with a life-size bronze statue of the national hero. On 27 January, 1953, following Fulgencio Batista's coup d'état, students led by political activist Fidel Castro marched with flaming torches from the Universidad de La Habana (p121) to the

quarry to commemorate the centenary of Martí's birth and demand that Batista step down; La Marcha de las Antorchas is repeated on 27 January each year. Appropriately, the site is now overseen by the Universidad de La Habana.

> **A corner of the limestone quarry has been turned into a garden with a life-size bronze statue of the national hero.**

JOSÉ MARTÍ

Born to Spanish parents in Havana in 1853, José Martí (below) was already taking part in anti-Spanish conspiracies by the time he went to secondary school. This led to his being deported in 1868, and exiled in 1878. Known for his vigorous writing style, he was also a Modernist poet, an activist, a politician and a sensitive interpreter of the impulses of the human soul. In 1895, when he died in battle at Boca de dos Ríos, José Martí was only 42, but he had already been an influential figure in the revolutionary struggle and written poems, articles and essays that would be the envy of any author.

33

Brands of cigars
are produced
in Cuba.

Fábrica de Tabacos
H Upmann

📍T3 🚇Belascoain (Padre
Varela), 852 e/ Desagüe
📞7879 3927

Although bearing the name
of H Upmann – a German
who settled in Cuba in 1844
and founded the eponymous
cigar brand – this factory
was in fact built in 1914 by Cuesta
Rey & Co., whose name adorns
the gable. Confusingly, locals
refer to it as the Fábrica El
Rey del Mundo – a cigar
brand previously made at
this site – or Fábrica Romeo
y Julieta, a name it earned
when it was nationalized. As
of 2015, the factory was
renamed Fábrica Antonio
Briones Montoto, after a
revolutionary hero, but few

use this name today.
As with all Cuba's state-run
cigar factories, this factory
produces a variety of different
brands, but its tours set it
apart from La Corona Cigar
Factory and Real Fábrica de
Tabacos Partagás, the other
two *fábricas* which are open
for visits in Havana. The tour
takes in the sorting room,
packaging room and rolling
room, where you can peer
over the shoulders of the
torcedores (rollers).

12

Avenida Carlos III

📍R4

Laid out in 1850 during a
redevelopment of the city
under the supervision of
Captain Miguel de Tacón, this
boulevard (its official name
is Avenida Salvador Allende)
was designed to enable
troops and military vehicles
to travel from the Castillo
del Príncipe – built on the
Aróstegui hill in the late
1700s – to their parade
ground in the present-day
Parque de la Fraternidad
(p99). The middle section of
the boulevard was reserved

↑ The Grand National
Masonic Temple on
Avenida Carlos III

for carriages, while the two
pleasant avenues on either
side, with their benches, trees
and fountains, were designed
for pedestrians. First named
Alameda de Tacón or Paseo
Militar, the thoroughfare was
renamed Avenida Carlos III in
honour of the Spanish king
who encouraged Cuban
commerce and culture during
the 18th century.
   One of the most unique
buildings on the street is the
Grand National Masonic
Temple, which was built in
the mid-1900s and has a
globe on its roof.

Workers grading tobacco
in the packaging room of the ↑
Fábrica de Tabacos H Upmann

↑ A farmworker picking tobacco plants in the Valle de Viñales

CUBAN CIGARS

Cigars were used by the indigenous Indians and are now an inextricable part of Cuba's culture and history. After Columbus's voyage, tobacco, then regarded in Europe as having therapeutic qualities, was imported to Spain and, later, the rest of the world.

HOW CIGARS ARE MADE

Cigar manufacturing is a real skill that Cubans hand down from generation to generation. The tobacco plant *(Nicotiana tabacum)* is harvested between November and February. The leaves are tied in bunches and then dried in barns for 45 to 60 days. They are then transported to a *fábrica* (factory) where a *torcedor* (cigar roller) makes them into cigars. The *capote* (wrapper leaf) is rolled around the *tripa* (filler leaves), which have been selected for their flavour. This in turn is covered by the *capa* (the smooth leaf on the outside of the cigar). The cigar is then trimmed.

TOP 5 BRANDS OF CUBAN CIGARS

Montecristo
This best-selling brand earned its name because the novel *The Count of Monte Cristo* was often read by a lector on the cigar rolling floor.

Cohiba
The Cohiba was created for Fidel Castro in 1966 and was not available to the general public until 1982.

Partagas
This brand was established in Havana in 1845 *(p100)*.

Romeo y Julieta
Named after Shakespeare's play, this was Winston Churchill's favourite brand.

H Upmann
Boxes of these cigars depict the seven gold medals that have been awarded to the brand.

←
A *torcedor* rolling a *capote* around the *tripa* of a cigar by hand

⑬ Barrio Chino

🔲 S3

The Chinese quarter of Havana, the Barrio Chino, now occupies a small area defined by calles San Nicolás, Dragones, Zanja and Rayo. Its heyday was during the early 1900s, when Barrio Chino was home to around 10,000 Chinese people; it was the largest Chinatown in Latin America. The bustling area contained numerous Chinese businesses – including four Chinese-language newspapers – as well as community and cultural associations, which ran communal spaces such as the Chung Wah Casino. Much of the Cuban-Chinese population left after the

Did You Know?

Before the revolution, the Shanghai Theatre in Barrio Chino was the centre of Havana's red light district.

Cuban revolution in 1959, when businesses were nationalized by the Communist government.

Today, Barrio Chino is more of a historical record than a thriving Chinatown. All the Chinese shops are concentrated in the so-called Cuchillo de Zanja area (around the Zanja and Rayo crossroads). The architecture is not particularly characteristic,

except for the quarter gate, which is topped by a pagoda roof. Another, much more impressive portico, in the Ming and Ching styles, was constructed in 1998 at the corner of Calle Dragones and Calle Amistad. It is almost 19 m (62 ft) wide and was donated to Cuba by the Chinese government.

The Barrio Chino is also home to the Iglesia de la Caridad, dedicated to Cuba's patron saint *(p259)*. The church has a popular statue, of a Virgin with Asian features, which was brought here in the mid-1950s.

THE CHINESE COMMUNITY IN HAVANA

The first Chinese people arrived in Cuba in the mid-1800s to work in the sugar industry and were treated like slaves. Eventually gaining their freedom, they began to cultivate small plots of land in Havana, and in one of these, near the present-day Calle Salud, they grew Cuba's first mangoes. This fruit was an immediate and spectacular success with the local population. Chinese restaurants began to appear in the area after the second wave of Chinese immigrants arrived from California (1869-75), armed with their American savings. While maintaining their own cultural traditions, the Chinese community has embraced their Cuban identity, sharing in the island's lot and contributing to its development. A black granite column at the corner of Calle Linea and Calle L remembers the Chinese who fought for Cuban independence.

⑭ Edificio Cuban Telephone Company

🔲 T3 🏠 Calle Águila, 153, esq Dragones 📞 7860 7574 🕐 Sat & Sun

This was the tallest building in Havana at the time of its inauguration, in 1927, as the headquarters of the United States-owned Cuban American Telephone and Telegraph Company. Designed by architect Leonardo Morales, it is an astonishing example of flamboyant Spanish Plateresque architecture, towering 62 m (203 ft) over Barrio Chino, with its stepped façade ascending to an elaborate tower, which gleams in the light. Today, the ornate structure houses the offices of ETECA, the state-run Cuban telephone company.

Visitors to the building head straight for the Museo de la Telecomunicaciones on the ground floor. Relating the history of the telephone, the museum features interactive exhibits, including a functioning switchboard dating from 1910 and many other antique devices.

The magnificent altar of the Neo-Gothic Iglesia del Sagrado Corazón

↑ The grand exterior of the Edificio Cuban Telephone Company

Iglesia del Sagrado Corazón

S4 **Avenida Simón Bolívar (Reina), 463** **7862 4979** **7:30am–6pm Mon-Sat, 8am-noon & 3-5pm Sun**

Although incongruously hemmed in between apartment buildings, with its distinctive white steeple rising above the surrounding buildings of Centro Habana, the Church of the Sacred Heart of St Ignatius of Loyola can be seen from much of the city. The 77-m- (253-ft-) high spire, the tallest in Cuba, is topped by a 4-m- (13-ft-) high bronze cross. Colloquially known as Iglesia de la Reina, the church was designed by architect Eugenio Dediot in 1914, on the order of the Jesuit priest Luis Gorgoza, and is a rare example of the Neo-Gothic style in Cuba. It was consecrated in 1923 and has been holding services every day (at 8am and 9pm) since.

Dominating the façade is a figure of Christ resting on three columns decorated with a capital depicting the parable of the prodigal son, with 32 gargoyles inset on either side. The interior, with triple naves supported by six columns to each side and a floor inlaid with stone and mosaic glass tiles, has 69 elaborate stained-glass windows narrating the life of Christ, as well as a wealth of stuccowork and pointed arches. A Byzantine-style Sacred Heart with sculptures of saints and prophets is on the high altar. Crafted of alabaster, wood and bronze, it was made in Madrid.

EAT

La Guarida

Featured in the film *Fresa y Chocolate*, La Guarida claims to be Cuba's most famous restaurant and has served celebrities including Beyoncé. Set in a dilapidated tenement building, it serves superb Cuban fusion fare.

S2 **Calle Concordia, 418** **laguarida.com**

$$$

Casa Miglis

This Swedish-owned *paladar* serves international fusion dishes. Look out for the Swedish design touches inside this personality-filled townhouse.

S2 **Calle Lealtad, 120** **casamiglis.com**

$$$

Havana's Barrio Chino bathed in golden sunlight

↑ Salvador González Escalona's famous mural, with its Santería symbols

16

Callejón de Hamel

R2

This narrow, colour-drenched, two-block-long *callejón* (alley) in the working-class Cayo Hueso quarter is a curious open-air living art installation, cultural venue and visually stunning expression of Afro-Cuban ethnology. Its name derives from a legendary French-German resident called Fernando Belleau Hamel, a wealthy trader who owned much of this area and built housing for workers here in the early 20th century.

In 1990, self-taught artist Salvador González Escalona began decorating the alley outside his home with surreal street art infused with Santería symbols *(p76)*. His inspiration came from a desire to pay homage to his multi-ethnic cultural roots and his work represents all the religious cults and movements of African origin that are still active in Cuba today.

Extending for 200 m (656 ft), the murals cover entire building façades. The alley is studded with shrines to the orishas of Santería; images of African gods and Abakuá devils; a *Nganga*, one of the large cauldron-like pots used in Palo Monte, the religion of former Bantu slaves from the African Congo; and sculptures comprising bathtubs, typewriters and other repurposed objects.

Every Sunday at noon, Callejón de Hamel explodes with vivacious rumba performances, pulsating with the beat of *tambores* (drums), rhythmic chants and frenetic dancing, attracting locals and tourists alike. Residents have set up small bars, restaurants and shops selling hand-crafted religious objects along the street. González's own grotto-like home has been transformed into an art-festooned gallery.

One block to the east, the curvaceous Edificio Solimar apartment complex, designed in 1944 by Manuel Copado, is an astounding example of "Streamline" Art Deco.

 HIDDEN GEM
Copper Church

At Calle Manrique 570, you'll find the 19th-century Iglesia Nuestra Señora de la Caridad del Cobre (Church of Our Lady of Charity of Copper). Admire the Romanesque façade and then step inside to see the splendid gilt altar. The church draws both Catholics and adherents of Santería.

DRINK

Sia Kara
Highly regarded for its mojitos, this trendy bohemian bar occupies a loft-style lounge complete with off-beat furnishings.

U3 ☐ Calle Industria, 502 ☎ 7867 4084

La Guarida
After dining at La Guarida *(p105)*, head to the chic rooftop lounge bar for a cocktail.

S2 ☐ Calle Concordia, 418 ☐ laguarida.com

Nazdarovie
This Russian-themed bar-restaurant overlooks the Malecón.

U1 ☐ Malecón, 24 ☎ 7860 2947

Sloppy Joe's
Made famous by *Our Man in Havana*, this legendary bar is true to the 1918 original.

U2 ☐ Avenida Zulueta Calles Animas ☎ 7866 7157

THE MALECÓN

No other place represents Havana better than the Malecón, and no other place thrills tourists and locals so much. This seafront promenade winds for 7 km (4 miles) alongside the city's historic quarters, from the colonial centre to the skyscrapers of Vedado, charting the history of Havana from past to present.

The Malecón boasts some of the city's most unique architecture, including the "Ataud" (the coffin), a 1950s skyscraper whose name derives from the shape of its balconies, and the Caryatid building, which has Art Deco-style female figures supporting the loggia. Look out for the Monumento a las Víctimas del Maine *(p120)*, which stands in one of the wide stretches on the edge of Vedado. The area between Prado and Calle Belacoaín is known for its pastel buildings, faded in the sun and salty air. The Havana seafront is especially magical at sunset, when the colours of these buildings are accentuated.

↑ The imposing Monumento a las Víctimas del Maine

Timeline

1901

⏶ The Castillo de la Punta was identified as the starting point of the Malecón.

1902

⏶ The open space in front of the Prado was completed.

1921

⏶ After expansion, the Malecón stretched as far Calle 23.

1950s

⏶ As the fastest road in the city, traffic takes over the Malecón.

↑ People relaxing in front of the Malecón's ubiquitous pastel buildings

A SHORT WALK

AROUND THE PARQUE CENTRAL

Distance 2 km (1 mile) **Time** 25 minutes
Nearest bus stop Parque Fraternidad

Lying on the border of the old city and Centro Habana, between the Capitolio and the Prado promenade, the Parque Central was designed in 1877 after the old city walls were demolished. A statue of Isabella II was put in the middle of the square but was later replaced by one of José Martí. The park is surrounded by 19th- and 20th-century monumental buildings and adorned with palm trees. The heart of the city centre and a popular meeting place, it is a delightful place for a stroll. Towards evening, when the air is cooler, people gather here to talk until the small hours of the night about baseball, music and politics.

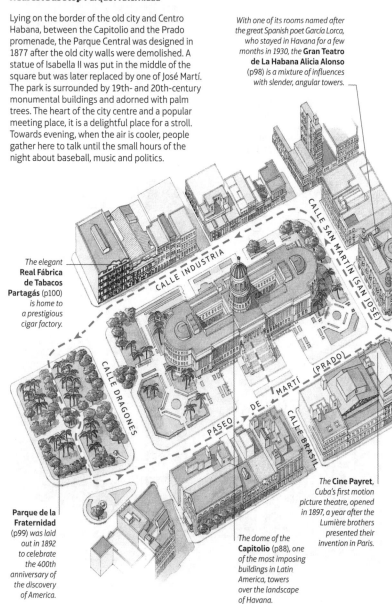

With one of its rooms named after the great Spanish poet García Lorca, who stayed in Havana for a few months in 1930, the **Gran Teatro de La Habana Alicia Alonso** *(p98) is a mixture of influences with slender, angular towers.*

The elegant **Real Fábrica de Tabacos Partagás** *(p100) is home to a prestigious cigar factory.*

Parque de la Fraternidad *(p99) was laid out in 1892 to celebrate the 400th anniversary of the discovery of America.*

The dome of the **Capitolio** *(p88), one of the most imposing buildings in Latin America, towers over the landscape of Havana.*

The **Cine Payret**, *Cuba's first motion picture theatre, opened in 1897, a year after the Lumière brothers presented their invention in Paris.*

↑ Elegant buildings and vintage cars along the popular Paseo del Prado

CENTRO HABANA AND PRADO

Locator Map
For more detail see p86

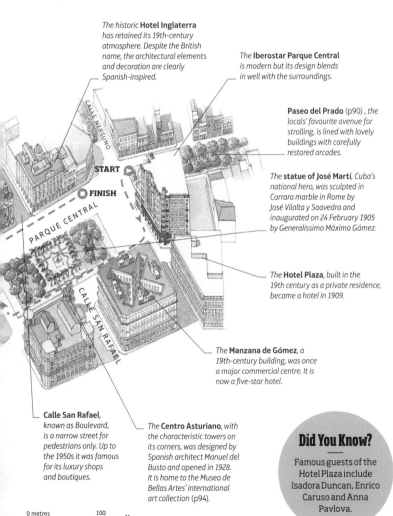

The historic **Hotel Inglaterra** *has retained its 19th-century atmosphere. Despite the British name, the architectural elements and decoration are clearly Spanish-inspired.*

The **Iberostar Parque Central** *is modern but its design blends in well with the surroundings.*

Paseo del Prado (p90) *, the locals' favourite avenue for strolling, is lined with lovely buildings with carefully restored arcades.*

The **statue of José Martí***, Cuba's national hero, was sculpted in Carrara marble in Rome by José Vilalta y Saavedra and inaugurated on 24 February 1905 by Generalissimo Máximo Gómez.*

The **Hotel Plaza***, built in the 19th century as a private residence, became a hotel in 1909.*

The **Manzana de Gómez***, a 19th-century building, was once a major commercial centre. It is now a five-star hotel.*

CALLE NEPTUNO

START ▶

● **FINISH**

PARQUE CENTRAL

CALLE SAN RAFAEL

Calle San Rafael*, known as Boulevard, is a narrow street for pedestrians only. Up to the 1950s it was famous for its luxury shops and boutiques.*

The **Centro Asturiano***, with the characteristic towers on its corners, was designed by Spanish architect Manuel del Busto and opened in 1928. It is home to the Museo de Bellas Artes' international art collection (p94).*

Did You Know?

Famous guests of the Hotel Plaza include Isadora Duncan, Enrico Caruso and Anna Pavlova.

0 metres 100
0 yards 100
↗ N

VEDADO AND PLAZA

The name Vedado ("prohibited") arose because in the 1500s, in order to have full view of any pirates approaching, it was forbidden to build houses and streets here. By the 19th century, however, the city needed this space to expand. The unusual grid plan of Vedado was the design of the engineer Luis Yboleón Bosque in 1859. It called for pavements 2-m (6-ft) wide, houses with a garden and broad straight avenues. In the late 19th and early 20th century the quarter was enlarged, becoming a prestigious residential area for many of the city's leading families and, today, it continues to be one of the most affluent areas of Havana.

Vedado has two different roles. It is Havana's modern cultural and political centre, with the Plaza de la Revolución at its heart; and it is also a historic quarter with a wealth of gardens and old houses with grand colonial entrances.

VEDADO AND PLAZA

Must Sees
1 Necrópolis de Colón
2 Memorial José Martí

Experience More
3 Plaza de la Revolución
4 Casa de las Américas
5 Parque Coppelia
6 Monumento a las Víctimas del *Maine*
7 US Embassy
8 Universidad de La Habana
9 Museo de Artes Decorativas
10 Museo Napoleónico
11 Parque John Lennon
12 Quinta de los Molinos

Eat
1 Café Laurent
2 La Chuchería
3 El Cocinero

Drink
4 Sarao
5 Fábrica de Arte
6 Café Madrigal
7 La Esencia

Stay
8 Hotel Nacional
9 Hotel Habana Libre
10 Casa Jorge Coalla Potts
11 Casa Blanca

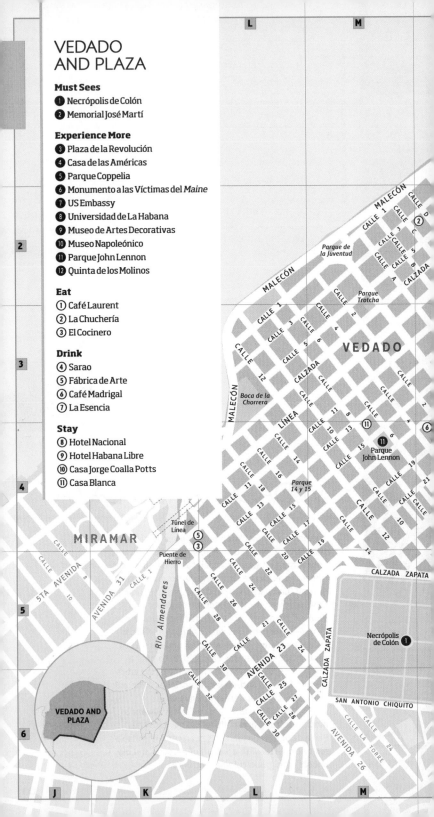

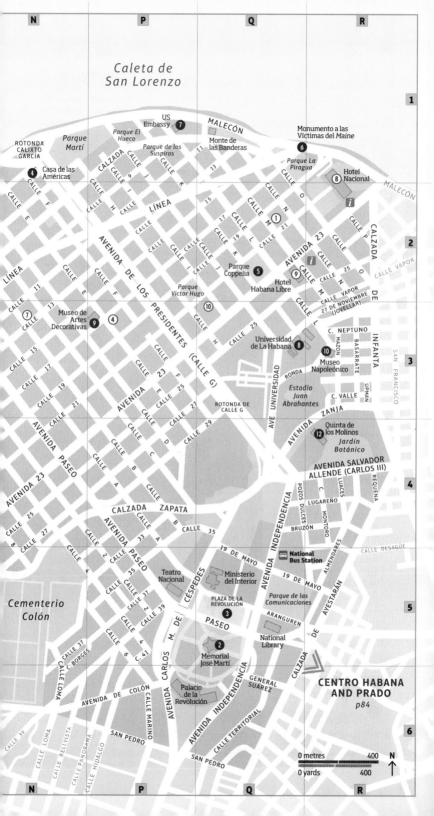

NECRÓPOLIS DE COLÓN

Did You Know?

A person who enjoys visiting graveyards is called a taphophile.

◉ M5 ⌂ Calle Zapata esq Calle 12 ☎ 7830 4517 ⏰ 8am–5pm daily

Havana's monumental Columbus Cemetery is one of the largest in the world, with 53,360 plots, where some two million people have been buried.

Built between 1871 and 1886, the cemetery was designed in the 1860s by the Spanish architect Calixto de Loira, who based the layout on the rigorously symmetrical plan of Roman military camps. Because of the many sculptures and monuments in different styles – from eclectic to the boldest expressions of contemporary art – the Necrópolis has been proclaimed a national monument. Although it is full of fascinating funerary art, it is still the cemetery for, and of, Havana's citizens.

LA MILAGROSA

"The Miraculous One" is the tomb of Amelia Goyri de la Hoz, who died in childbirth in 1901. She and the child were buried together. According to legend, a few years later the tomb was opened and she was found intact, holding her baby in her arms. Amelia became a symbol of motherly love, the protector of pregnant women and newborn children. Future mothers pilgrimage to her tomb to ask for her blessing.

[1] Monumento a los Bomberos, a monument to the 25 firefighters who died in an 1890 fire, stands near the Capilla Central. The red-roofed chapel sits in the middle of Avenida Colón, the cemetery's main avenue.

[2] This delicate 1950s marble bas-relief – La Piedad de Rita Longa – adorns the black marble tomb of the Aguilera family.

[3] The cemetery's main entrance is topped by a statue in Carrara marble of the three theological virtues – Faith, Hope and Charity – sculpted in 1904 by José Vilalta de Saavedra.

↑ An angel-topped tomb and many other graves in the Necrópolis de Colón

2 ⊘ Ⓜ️ 🛍️

MEMORIAL JOSÉ MARTÍ

📍 Q5 🏛️ Plaza de la Revolución 📞 7882 0906
🕐 9:30am–4:30pm Mon-Sat

Havana's tallest structure, this striking monument is a fitting tribute to Cuba's national hero, the intellectual and independence advocate José Martí *(p101)*, whose statue kneels at the foot of the tower in a meditative pose.

Work on this monument, located in the middle of the Plaza de la Revolución, began in 1953, on the 100th anniversary of the birth of Cuba's national hero, and was finished in 1958. It consists of a 109-m (358-ft) tower representing a five-pointed star and is built of grey marble from the Isla de la Juventud. At the base of the tower, the 18-m- (59-ft-) high white marble statue of José Martí was carved on site by Juan José Sicre. The actual Martí Memorial is in the interior of the base. The foot of the monument also houses two rooms containing manuscripts, portraits and mementos of Martí, while a third room describes the history of the monument and a fourth puts on contemporary art exhibitions. The Sala de Actos is an auditorium used for concerts, lectures and poetry readings. The real highlight, however, is the mural in the lobby which uses pithy quotations from Martí.

Did You Know?

The monument stands on a hill 30 m (100 ft) above sea level.

The towering Memorial José Martí, fronted by a statue of the national hero ↑

GREAT VIEW
On High
On clear days, the mirador on top of the tower, which is the highest point in Havana, affords views over the entire city. You can even see the sea from here.

↑ The iconic image of Che Guevara glowing at dusk

↑ The view from the memorial taking in the Palacio de la Revolución

EXPERIENCE MORE

③
Plaza de la Revolución

Q5

Plaza de la Revolución, Cuba's political, administrative and cultural centre since 1959, was designed in 1952 under the Batista regime. Formerly the Plaza Cívica, it was renamed following Fidel Castro's victory.

The sober monumental architecture wins no beauty prize, but the square is an important place. Here were held the first mass rallies after the revolution and festivities for the campaign against illiteracy in 1961. Military parades and official celebrations have often seen more than a million people gather, as speakers take their place on the podium next to the statue of José Martí.

A huge steel sculpture of Che Guevara adorns the exterior of the Ministry of the Interior, accompanied by the words *Hasta la victoria siempre* (Always strive for victory). To the east, the Ministerio de Información y Comunicaciones has a similar metal image of Comandante Camilo Cienfuegos, with the slogan *Vas bien Fidel* (You're doing well, Fidel).

EAT

Café Laurent
Located in an upscale penthouse, this restaurant serves delicious nouvelle Cuban cuisine.

Q2 **Calle M 257**
7832 6890

ⓈⓈⓈ

La Chuchería
This Miami-style sports bar on the Malecón has Havana's best pizza.

N2 **Avenida 1ra e/ C y D** **7830 7908**

ⓈⓈⓈ

El Cocinero
Sumptuous restaurant serving gourmet fare and tapas, with an open-air rooftop bar.

K4 **Calle 26 e/ 11 y 13**
elcocinerocuba.com

ⓈⓈⓈ

↑ The striking interior of the Parque Coppelia ice cream parlour

④
Casa de las Américas

 N1 🏛 Calle 3ra, esq G ⏰ 8:30am–4pm Mon-Fri 📅 1 Jan, 1 May, 26 Jul, 10 Oct, 25 Dec 🌐 casa.cult.cu

On the Malecón, beyond the Monumento a las Víctimas del *Maine*, there is a kind of secular temple, with a bell tower but no cross. This is the Casa de las Américas, a cultural institution, which was built in just four months following the triumph of the Cuban revolution. Haydée Santamaría, one of the heroines of the struggle, founded the institution with the aim of promoting exchanges among artists and writers across the American continent.

The centre features the Arte Nuestra América, the world's most comprehensive collection of Latin-American painting and graphic art, with contemporary works dating from the 1960s to the present day.

→
Detail from the lofty monument to the *Maine* victims

⑤
Parque Coppelia

Q2 🏛 Calle 23 y L 📞 7832 6149 🚪 Mon

Occupying an entire block at the top of La Rampa, the world's largest ice cream parlour was created in 1966 by Fidel Castro and fellow revolutionary Celia Sánchez (who named it after her favourite ballet) to offer an affordable indulgence for the masses. *La catedral de helado* (the ice cream cathedral) is a two-storey domed Modernist pavilion – which looks like a futuristic church-cum-flying saucer – able to seat hundreds at a time at communal tables. Despite the building's huge capacity, queues often extend around the block.

⑥
Monumento a las Víctimas del Maine

 R1 🏛 Malecón y Calle 17

This Neo-Classical monument was erected in 1925 to honour the 266 US sailors killed when the USS *Maine* exploded in Havana harbour in 1898, triggering the Spanish–American War. It comprises two ship's cannons tethered by an anchor chain at the base of twin Corinthian columns.

→
Students in the college library at the University of Havana

> INSIDER TIP
> **Get the Scoop**
>
> Coppelia is all about the shared experience. Don't let a queue director steer you toward a "tourist section" offering instant service at a higher price. Stay in line and you will pay less for your ice cream and can sit with the locals at one of the communal tables.

A bronze eagle that topped the monument was toppled by a mob after the failed Bay of Pigs invasion of 1961 *(p177)*. A plaque added by the Castro government reads: "To the victims of the *Maine*, who were sacrificed by imperialist voracity in its eagerness to seize the island of Cuba."

⑦
US Embassy

 P1 🏛 Malecón y L 🌐 cu.usembassy.gov

The handsome Modernist US Embassy has a commanding position on the Malecón. The sparsely elegant 1953 building of Jaimanitas stone was closed in 1961 when the US severed relations with Cuba. In 1977 it reopened as the US Interests Section, and became the US Embassy again on 20 July 2015, after President Obama renewed diplomatic relations.

The embassy looks east over 138 huge flagstaffs erected in 2006 to block anti-Castro messages posted by the Embassy. Beyond these, the Tribuna Abierta Anti-Imperialista (Anti-Imperialist Open Platform) is an ugly contrivance laid out in 1999 for anti-US demonstrations.

8

Universidad de La Habana

🗺 Q3 📍 Calle 27 de Noviembre (Jovellar) y Ronda

The University of Havana was founded under the auspices of a papal bull in 1728 and was initially in the Dominican monastery of St John Lateran, in the heart of La Habana Vieja. In 1902, a few days after the proclamation of the Cuban Republic, it was moved to the Vedado area.

The new university was built between 1906 and 1940. In front of the main entrance is the Alma Mater, the symbol of the university. This statue, of a woman with her arms outstretched in a gesture of welcome, was cast in 1919 in New York by the Czech sculptor Mario Korbel. In 1927 it was installed at the top of the

138

Flags placed at the US Embassy in 2006 for the years since the independence effort began in 1868.

broad granite stairs here. The grand entrance overlooks Calle San Lázaro, which broadens into a plaza where the ashes of Julio Antonio Mella – the Marxist leader of the Havana student movement in the 1920s – are kept.

The Science Faculty is home to the Felipe Poey Museum of Natural History, but the highlight here is the **Museo Antropológico Montané**, in the Mathematics Department. Founded in 1903, it displays exceptional Pre-Columbian finds from Cuba, such as the Idolo de Tabaco found on the island's eastern tip, the Idolo de Bayamo, one of the Caribbean's largest stone sculptures, and the Dujo de Santa Fe, a wooden ceremonial seat.

The oldest building is the austere Great Hall, housing allegorical paintings by Armando Menocal. It also contains the old University of San Gerónimo bell and the remains of Félix Varela, the Cuban philosopher and intellectual, brought to Cuba in 1911 from Florida, where he had died.

Museo Antropológico Montané

Felipe Poey Bldg, Plaza Ignacio Agramonte **📞 7877 4221** **🕘 9am-2pm Mon-Fri 🚫 1 Jan, 1 May, 26 Jul, 10 Oct, 25 Dec**

DRINK

Sarao

This chic, neon-lit nightclub draws Havana's trendsetters. Dress to impress.

🗺 P3 📍 Calles 17 y E **📞 7832 0433**

Fábrica de Arte

Boasting several bars, this eclectic entertainment venue is always buzzing. Arrive early to avoid long queues.

🗺 K4 📍 Calle 13, 61 **📞 7838 2260**

Café Madrigal

This bohemian, LGBT-friendly bar is found in the home of a renowned cinematographer. It serves great cocktails and plays great music.

🗺 N4 📍 Calle 17, 809 **📞 7831 2433**

La Esencia

A hugely popular bar in a Neo-Classical mansion, La Esencia is populated by Havana's *farándula* (in-crowd).

🗺 N3 📍 Calle B, 153 **🌐 esenciahabana.com**

Museo de Artes Decorativas

N3 **Calle 17, 502**
7832 0924 **9:30am–4pm Tue–Sat** **1 Jan, 1 May, 25 Dec**

The wonderful Museum of Decorative Arts is housed in the former residence of one of the wealthiest Cuban women of the 20th century: the Countess de Revilla de Camargo, sister of José Gómez Mena, the owner of the Manzana de Gómez (p111). A patron of the arts, she hosted gatherings of the era's noted intellectuals and celebrities.

The mansion was built in 1927, and is well worth a visit for its French Rococo-Louis XV furnishings, as well as for the inner gardens.

The collection of more than 33,000 works of art reveals the sophisticated and exotic tastes of the ruling classes and wealthy collectors of the colonial period. Major works of art on display here include two paintings by Hubert Robert, *The Swing* and *The Large Waterfall at Tivoli*, and two 17th-century bronze sculptures in the foyer.

The main hall on the Louis XV-style ground floor has 18th-century Chinese vases, Meissen porcelain, a large Aubusson carpet dating from 1722 and paintings by French artists. The dining room has walls covered with Italian marble as a backdrop to a collection of clocks.

A bedroom on the ground floor holds a collection of Chinese screens, while the Countess's room features a small desk that once belonged to Marie Antoinette.

Last, but not least, is the fabulous pink marble Art Deco bathroom, which should not be missed.

The sumptuous main hall of the beautiful Museo de Artes Decorativas *(inset)*

THE MOB IN HAVANA

In December 1946, mobsters Meyer Lansky and "Lucky" Luciano led a mafia summit in the Hotel Nacional with the aim of turning Havana into a criminal empire. When, in 1952, Batista enacted a coup, he gave the mob free rein for a cut of the profits. Laundered money from casinos, drugs and prostitution paid for many of Vedado's high-rises. Following the revolution, the mob was kicked out of Cuba.

Museo Napoleónico

R3 **Calle San Miguel, 1159, esq Ronda** **7879 1412, 7879 1460** **9:30am–5pm Tue–Sat, 9:30am–noon Sun**

The surprising presence of a Napoleonic museum in Cuba is due to the passion of sugar magnate Julio Lobo. For years he sent his agents

all over the world in search of Napoleonic mementos. In 1959, when Lobo left Cuba, the Cuban government bought his collection.

Every room in this curious museum contains fine examples of imperial-style furniture as well as surprising Napoleonic memorabilia, including one of the emperor's teeth and a tuft of his hair. There are two portraits, one by Andrea Appioni, painted in Milan during Napoleon's second Italian campaign, and another by Antoine Gros, plus his death mask, cast two days before Napoleon's death by Francesco Antommarchi, the Italian physician who had accompanied him to the island of St Helena and who later settled in Cuba.

The restored mansion was built in the 1920s by Oreste Ferrara, counsellor to the dictator Gerardo Machado, who furnished it in a Neo-Florentine Gothic style.

← The former Beatle, in casual repose in Parque John Lennon

Parque John Lennon

M4 **Calles 17 y 6**

It's ironic that a life-size bronze effigy of John Lennon sits, legs crossed, on a cast-iron bench in a park named in his honour, as music by The Beatles was once banned in Cuba. Nonetheless, the statue was unveiled in 2000 by sculptor José Villa in Fidel Castro's presence on the 20th anniversary of Lennon's death. A slab at Lennon's feet is inscribed in Spanish with the "Imagine" lyric "People say I'm a dreamer, but I'm not the only one." A *custodio* (guardian) cares for a pair of spectacles, which are placed on Lennon's face when visitors approach.

Quinta de los Molinos

R4 **Avenida Carlos III (Salvador Allende) e/ Infanta y Calle G** **7873 6510** **10am-noon Thu-Sun**

A typical 19th-century villa in the Vedado quarter, this is a verdant retreat amid the bustle of the city. It was built as the summer residence of the captains-general in 1837 and stands in a leafy area with two *molinos* (tobacco mills). Built by royal decree, the mills were operated in the 19th-century, powered by waters from the city's aqueducts.

Following an ambitious restoration project, the rambling grounds around the villa are now home to lush botanical gardens, which are crisscrossed with pathways. The gardens contain a wealth of plant life, including many indigenous Cuban species. A colourful butterfly house is also situated at the rear end of this oasis.

PICTURE PERFECT
Imagine all the Pictures

To get an iconic selfie, sit on the bench next to the statue of John Lennon and pretend to chat to him. Don't forget to ask the *custodio* to place Lennon's glasses on his face before snapping.

STAY

Hotel Nacional
Havana's grand-dame hotel has bags of character.

R1 **Calles 21 y O** **hotelnacionalde cuba.com**

$$$

Hotel Habana Libre
Modernist high-rise with chic rooms.

Q2 **Calles L y 23** **meliacuba.com**

$$$

Casa Jorge Coalla Potts
A lovely two-room *casa* with friendly hosts.

Q3 **Calle I, 456, Apto 11** **havana roomrental.com**

$$$

Casa Blanca
Two-room B&B in a gracious old mansion.

M4 **Calle 13, 917** **7833 5697**

$$$

A SHORT WALK
VEDADO

Distance 3.5 km (2 miles) **Time** 30 minutes
Difficulty Relatively flat; plan stops for
the middle of the day **Nearest bus stop**
Calles 21 y L

This walk takes in the broad avenues typical
of Vedado, providing a taste of the district's
odd architectural mix of 1950s high-rises and
crumbling Neo-Classical mansions. There is
only one museum on this route (Vedado has
few conventional attractions), leaving you free
to simply stroll and look around. Avenida 23,
modern Havana's most well-known street,
is the main reference point for the walk,
particularly the first few blocks,
which is known as La Rampa.

Locator Map
For more detail see p114

CENTRO HABANA
AND PRADO

Parque
Martí

ROTONDA
CALIXTO
GARCÍA

Ministerio
de Relaciones
Exteriores
de Cuba

Casa de las
Américas

MALECÓN

AVENIDA DE

Museo de la Danza

Parque de
la Juventud

*The mansion on the
corner with Calle Línea
houses the* **Museo de la
Danza***, run by the famous
ballerina Alicia Alonso. It
displays mementos of
iconic ballet dancers.*

*Continue along Calle
Línea to the junction
with Avenida Paseo.
This long boulevard
is lined with elegant
ministries and public
administration offices.*

Parque
Trotcha

CALZADA

LÍNEA

AVENIDA PASEO

The **Casa de la
Amistad***, at No 406,
is a cultural centre.
It once belonged to
Catelina Lasa, grande
dame of Havana.*

*Follow Calle 17 west past
several striking centenary
mansions to reach* **Parque
John Lennon** *(p123). Sit
beside the statue of the
singer on the bench.*

Parque
John Lennon

Casa de la
Amistad

*Walk to Calle 23 y 12 to end
at the* **Cuban Institute
of Cinematographic Arts
and Industry (ICAIC)***,
which has a contemporary
art gallery.*

FINISH

Cuban Institute
of Cinematographic
Arts and Industry (ICAIC)

0 metres   400
0 yards   400

N

AVENIDA 23

CALZADA ZAPATA

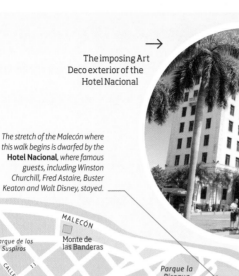

→ The imposing Art Deco exterior of the Hotel Nacional

The stretch of the Malecón where this walk begins is dwarfed by the **Hotel Nacional**, *where famous guests, including Winston Churchill, Fred Astaire, Buster Keaton and Walt Disney, stayed.*

MALECÓN

Parque el Hueco

CALZADA

Parque de los Suspiros

Monte de las Banderas

Parque la Piragua

CALLE J

CALLE K

CALLE 11

CALLE 13

LÍNEA

CALLE 15

Edificio FOCSA

Hotel Capri

Hotel Nacional

START

CALLE I

CALLE 17

CALLE 19

CALLE K

CALLE 21

CALLE

CALLE

CALLE

CALLE L

CALLE M

CALLE N

CALLE O

AVENIDA 23

Parque Coppelia

Hotel Habana Libre

LOS PRESIDENTES

Parque Víctor Hugo

Parque El Quijote

CALLE H

(CALLE G)

Head briefly south to reach **La Rampa** *(the stretch of Avenida 23 sloping uphill between the seafront and Calle L). Modern and lively, lined with restaurants and bars with old-fashioned neon signs, La Rampa would pass for a typical 1950s street.*

In the middle of the park at the corner of Calle 23 and L is **Parque Coppelia** *(p120), a large futuristic building. There are always queues at this ice-cream parlour.*

At the intersection with Calle J is the **Parque El Quijote**, *a tree-shaded area with a modern statue of a nude Don Quixote on horseback by Sergio Martínez.*

The tour continues by turning right at Calle G (Avenida de los Presidentes), a wide, tree-lined avenue with luxurious late-19th-century French-style mansions and 1950s high-rise apartments.

↑ An old-fashioned classic American car cruising on La Rampa

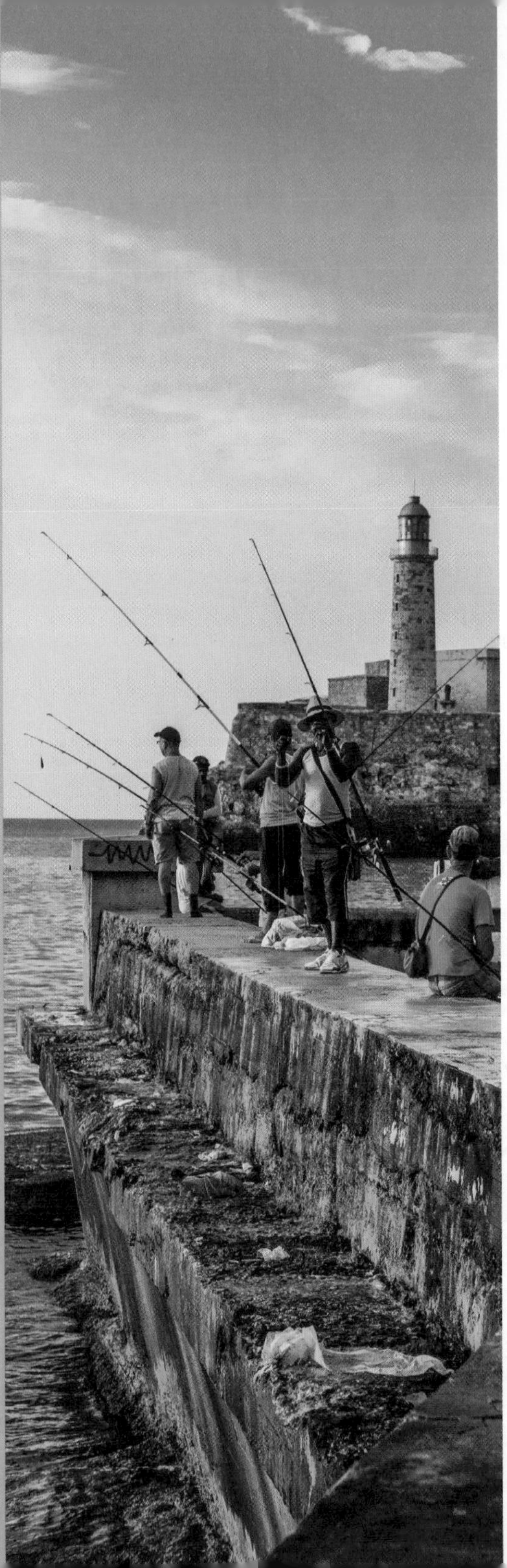

Fishermen preparing their rods on the walls of Havana's harbour

Experience

1. Instituto Superior de Arte
2. Ciudad Escolar Libertad
3. Cubanacán
4. Fusterlandia
5. Kcho Estudio Romerillo
6. Castillo del Morro
7. San Carlos de la Cabaña
8. Casablanca
9. Regla
10. Guanabacoa
11. Cojímar
12. Playas del Este
13. Alamar
14. Museo Ernest Hemingway
15. Santa María del Rosario
16. Parque Lenin
17. Santuario Nacional de San Lázaro
18. Santiago de las Vegas
19. Jardín Botánico Nacional

BEYOND
THE CENTRE

Havana sprawls well beyond its centre. The Miramar quarter, lying to the west of the city, was a glamorous area home to mansions and country clubs in the early 1950s and it retains its elegant air. To the east are the Castillo del Morro and San Carlos de La Cabaña defence fortresses – evidence of Havana's strategic importance in the 16th century. The Spanish saw the city as the "key to the New World" and, consequently, it was constantly threatened by buccaneers. You'll also find many of Ernest Hemingway's favourite haunts here, including Finca La Vigía – the villa where he wrote some of his best novels – and the fishing village of Cojímar.

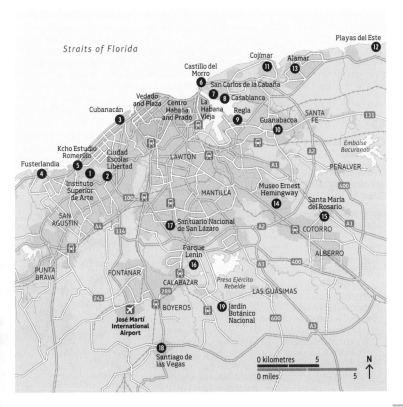

EXPERIENCE

❶ Instituto Superior de Arte

🏠 Calle 120, 1110 at 9na (Havana) 🌐 isa.cult.cu

After the revolution, Fidel Castro denounced golf as "bourgeois" and in 1961, after playing a round with Che Guevara at the former Havana Country Club, the grounds were converted into a campus for the Instituto Superior de Arte. Cuban architect Ricardo Porro and Italian architects Vittorio Garatti and Roberto Gottardi were hired to design faculties of music, ballet, modern dance, and visual and plastic art. But the domed, sinuous red-bricked complex was never completed – both the concept of a school for the arts and the design itself fell out of favour in 1965 and were abandoned.

Advance permission is needed to enter, but there are good views of the complex from calles 15 and 134.

❷ Ciudad Escolar Libertad

🏠 Avenidas 31 y 100 (Havana) 📞 7260 8054 🚫 Sun

During the US occupation of Cuba (1898–1902), the military

↑ Cars parked in front of a hotel on a street in the neighbourhood of Cubanacán

government chose Camp Columbia, in the Marianao district inland of Miramar, as its headquarters. Here, Fulgencio Batista enacted his 1933 and 1952 *coups d'état*, and fled Cuba on 31 December 1958; the camp was famously bombed on the eve of the Bay of Pigs invasion (*p177*).

Castro turned the site into Ciudad Escolar Libertad, an educational centre and head-quarters of the national literacy campaign. The on-site Museo de la Campaña de Alfabetización tells the story.

Plaza Finlay, outside the entrance, is pinned by a monument (El Obelisko) resembling a syringe to honour Dr Carlos Finlay, who identified the species of mosquito that causes yellow fever. The curved Art Deco buildings are carved with impressive bas-reliefs.

❸ Cubanacán

🏠 Havana 🚌

Rising inland to the west of Miramar, Cubanacán is the city's most exclusive residential area. Colloquially called "Havana's Beverly Hills", it was developed from the 1920s onwards with winding tree-lined boulevards graced by flamboyant mansions and stunning Modernist homes. Most of the residents fled Cuba after the revolution and the area is now home to foreign ambassadors and members of Cuba's governmental and military elite, while other buildings serve as *protocolos* (homes rented only to VIP guests).

The extravagant 1910 Beaux Arts mansion of the Marqués de Pinar del Río is the unlikely venue for the

Fábrica El Laguito, the principal factory making Cohiba cigars. Nearby, the austere Palacio de las Convenciones, built in 1979, is Cuba's main conference venue and host to the biannual sitting of the Asamblea Nacional del Poder Popular.

④

Fusterlandia

Calle 226 y Avenida 5ta (Havana) **☎** 7271 2932

Once a fishing and military community on the western edge of Havana called Jaimanitas, Fusterlandia gained its new name as a result of the mosaic work of Cuban artist José Fuster. By ornamenting his home town, Fuster launched this

remarkable artistic community project. Fusterlandia is now covered with flamboyant and naïve ceramic artwork. You'll see it on walls, pavements and dozens of homes. Although inspired by Gaudí, Picasso and Romanian artist Constantin Brâncuşi, Fuster's themes are purely Cuban: palm trees, crocodiles, cockerel, couples making love. Don't miss the Casa-Estudio Fuster (the artist's surreal home and studio) which has the most astounding adornment.

Fidel Castro's home was nearby, connected by tunnel to the Jaimanitas naval facility at Punta Cero. Avenida 5ta between calles 188 and 250 is still a no-photography zone.

⑤

Kcho Estudio Romerillo

Avenida 7ma e/ 120 (Havana) **☎** 7208 0965

World-renowned artist Kcho (Alexis Leiva Machado), recipient in 1995 of the UNESCO Prize for Promotion of the Arts, created this cultural complex in 2014. It includes a working foundry, pottery, carpentry workshop, library

SHOP

Casa-Estudio Fuster
Fuster's naïve ceramics and paintings can be bought at the artist's studio. Big canvases fetch thousands of dollars, but small items start at $35.

Avenida 1ra y 226 (Havana) **☎** 7271 2932

experimental graphics workshop, theatre, computer room, and various art galleries. There are guided tours by appointment, and visitors can join the free community arts classes.

Spilling onto neighbouring streets, the Museo Orgánico Romerillo community project studs pavements and grassy boulevard medians with installations, adding colour and vitality to the sub-district of Cubanacán. The project has engaged local residents, who cleaned up rubbish dumps and helped them become pleasant parks.

← The enticing, colourful entrance to Fusterlandia, adorned with mosaics

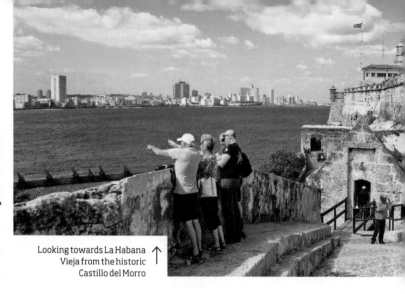

Looking towards La Habana Vieja from the historic Castillo del Morro

Castillo del Morro

📍 Carretera de la Cabaña, Habana del Este (Havana)
📞 7862 0617 🕐 9am–6pm daily

Construction of this fortress, which was designed by the Italian military architect Giovanni Bautista Antonelli, began in 1589 at the request of the governor Juan de Texeda. The function of the Castillo de los Tres Reyes del Morro (its full title) was to detect the approach of any enemy. Various treasures of the New World were regularly concentrated in the port when ships were docked in Cuba on their voyage to Spain, and it was necessary to protect them.

The original lighthouse on the "Morrillo", the highest point of the hill, was rebuilt several times, until General Leopoldo O'Donnell ordered a new one to be built in 1845. This still stands today. It is made of stone, and has its original lamp, with rays that shine for a radius of 30 km (20 miles). Today the fortress and the neighbouring San Carlos de La Cabaña fortification form the Parque Histórico-Militar Morro Cabaña. Many tourists and locals come to admire the magnificent view of the city and port of Havana.

Access to the castles is through an impressive gallery, where plaques indicate the spot where the British opened a breach in 1762, taking the Morro and all of Havana after a 40-day siege.

On the northern side, the Plataforma de la Reina has defence walls and steps leading to the upper terrace. From here visitors can gain an overall view of the fortress.

THE CAÑONAZO

Every evening, at 9pm exactly, the "Cañonazo" ceremony is held in La Cabaña fortress. On the hour, a volley of cannon shots is fired by a group of young soldiers of the Revolutionary Armed Forces, dressed in 18th-century uniforms. This theatrical ceremony recalls the colonial period, when shots were fired at the end of each day to tell citizens that the city gates were closed and access to the bay had been blocked.

San Carlos de La Cabaña

📍 Carretera de la Cabaña, Habana del Este (Havana)
📞 7862 0617 🕐 9am–10pm daily

After the British conquest of Havana in 1762, it was 11 months before the Spaniards

of French military schools, but with detailing by the Spanish engineer Silvestre Abarca. With its crown-shaped plan, the structure is considered a fine example of a bastion-type fortification.

A visit to the fortress is a journey through history. The central thoroughfare leads to the Baluardo di San Ambrosio bastion and the Terraza de San Agustín, where the poet Juan Clemente Zenea was executed for his separatist ideas in 1871. In the same area are some Soviet nuclear missiles, left over from the 1962 Cuban Missile Crisis (p54).

The Museo Monográfico illustrates the history of the fortress through documents and photographs. The Museo de Armas y Fortificaciones is a military museum. The one museum not to miss is the Comandancia del Che: on 3 January 1959 the *barbudos* (as Castro and his bearded revolutionaries were known) occupied La Cabaña and set up their headquarters in what was once the Spanish military governor's residence. Today it is a museum containing various items that belonged to Che Guevara, including his weapons, glasses and camera.

Did You Know?

A chain between Castillo del Morro and Castillo San Salvador de la Punta used to block the harbour.

regained the capital. The bitter experience of foreign occupation convinced them of the need to fortify the hill dominating the port, so, in 1763, construction began on the new Cabaña fortress. No fewer than 4,000 men laboured on the project, including Mexican and Indian prisoners brought from the Yucatán peninsula in conditions of semi-slavery.

The new fortification cost 14 million pesos, a sum so large that, according to an old legend, King Carlos III of Spain on hearing of the expense asked for a spyglass and reputedly said: "Such an expensive construction should be visible from Madrid."

La Cabaña, which extends for more than 700 m (2,300 ft) along the entrance canal of the bay, is a huge 10-ha (25-acre) polygon designed in keeping with the principles

→

The gleaming white *Cristo de La Habana* statue in Casablanca

---

DRINK

Casa de la Música
One of Havana's hottest salsa venues, Casa de la Música hosts top bands. Upstairs, Disco Tun Tún has dancing till dawn.

📍 Calle 20 Avenida 35 (Havana) 📞 7204 0447 🕒 Mon & Tue

Espacios
This private club is popular with the party crowd. It has an outdoor space for live music, as well as indoor lounges.

📍 Calle 10 513 e/ Avenida 29 y 31 (Havana) 📞 7202 2921

The revolutionary's original office, which has been left intact, is also open to visitors.

8

Casablanca

📍 Havana 🚢 From Muelle de Luz, La Habana Vieja, every 15 mins; 7794 5466 📍

This fishing village was built in the 1700s on the other side of the Bay of Havana from the city. It is best known for the huge *Cristo de La Habana*, an 18-m- (60-ft-) tall white marble statue of Christ, which looms over the village. The work of the Cuban sculptor Jilma Madera in 1958, it was commissioned by President Batista's wife, Marta, who had made a vow to finance a large statue of Christ if her husband survived the 1957 attack by students on the presidential palace. Ironically, the statue was completed a week before the revolution. It can be seen from many parts of the city and is familiar to all Cubans.

EXPERIENCE Beyond the Centre

9
Regla

🅰 Havana 🚢 From Muelle de Luz, Habana Vieja, every 30 mins; 7794 5466

Regla lies on the east coast of the Bay of Havana, a few minutes by ferry from Muelle de Luz. The town was founded in 1687 and over the years grew in economic importance as a fishing port and centre for huge sugar warehouses. In the 19th century freed slaves settled in Regla, and there is still a strong Afro-Cuban culture here today.

The church of Nuestra Señora de la Virgen de Regla was built here in 1687. A modest structure, it stands on a small hill from which there are scenic views of the bay of Havana. The humble interior includes an ornate golden altar incorporating the figure of the dark-skinned Virgin, dressed in ornate blue robes.

The Liceo Artístico y Literario – the town's centre for art and literature – was opened by José Martí in 1879 with a famous speech on Cuban independence.

10
Guanabacoa

🅰 Havana 🚌

After its foundation in 1607, this town became a port of call for slave traffic, which explains its fame as a city associated with Afro-Cuban culture. Its name, of Indian origin, means "land of many waters": there are several springs in this area which at one time encouraged wealthy Habaneros to build homes here. Today, the town is proud of its colonial houses and of having been the birthplace of three leading 20th-century

Statues in alcoves lining the walls of Nuestra Señora de la Virgen de Regla church (inset)

PICTURE PERFECT
A Water Landscape

As well as being a convenient way to get to Regla, the ferry from Muelle de Luz grants breathtaking views of Havana from the water. Cross at sunset and point your lens at the capital's Instagram-ready skyline.

Cuban musicians: pianist and composer Ernesto Lecuona, singer Rita Montaner and *chansonnier* Ignacio Villa, better known as Bola de Nieve.

Guanabacoa has several interesting churches. Of these, the Ermita de Potosí in particular is well worth a visit. Built in 1644, it is one of the oldest and most original colonial-period churches.

The interesting **Museo Municipal de Guanabacoa**, in a well-restored colonial house, illustrates the history of the town. The dominant figure is that of Pepe Antonio, the local hero in the struggle against the British in the 18th century. The museum places particular emphasis on the Santería and

→ A classic car parked by the water in front of Cojímar's 17th-century fort

Palo Monte religions and on the rituals of the Abakuá cult. An impressive piece in this section is the *Mano Poderosa*, a multicoloured wooden sculpture that stands approximately 1 m (3 ft) high. According to legend, it once belonged to a woman who was able to make contact with the dead. Traditional Afro-Cuban dance is sometimes held in the courtyard.

Museo Municipal de Guanabacoa

⊛ ⊛ 🏠 Calle Martí 108, e/ Quintin Banderas y E V Valenzuela 📞 7797 9117 🕒 9am–5pm Mon–Sat, 9am–1pm Sun

---

Cojímar

🏠 Havana

A charming village with single-storey wooden houses Cojímar was once inhabited only by fishermen. Now there are also escapees from the capital, including writers and artists, who have chosen to leave for a more peaceful life.

In the 1950s however, there was only one author to be seen on the streets of Cojímar: Ernest Hemingway *(p135)*. Many of the local fishermen were Hemingway's friends and he liked to play dominoes and drink rum while listening to their stories. He made this village the setting for his famous novel *The Old Man and the Sea*.

In the small square named after Hemingway there is a monument featuring a bust of the author – a faithful copy of the one in El Floridita *(p73)*. It is here thanks to the author's fishermen friends, who donated anchors, hooks and tools to pay for the casting.

Nearby, on the seafront, is a small fort, which was built as the easternmost defence point of Havana in 1646. It was designed by Giovanni Bautista Antonelli, architect of the Castillo del Morro *(p130)*.

Cojímar is also the home of Hemingway's favourite restaurant, La Terraza *(Calle Real 161)*. It makes much of its connection with the author, and photos of him adorn the walls. The restaurant is as elegant and well run as it was during Hemingway's time. The cocktail lounge has a splendid wooden bar and is an ideal spot to enjoy a drink.

> **Many of the local fishermen were Hemingway's friends and he liked to play dominoes and drink rum while listening to their stories.**

12
Playas del Este

 Havana

Havana is one of the few cities in the world to have sizable beaches only a 20-minute drive from the city centre. Easy to reach via a good, fast road, the Playas del Este consist of a stretch of about 10 km (6 miles) of fine sand and crystal-clear water, lined with hotels, villages and tourist facilities. The beaches can offer a good compromise for people who want to spend some of their holiday at the seaside during their visit to Havana. Bear in mind, however, that this area is also a popular haunt of *jineteros* (touts promoting hotels and restaurants), though in places security guards have been drafted in to deter them.

Did You Know?

Alamar is a centre for rap and hip-hop and hosts Cuba's annual Festival de Rap Cubano in August.

Arriving from central Havana, the first beach you'll reach is Bacuranao, a peaceful spot and a favourite with families. The loveliest place on the riviera is Santa María del Mar. It has the best beach, lined with pine and coconut trees, as well as some hotels and sport facilities, and is therefore very popular with tourists. Guanabo is a more traditional spot, with small houses, local restaurants and shops; at weekends this is the liveliest place along the coast when Habaneros arrive by the hundred. The Bajo de las Lavanderas, close to the shore, is a delight for scuba and skin divers, and deep-sea fishing trips can be arranged at the Marlin Náutica kiosks (*p41*) on the beaches.

A small island, Mi Cayito, lies at the mouth of the Itabo river. It has a lively beach which is popular with the local LGBT community.

13
Alamar

 Havana

A vast post-revolutionary urban complex 5 km (3 miles) east of the Havana harbour tunnel, Alamar at first sight

 GREAT VIEW
Sundown Style

Enjoy a sundown with a sundowner at the Mirador de Bello Monte, a hilltop bar off the Vía Blanca highway. This well-known spot has panoramic views over the white sands and iridescent sea of the entire length of the Playas del Este.

looks ghastly, with hundreds of identical Soviet-style pre-fabricated blocks of flats arranged without logical order. Most of the builders were unskilled volunteers who formed "micro-brigades" to construct units they would then occupy. Some 100,000 people live here.

First impressions aside, Alamar is not without off-beat charm. Don't miss **Oraniponico Alamar,** an organic farm to the west of the town, which is run as a private cooperative on land leased rent-free from the state. It's fascinating, and has tours in English. Nearby is one of Havana's most colourful markets.

Finding any Alamar address is like navigating the minotaur's maze, but ask a local to direct

Sailing boats and kayaks on the sands of Playas del Este

you to Jardín de los Afectos (*Calle 7ma and 171, Zona 10*), which has funky art made from recycled miscellany by artist Gallo Portieles.

Oranipónico Alamar
 Avenida 5ta
farmcuba.org

Museo Ernest Hemingway

Calle Vigía (Havana)
San Francisco de Paula
7692 0176 **10am–4:30pm Mon-Sat**

Finca La Vigía is the only home Ernest Hemingway ever had outside the US, and he lived here, between various foreign trips, for almost 20 years.

The villa, built in 1887 to a design by Catalan architect Miguel Pascual y Baguer, was bought by Hemingway in 1940. It was made a public museum in 1962, as soon as news of the writer's suicide in the US reached Cuba. To protect the interior, visitors are not allowed inside, but the rooms can be viewed through the windows and doors to the garden, which are thrown open but roped off, except on rainy days.

Everything in Finca La Vigía is in the same meticulous order it was in when Hemingway lived here. There is his library with more than 9,000 books; various hunting trophies from African safaris hanging in the living room; personal possessions, such as his weapons and typewriter; and valuable artworks, including a ceramic plate by Picasso.

Two curious features in the garden are the pet cemetery (Hemingway had about 50 cats during his lifetime) and the *Pilar*, the author's fishing boat, which was transferred from Cojímar (*p133*) to the museum and placed in a specially built pavilion in the former tennis court. The *Pilar* was a comfortable and fast boat made of black American oak, and the author loved ploughing through the waves on fishing expeditions with his friend Gregorio Fuentes. The boat became infamous as, during World War II, Hemingway used it to patrol the sea north of Cuba, on the lookout for Nazi submarines that were trying to sink ships laden with sugar intended for the Allied troops.

HEMINGWAY IN CUBA

The great American author fell in love with Cuba on his first visit in 1932, attracted initially by the marlin fishing. It was not until 1939, however, that he decided to move to the island, initially residing in the Ambos Mundos hotel in La Habana Vieja before purchasing Finca La Vigía, a quiet villa outside the city. He wrote a number of his most famous novels there, and considered himself a Cuban. He returned to the US in 1960 after the Cuban revolution of 1959.

Santa María del Rosario

Havana **Cotorro**

Near Hemingway's villa is the village of Santa María del Rosario, founded in 1732 and home to the church of the same name (also known as Catedral de los Campos de Cuba), notable for its splendid *mudéjar* ceilings.

The church, designed in 1760–66 by José Perera, has an austere façade similar to Spanish missions in the western US, while the interior has some unusually lavish elements, such as the gilded high altar, and paintings by Nicolás de la Escalera, one of Cuba's early artists.

↑ The living room, lined with Hemingway's African hunting trophies, at Finca La Vigía

Huge carved granite monument to Lenin in the park that bears his name

Parque Lenin

Calle 100 y Cortina de la Presa, Arroyo Naranjo (Havana) 7644 2810 10am-5pm Wed-Sun

Located 20 km (12 miles) south of Central Havana and occupying 7.5 sq km (3 sq miles), Lenin Park was created in the 1970s, under the orders of Celia Sánchez, as an amusement park for children and a green area for an expanding city. Ever since it was created, Parque Lenin has been the largest recreation area in all of Havana.

Russian architect Lev Korbel designed the vast monument honouring the Soviet leader. Weighing 1,200 tons and 9 m (30 ft) high, it was completed in 1982 under the supervision of park designer Antonio Quintana Simonetti.

Habaneros love to walk here among the palm, cedar, pine and araucaria trees. On top of its natural beauty, the park is also home to many attractions including the original fairground rides, which have an old-fashioned air, a freshwater aquarium, stables, outdoor cinema, art gallery, swimming pools, café and Las Ruínas restaurant.

The latter occupies a 1960s building that incorporates the crumbling walls of an old plantation house.

Nearby, among gardens and tree-lined paths, is the largest exhibition centre in Cuba, **ExpoCuba**, which hosts events all year. In autumn the famous Feria Internacional de La Habana offers an overview of Cuba's economic and socio-political life.

ExpoCuba
7697 4252

Santuario Nacional de San Lázaro

Calzada de San Antonio Km 23, El Rincón, Santiago de las Vegas (Havana) 7683 2396 7am-5pm daily

This sanctuary, dedicated to St Lazarus, the patron saint of the sick, lies in the small village of El Rincón, outside Santiago de las Vegas. Appropriately, it is located next to an old lepers' hospital, which now specializes in dermatology.

In Afro-Cuban religions Lazarus, from the Bible, corresponds to Babalú Ayé. Both Lazarus and Babalú Ayé are represented in folk iconography as old men dressed in tatters and covered with sores. In the case of the African saint, the skin disease was supposedly punishment from Olofi, the father of all the gods, for the saint's adulterous and libertine past.

On the saint's feast day, 17 December, the simple white sanctuary welcomes thousands of worshippers, many of whom have crawled from Havana. They flock here to make vows and

→
People strolling past the Santuario Nacional de San Lázaro

requests to St Lazarus (called *milagroso* or "the miraculous one"), or to ask for his healing powers. The pilgrims light candles, leave fragrant flowers and make offerings at the sanctuary's altars. The water from the fountain to the right of the sanctuary is considered by believers to miraculously cure diseases and ease pain.

 18

Santiago de las Vegas

 Havana

Most people simply pass through Santiago de las Vegas without stopping while en route to, or from, José Martí International Airport or the Santuario Nacional de San Lázaro, in nearby Rincón. But this town, which is connected to Havana via the multi-lane Avenida de Boyeros, is also the gateway to the hilltop Mausoleo de General Antonio Maceo Grajales, at El Cacahual. The avenue winds uphill to this impressive site where the Wars of Independence hero – known as "Titan of Bronze" – is buried beneath a marble tomb with bas-reliefs of his image and that of other Mambises (independence fighters).

> **Both Lazarus and Babalú Ayé are represented in folk iconography as old men dressed in tatters and covered with sores.**

The general was killed nearby at the Battle of San Pedro on 7 December 1896. A small museum recalls details of Maceo's life.

The town itself is graced by the Parque Juan Delgado, which is overlooked by a handsome church, dating from 1694, and a statue of Colonel Juan Delgado González, who bravely retrieved Maceo's corpse.

19

Jardín Botánico Nacional

📍 **Carretera del Rocío Km 3, Calabazar, Arroyo Naranjo (Havana)** 📞 **7697 9159** 🕐 **9am–4pm daily** 🚫 **1 Jan, 26 Jul, 25 Dec**

This huge 6-sq-km (2-sq-mile) botanical garden, set in an area of woods and cultivated fields, contains plants from all over the world. The gardens are divided into zones by geography, and the Caribbean section, which takes up one-fifth of the garden,

has 7,000 flowering plants, half of them unique to Cuba. There are also curiosities such as the Archaic Woods, with descendants of ancient plants, and the Palmetum, with a large collection of palm trees.

The cactus area near the entrance is a must-see, but the most interesting part of the park is the Jardín Japonés, a Japanese garden with waterfalls and a pond with a gazebo. It was donated to Cuba by the local Asian community in 1989. Another fascinating sight is the orchid garden, with many varieties.

EAT

Corte del Principe
This authentic Italian restaurant serves divine dishes, such as beef carpaccio and homemade pasta.

📍 **Calle 9na y 74, Playa** 📞 **5255 9091**

$ $ $

Río Mar
This *paladar* is set in a fabulous 1950s home, with a terrace overlooking the Río Almandares. Order a seafood dish here.

📍 **Avenida 3ra y Final, La Puntilla** 📞 **7720 4838**

$ $ $

El Aljibe
An open-air state-run restaurant serving delicious all-you-can-eat roast chicken with white rice, black beans and all the trimmings.

📍 **Avenida 7ma y 24, Playa** 📞 **7204 1583**

$ $ $

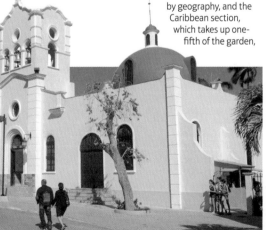

A LONG WALK
MIRAMAR

Distance 5 km (3 miles) **Time** 45 minutes
Difficulty Flat, easy ground; can be breezy
when walking alongside the sea **Nearest
bus route** HabanaBusTour route T2

Miramar is the most elegant part of Havana – as it was
before the revolution, when the city's richest inhabitants
lived here. Life in this quarter revolves around the Avenida
5, a broad, tree-lined avenue flanked by splendid early
20th-century villas that are now home to embassies and
institutions. On a walk through the quarter, you'll pass
these imposing mansions, as well as eclectic churches,
fascinating museums and lively stretches of beach.

Locator Map
For more detail see p126

↑ The striking tower of the Russian
Embassy, looming over Miramar

*Walk up Calle 28 to Avenida 3ra
("tercera") and pop inside the
Maqueta de La Habana to see
the 1:1,000 scale-model of the
entire city. It took ten years to
create this 144 sq m (1,550 sq ft)
reconstruction.*

*Avenida 1ra ("primera")
lacks the liveliness of the
Malecón, but the water is
clear and there are peaceful spots for sunbathing,
such as **Playita 16** (at the
end of Calle 16).*

*Rising over Avenida 1ra is the
stark tower of the former Soviet
Embassy. Today, the **Russian
Embassy** is topped by a thinner
tower containing intelligence-
gathering devices.*

CALLE 28

Maqueta de
La Habana

CALLE 36
CALLE 36A
CALLE 38
CALLE 40
CALLE 40A
CALLE 42
3RA AVENIDA
CALLE 34
CALLE 32

5TA AVENIDA

CALLE 36A
CALLE 38
CALLE 40

1RA AVENIDA
1RA A
CALLE 60
3RA A

1RA AVENIDA
3RA AVENIDA

Acuario
Nacional
de Cuba

Russian
Embassy

🔴 **FINISH**

Iglesia de
San Antonio
de Padua

*Walk down Calle 60 to return
to Avenida 5ta and end your
walk at the **Iglesia de San
Antonio de Padua**. Built in
1949, it is a sombre Neo-
Romanesque structure.*

The **Almendares** river earned its name in the 17th century when a sick Spanish bishop called Almendáriz fully recovered after a stay along its banks.

Begin your walk on the west side of the tunnel under the Almendares river, where **Avenida 5** begins. This broad avenue is known as "Embassy Row".

At the corner with Calle 2 is the restored **Casa de las Tejas Verdes** (House of the Green Tiles), which is now a centre devoted to architecture. The house is open for guided visits.

At Calle 10, Avenida 5ta is pinned by the **Reloj de Quinta Avenida**, a 22-m- (72-ft-) high Spanish Renaissance clock tower.

Playita 16

1RA AVENIDA

CALLE 2

CALLE 4

CALLE A

CALLE 10

CALLE 12

CALLE 14

CALLE 16

1RA AVENIDA

3RA AVENIDA

CALLE 18

CALLE 20

CALLE 22

CALLE 24

CALLE 26

CALLE 30

Almendares

Avenida 5ta
Fuente de las Américas
▶ **START**

Casa de las Tejas Verdes

5TA AVENIDA

CALLE 8

AVENIDA 31

CALLE 10

CALLE 12

CALLE 14

Reloj de 5ta Avenida

Memorial de la Denuncia

Iglesia de Santa Rita de Casia

Dividing Avenida 5ta is the **Fuente de las Américas**, a white fountain made from Carrara marble. Erected in 1929, it has four Nereids holding giant oyster shells that ephemerally spout water.

At the corner of Calle 14, the **Memorial de la Denuncia** (Museum of the Complaint) displays exhibits denouncing US aggression against Cuba.

| 0 metres | 400 |
| 0 yards | 400 |

N ↑

Further down the Avenida, at the corner of Calle 26, is the modern **Iglesia de Santa Rita**, with three distinctive tall arches on its façade. Pop in to see the statue of St Rita by Cuban sculptress Rita Longa, to the left of the entrance.

→
Relaxing beside the Río Almendares, Miramar's river boundary

EXPERIENCE CUBA

Strolling along the beach at Varadero

Western Cuba 142

Central Cuba – West 166

Central Cuba – East 194

Eastern Cuba 226

WESTERN CUBA

Colonized in the 16th and 17th centuries by Europeans, mainly from the Canary Islands, Western Cuba retains its traditionally agricultural air. According to the inhabitants of Santiago de Cuba, Pinar del Río and Artemisa provinces are the least "revolutionary" parts of Cuba. They form the island's most rural region, populated by white farmers who have never been known for their warlike passion. But, despite this reputation, Western Cuba was the scene of several battles against the Spanish in the late 1800s, and there was in fact a revolutionary front here in 1958.

Historically, Pinar del Río province has preferred to concentrate its efforts on producing what they claim is the best tobacco in the world. Tobacco fields are scattered among the Sierra del Rosario and Sierra de los Órganos ranges, which are barely 600 m (1,970 ft) above sea level – not high enough to be mountains yet tall enough to create a breathtaking landscape. The Sierra del Rosario, and the Guanahacabibes peninsula in the far west, are UNESCO world biosphere reserves, emphasizing conservation-conscious ecotourism.

Ecotourism is less of a priority on Cayo Largo, a long-established island resort with numerous hotels. This island forms part of the Archipiélago de los Canarreos, in the Caribbean Sea, which is made up of 350 *cayos* or keys and provides excellent diving opportunities.

WESTERN CUBA

Must Sees

1 Las Terrazas

2 Valle de Viñales

3 Isla de la Juventud

Experience More

4 Soroa

5 San Diego de los Baños

6 Parque Nacional La Güira

7 Pinar del Río

8 Viñales

9 Vuelta Abajo

10 Cayo Levisa

11 Rancho La Guabina

12 María La Gorda

13 Parque Nacional Península de Guanahacabibes

14 Cayo Largo

←

1 The pool at Hotel Los Jazmines in Viñales.

2 Diving in María La Gorda.

3 A street in La Habana Vieja.

4 Mural de la Prehistoria in Valle de Viñales.

Western Cuba is captivating, with its sensational scenery, breathtaking beaches and a plethora of exciting eco-activities on offer. Here, we show you how to take a perfect 5-day trip to the west, starting in Havana.

5 DAYS
In Western Cuba

Day 1

Morning From the capital, drive to Las Terrazas (p148). Spend the morning hiking the trails here, before savouring a Cuban lunch at La Fonda de Mercedes (p156).

Afternoon Admire the wealth of artwork that Las Terrazas has inspired at the studios of Henry Aloma and Lester Campa. Then, spend the night at Hotel Moka (p163) to appreciate fully this unique community.

Day 2

Morning The orchid garden at Soroa (p156) is a short drive away, and makes for a fascinating visit. Exit the autopista at Entronque de Herradura and take the scenic road over the Sierra del Órganos to Cueva de Los Portales (p157) – a cavern that Che Guevara used as his headquarters.

Afternoon Once you reach Viñales (p162), have lunch at swanky 3J Tapas Bar (p165). After exploring the grand buildings around Parque Martí, take a dip in the infinity pool at Hotel Los Jazmines (p163).

Day 3

Morning There's no shortage of things to see and do in the Valle de Viñales, with the most popular activities being horseback riding and hiking. After exploring the valley, dine on a delicious lunch of traditional *criolla* dishes at Finca Agroecológico El Paraíso (p165).

Afternoon Explore the fantastical Gran Caverna de Santo Tomás (p151), taking in the exquisite stalactites and stalagmites. Paladar Buena Vista is the perfect place for a panoramic sunset dinner (p165).

Day 4

Morning Head south via the sleepy town of Pinar del Río into the Vuelta Abajo (p162) tobacco growing region. You'll drive through miles of leafy plantations before you reach your destination – Finca Pinar El San Luis. Call (48) 797 470 to arrange a guided tour and lunch here at Cuba's most famous tobacco farm.

Afternoon Parque Nacional Península de Guanahacabibes (p164) is at Cuba's western tip. Snorkel at María La Gorda, before spending the night at Villa Cabo San Antonio (www.gaviotahotels.com).

Day 5

Morning If scuba diving isn't for you, head on a guided excursion of the national park arranged through EcoTur (p275). Be sure to keep an eye out for *tocororó*, with its red, blue and white plumage.

Afternoon Following a fresh seafood lunch at a local beachfront *paladar*, depart for Havana. You'll be back in the capital with enough time to indulge in a delectable rum-based cocktail at the iconic Sloppy Joe's (p108).

① 🍴 🏠 🛍️

LAS TERRAZAS

🗺️ C1 🏠 Artemisa 🚌 From Havana to Viñales ℹ️ Rancho Curujey, Las Terrazas; www.lasterrazas.cu

This unique community, in the Sierra del Rosario, was created in 1971 around a lake as part of a reforestation project. One of Cuba's premier ecotourism sites, it has trails, coffee plantations and artists' studios.

Almost as soon as it was created, the eco-village was colonized by artists who were drawn to the community by its ethos and natural beauty and there are plenty of artists' studios to explore. A short distance from the village lies the perfectly preserved Cafetal Buenavista – an old coffee plantation. This is the perfect spot for lunch as its restaurant overlooks the plant-punctuated hillside.

Las Terrazas is characterized by its natural beauty. It is surrounded by scenic trails, where brightly coloured birds sing from the trees. The Sendero Las Delicias is a 3-km (2-mile) hike that runs from Cafetal Buenavista to a thatched *ranchón* (snack bar). Here, the Río San Juan tumbles over rocky tiers and jade-coloured pools form the Baños del Río San Juan.

INSIDER TIP
Watch the Birdie

The 6-km- (4-mile-) long Sendero La Serafina is a great trail for bird-watching. Here, there is a strong likelihood of seeing the island's endemic species, including Cuban trogon *(tocororo)*, the colourful Cuban tody and the Cuban solitaire, which has a beautiful voice.

Las Terrazas sitting on its scenic lake, near the Baños del Río San Juan cascades *(inset)*

1 The Cuban trogon, or *tocororo*, is the island's national bird because its colours mimic those of the Cuban flag.

2 There are plenty of opportunities for boat rides on Las Terrazas's lake.

3 Founded in 1801 by French settlers from Haiti, Cafetal Buenavista is Cuba's oldest coffee plantation. Here, you can visit the ruined slave quarters, the terraces where the coffee beans were dried and a grinding stone once powered by oxen. The plantation's stone mansion is now a restaurant, serving traditional Cuban fare.

Did You Know?

Las Terrazas is named for the area's hillside terraces – the result of deforestation.

ARTIST STUDIOS IN LAS TERRAZAS

It is not hard to see why so many artists have made scenic Las Terrazas their home and there are plenty of studios here in which to browse or buy their highly creative works. Cluttered with canvases, paintbrushes and paint, the studio of acclaimed artist Lester Campa displays his detailed landscapes, which are inspired by the deforestation of his adopted community. Henry Alomá's studio also reflects the landscape of Las Terrazas. It is a veritable zoo of fascinating surrealist creatures, particularly birds, which are often presented as macabre, almost hallucinogenic, allegorical statements.

VALLE DE VIÑALES

🅰B2 🏠 Viñales (Pinar del Río) 🚌 Salvador Cisneros 63, (48) 793 112; connections with Havana, Cienfuegos, Pinar del Río, Trinidad, Varadero
ℹ️ Cubanacán Viajes, Salvador Cisneros 63c, Plaza Viñales, (48) 796 393; Infotur, Salvador Cisneros 63c, (48) 796 263

A unique landscape awaits visitors to the Viñales Valley. With caves, murals and hot springs, there is plenty to experience in the valley, besides the bizarre *mogotes*.

Resembling sugar loaves, *mogotes* are gigantic karst formations, characteristic of the valley. They are like stone sentinels keeping watch over the corn and tobacco fields, the red earth with majestic royal palm trees and the farmhouses with roofs of palm leaves. According to legend, centuries ago some Spanish sailors who were approaching the coast thought the profile of the *mogotes* they glimpsed in the fog looked like a church organ. Hence the name Sierra de los Órganos, given to the network of hills in this area.

The *mogotes* are all that remains of what was once a limestone plateau. Over a period lasting millions of years, underground aquifers eroded the softer limestone, giving rise to large caverns whose ceilings later collapsed, forming the hollow *mogotes*, with their vast internal caverns. Take a tour of the caves via the Centro de Visitantes *((48) 796 144)*.

Riding a horse *(inset)* through the lush, *mogote*-punctuated Valle de Viñales ↑

Did You Know?

Painter González used cracks in the rock to create special effects of light and colour in his mural.

① Between 1959 and 1962, Cuban artist Leovigildo González, a pupil of the Mexican artist Diego Rivera, painted the history of evolution – from ammonites to *Homo sapiens* – on the face of a *mogote*.

② The Iglesia del Sagrado Corazón de Jesús is a pretty church, with a distinctive blue door, in the town of Viñales.

③ The Gran Caverna de Santo Tomás is the largest network of caves in Latin America, with 46 km (29 miles) of galleries and up to eight levels of communicating grottoes.

PICTURE PERFECT
Mogotes

For the best panoramic vistas of the iconic *mogotes*, head to the *mirador* (lookout) beside the Hotel Los Jazmines *(p163)*. Sunrise and sunset are particularly rewarding times to snap that striking shot.

↑ The palm-tree fronted shore of the Isla de la Juventud

3

ISLA DE LA JUVENTUD

🅰C3 🏠 Isla de la Juventud 🚌 Rafael Cabrera Mustelier, Carretera La Fé, Km 5, (46) 322 300 ⛴ Daily catamaran from Batabanó, lasting 2-3 hours; call (46) 324 415 for information ℹ Ecotur; (46) 327 101

The naturalist Alexander von Humboldt described this island as an abandoned place, Batista wanted to turn it into a paradise for rich Americans, while Fidel Castro repopulated it with young people, built universities and changed its name to the Isla de la Juventud (Isle of Youth). The result is an unspoiled isle of wonders.

① Nueva Gerona

Surrounded by hills that yield multicoloured marble, the small, peaceful town of Nueva Gerona was founded in 1830 on the banks of Las Casas river by Spanish settlers. These colonists came from American countries that had won their independence.

The town is built on a characteristic grid plan. A good starting point for a visit to Nueva Gerona is Calle 39, the graceful main street

flanked by coloured arcades. Here, you'll find the local cinema, theatre, pharmacy, post office, hospital, bank, and numerous bars and restaurants. This street ends at the Parque Central, Nueva Gerona's main square, where the Iglesia de Nuestra Señora de los Dolores stands. First built in Neo-Classical style in 1853, this church was totally destroyed by a cyclone in 1926 and rebuilt three years later in colonial style.

South of the Parque Central, the former City Hall building is now the home of the **Museo**

Municipal de Nueva Gerona. It displays many objects and documents concerning pirates and buccaneers – the main protagonists in the island's history – as well as mementos of the revolution. Another museum, the Casa Natal Jesús Montané, is dedicated solely to the struggle against Batista's dictatorship.

The **Museo de Historia Natural Antonio Núñez Jiménez** covers the natural history of the island, and there is a fine planetarium here as well, the only one in the world where the North Star can be seen together with the Southern Cross.

Museo Municipal de Nueva Gerona

🏛🏛 🏠 Calle 30, e/37 y Martí ☎ (46) 323 791 🕐 9am-4:30pm Tue-Sat, 8am-noon Sun

Museo de Historia Natural Antonio Núñez Jiménez

 Calle 41, esq 54, 4625 (46) 323 143 9am–5pm Tue–Sat, 8am–noon Sun

---

②

Presidio Modelo

4 km (2.5 miles) SE of Nueva Gerona, Reparto Delio Chacón (46) 325 112 8am–4pm Tue–Sat, 8am–noon Sun

On the road that connects the capital with Playa Bibijagua, a popular beach of black sand frequented by the inhabitants of Nueva Gerona, is Cuba's most famous penitentiary, which was converted into a museum in 1967. Originally built by Gerardo Machado, it was modelled on the famous panopticon (a prison laid out so inmates can be observed

by a single guard) in Joliet in the US. The prison consists of tiny cells in the interior of four enormous multistorey round cement blocks. In the middle of each stood a sentry-box from which guards could keep a close watch on all the prisoners. Guards circulated in underground galleries, never coming into contact with the prisoners above.

It was in the Presidio Modelo that the organizers of the attack on the Moncada army barracks in Santiago, led by Fidel Castro, were imprisoned in October 1953. They were liberated in an amnesty in May 1955.

At the entrance to the first pavilion is cell 3859, where Castro, despite his isolation, managed to reorganize the revolutionary movement, starting with the defence plea he made in court, "History Will Absolve Me".

"HISTORY WILL ABSOLVE ME"

At his "History Will Absolve Me" trial following the failed Moncada Barracks attack in 1953 (p238), Castro named José Martí (p101) as the attack's "intellectual author." Martí's vision of a fully literate, non-discriminatory, post-independence society informed Castro's revolution.

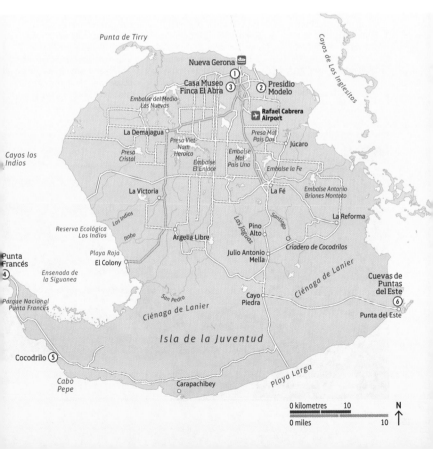

Casa Museo Finca El Abra

⌂ Carretera Siguanea Km 1.5 (5 km/3 miles SW of Nueva Gerona) ☎ 5219 3054 ⏰ 9am-5pm Tue-Sat, 9am-noon Sun

On the edge of the Sierra de las Casas is an elegant villa where, in 1870, the 17-year-old José Martí was held for nine weeks before being deported to Spain for his separatist views. A museum here displays photographs and documents relating to the national hero's presence on the island, but the rest of the villa is occupied by the descendants of the original owner, a rich Catalan.

PICTURE PERFECT
Underwater World

Owners of underwater cameras will find that the dive sites off Punta Francés are the perfect photography haunts. Keep your flash on, get close to your subject and set your camera to the highest resolution.

Punta Francés

🛈 Centro Internacional de Buceo; (48) 771 306

The 56 dive sites between Punta Francés and Punta Pedernales lie at the end of a shelf which gently slopes down from the coast to a depth of 20–25 m (65–82 ft), and then abruptly drops for hundreds of metres. This vertical wall is a favourite with passing fish, which literally rub shoulders with divers. While dives on the platform can be made by beginners, those along the shelf are more difficult and suited to divers with more experience.

Numerous great dive sights are peppered along this stretch of coast, but the following are among the most fascinating: La Pared de Coral Negro, which has an abundance of black coral as well as sponges as much as 35 m (115 ft) in diameter; El Reino del Sahara, one of the most beautiful shallow dives; El Mirador, a wall dive among sponges and large madrepores; El Arco de los Sábalos, the domain of tarpons; and Cayo Los Indios, where shipwrecks can be explored on the seabed at a depth of 10–12 m (33–40 ft).

All kinds of diving equipment can be rented from the Centro Internacional de Buceo (but it is advisable to take a 3-mm wet suit with you). From here boats take visitors to the dive sites. At noon, lunch is served at the jetty next to the stunning beach at Punta Francés.

The boat trip from the centre to Punta Francés, also known as Costa de los Piratas (the pirate coast), is a wonderful excursion for all diving abilities. Participants don snorkels, masks and fins to accompany professional divers exploring a French pirate's cave. Once back on dry land, you then trek to see nesting American crocodiles.

To the east of the Centro Internacional de Buceo is an area known as La Cañada, where Ecotur can arrange a guided walk through pine, palm and mango forests. The walk passes the "Jacuzzi of the Gods", a freshwater stream where walkers can bathe. The trail ends at the park ranger's house where home-roasted lamb and coffee is served to hikers.

↑ Scuba divers surveying a vibrant coral reef in a dive site near Punta Francés

HISTORY OF THE ISLAND

The Taíno and Siboney peoples knew of the Isla de la Juventud long before Columbus "discovered" it in 1494. The Spanish crown licensed the island to cattle breeders, but in practice handed it over to pirates, who used it as a hiding place for booty taken from Spanish ships.

After Nueva Gerona was founded in 1830, the island was used as a place of detention for Cuban nationalists, including José Martí. In 1953 Batista turned the island into a free zone where money could be laundered. The dictator also wanted to turn it into a holiday paradise for the rich. On New Year's night in 1958, a group of soldiers in the rebels' army took over the island during the opening ceremony of the Hotel Colony, and arrested the mafiosi in the hotel.

In 1966, after a devastating cyclone, the government planted new citrus groves on the island, creating work. In 10 years the island's population grew from 10,000 to 80,000.

 ### Cocodrilo

86 km (53 miles) SE of Nueva Gerona Ecotur; (46) 327 101

Formerly called Jacksonville, this fishing village was founded in the early 20th century by a small community from the British colony of the Cayman Islands in the Caribbean. Even now, a few of the villagers speak English as their first language. The British settlers introduced the Round Dance, a typical Jamaican dance, which blended with Cuban music to create Sucu Sucu. This danceform is still very popular among locals.

Did You Know?

Pirates hid their booty on the island because the waters were too shallow for Spanish ships.

 ### Cuevas de Punta del Este

59 km (37 miles) SE of Nueva Gerona Ecotur; (46) 327 101; www.ecoturcuba.tur.cu

Punta del Este, located on the southeastern tip of the island, has a stunning white-sand beach. It is, however, most famous for its seven caves, which were discovered in 1910 by a French castaway who took refuge here. On the walls of the caves are 235 drawings made by Siboneys in an age long before the arrival of Christopher Columbus.

The drawings in the largest cave – a series of red and black concentric circles crossed by arrows pointing eastward – probably represent a solar calendar. The complexity of these drawings led the Cuban ethnologist Fernando Ortíz, who studied them in 1925, to call them "the Sistine Chapel of the Caribbean".

Permits must be obtained in advance to explore the caves; wear insect repellant.

STAY

Tu Isla
This is the best private hotel in Nueva Gerona, with eight rooms (five with their own private bathrooms) and a superb garden restaurant. The rooftop bar hosts brilliant live music acts.

Calle 24 4510, Neuva Gerona (46) 509 128

Casa de la Alegría
Operated by attentive owners, this pleasant two-bedroom *casa particular* is a lovely place to stay on the island. One room is a secluded apartment.

Calle 43 3602, Nueva Gerona (46) 323 664

EXPERIENCE MORE

Soroa

C1 **Candelaria (Artemisa)** **Candelaria** **Hotel Soroa; (48) 523 788**

The town of Soroa lies 250 m (820 ft) above sea level in the middle of tropical forest in the Sierra del Rosario region. It was named after two Basque brothers, Lorenzo and Antonio Soroa Muñagorri, who, in around 1856, bought various coffee plantations in the area and soon became the proprietors of the entire territory. One of the estates in the valley, Finca Angerona, was in the 19th century the setting for a legendary love story involving the French-German Cornelius Sausse, who built the farm in 1813, and a Haitian girl, Ursule Lambert.

Soroa, today, is a small town with a hotel (Villa Soroa) and a number of tourist attractions. The most photographed is the Saltón, a spectacular waterfall on the Manantiales river, a 20-minute walk from the Villa Soroa. But the major sight here is the **Orquideario de Soroa**, an orchid garden which has been declared a national monument. It has one of the largest orchid collections in the world, with more than 700 species, 250 of which are endemic, in an area of 350 sq km (135 sq miles). The park, often visited by Hemingway, was founded in 1943 by a lawyer from the Canaries, Tomás Felipe Camacho. He had orchids sent here from all over the world in memory of his daughter, who had died at the age of 20 during childbirth, and his wife, who died shortly after.

Outside the town is the Castillo de las Nubes, a medieval-like construction built in 1940 for Antonio Arturo Sánchez Bustamante, the landowner of this area. The Castillo is a noted viewpoint, worth visiting for the marvellous views over the Sierra del Rosario alone.

← Bathers cooling off in the cascading Saltón waterfall near Soroa

EAT

La Fonda de Mercedes
This family-run restaurant serves traditional *criolla* meals, including delicious *ajiaco* stew.

C1 **Unit 9, Las Terrazas** **(48) 578 676**

 $\$$$\$$$\$$

El Galeón
Choose to sit on the shaded patio or on the pirate-themed rooftop. The grilled snapper is recommended.

C3 **Calle 24 4510, Nueva Gerona, Isla de la Juventud** **(46) 509 128**

 $\$$$\$$$\$$

Admiring the Cueva de los Portales, in the Parque Nacional La Güira

Orquideario de Soroa

⊛ 🏠 Carretera de Soroa Km 8 📞 (48) 523 871 🕐 8:30am–4:30pm daily

---

⑤
San Diego de los Baños

🅰 C2 🏠 Los Palacios (Pinar del Río)

This peaceful village on the slopes of the Sierra de los Quemados, about 5 km (3 miles) east of the Parque Nacional La Güira, was a major tourist and therapeutic centre a century ago. The thermal springs in the area, with their sulphurous water, were said to help cure rheumatism and skin diseases. It was promoted to US visitors as a "Saratoga in the Tropics" – a town near New York famed for its springs. Unfortunately the spa has been closed for several years, but the village retains a faded colonial charm. The peaceful plaza and Hotel Saratoga recall the town's erstwhile grandeur.

Did You Know?

Che Guevara wanted an altruistic society in which money could be eliminated.

---

⑥
Parque Nacional La Güira

🅰 C2 🏠 Los Palacios (Pinar del Río) ℹ Cueva de los Portales: Carretera San Andrès Km 14; (48) 750 486; 7am–6pm daily

Prior to the revolution, the rugged, remote and heavily forested 219 sq km (85 sq miles) that make up the Parque Nacional La Güira was one of the largest agricultural estates in the province of Pinar del Río. At its heart lies the landscaped grounds and former residence of the landowner Juan Manuel Cortina, a successful lawyer and notable politician. This was one of the first properties to be nationalized after Castro's rebel army seized power, forcing Cortina to flee Cuba in 1959 on charges of worker exploitation. He ended his days in Miami, where he died in 1970. His estate, Hacienda Cortina, is entered via mock medieval fortress gates. Though it lay derelict for many years, the estate is still in fairly good shape and includes the ruins of a medieval-style residence and an English garden with bronze lions, a small Chinese temple and Carrara marble statues of mythological figures including sphinxes and satyrs.

At the western edge of the park, but not accessible via Hacienda Cortina, is the Cueva de los Portales, a massive cavern in a *mogote* that was created by the Río Caiguanabo. Soaring to some 30 m (96 ft), this remote sanctuary was used by indigenous people as a refuge from the massacres that were waged by the Spanish in the early 16th century and swept through the island.

During the Cuban Missile Crisis of 1962, the cave became the headquarters of Che Guevara's Western Army. Built against one of the interior walls, amid dramatic dripstone formations, the room where Guevara had his office still contains his simple furniture. Note his narrow iron bed inside a natural recess in the rock wall. The site is a National Monument, and a guide will accompany your visit.

CUBAN MISSILE CRISIS

As a consequence of the failed Bay of Pigs invasion *(p177)*, President Kennedy became determined to eradicate Communism in Cuba. Concerned for the island's security, Castro requested that the Soviets install nuclear missiles. As a result, Kennedy was pressured by military hotheads to attack Cuba, while Castro urged Khrushchev to launch a nuclear strike on the US. After a tense 13 days, Khrushchev agreed to withdraw the missiles and Kennedy conceded not to invade Cuba.

❼ Pinar del Río

🅰B2 🚉 Pinar del Río
🚌 From Havana
🛈 Infotur, Hotel Vueltabajo, Calle Martí 103, (48) 759 381; Cubanacán, Calle Martí 109, esq Colón, (48) 750 178

In 1778, when the Cuban provinces were founded, the town of Nueva Filipina was renamed Pinar because of a pine grove in the vicinity, on the banks of the Guamá river. Nearby, General Antonio Maceo fought a number of battles in 1896–7 that were crucial to the Cubans' victory in the third war of independence.

Today, the pines no longer grow here, but the clean air and colonial atmosphere of Pinar del Río are unchanged. The capital of the western-most province in Cuba, the town can seem remote and old-fashioned. It has long been a centre for the cultivation and industrial processing of tobacco and is best utilized as a base for exploring the surrounding countryside. Although it is still largely untouched by hotel chains, the town does have numerous *casas particulares*. Watch out for *jineteros*, the aggressive touts who frequent the town offering accommodation help to travellers.

Pinar del Río is at its best in the carnival month of July and during November, when stages are set up throughout the city for the Nosotros

INSIDER TIP
Game Time

If visiting between November and April, check the local calendar to see if the Vegueros – Pinar del Río's baseball team – is playing any games at the Estadio Capitán San Luis. Take a hat, water and snacks. Enjoy the game!

CUBAN TOBACCO

The tobacco plant (*Nicotiana tabacum*) grows from small, round, golden seeds. Cuban tobacco seeds are in demand throughout the world, because their quality is considered to be so good. The plant reaches its full height in the three or four months from November to February. Like cigar-making (*p103*), tobacco growing is the result of age-old expertise handed down from generation to generation. Tobacco plants are quite delicate, and need skilful handling. There are two types: *Corojo*, grown in greenhouses, which has the prettiest leaves and is used as wrapper leaves for the cigars, and *Criollo*, which grows outdoors and provides the other leaves.

festival and colourfully dressed performers on stilts loom over the streets.

The most striking aspect about the historic centre of this small, orderly and peaceful town is the abundance of columns: Corinthian or Ionic, simple or decorated. It's easy to see from these architectural flourishes why Pinar del Río is known as the "city of capitals".

The most important buildings lie on the arcaded main street, Calle Martí (also known as Calle Real). In the Cultural Heritage Fund shop, at the corner of Calle Rosario, visitors can buy local crafts as well as art reproductions. In the evening, the Casa de la Cultura (at No 125) hosts shows and concerts of traditional music such as *punto guajiro* (from *guajiro*, the Cuban word for farmer), which is performed by a group playing different kinds of guitar, and is generally characterized by improvisation.

At Nos 172, 174 and 176 in Calle Colón, there are three

unusual buildings designed by Rogelio Pérez Cubillas, the city's leading architect in the 1930s and 1940s.

The somewhat extravagant Palacio Guasch is a mixture of Moorish arches, Gothic spires and Baroque elements. It was built in 1909 for a wealthy physician who had travelled widely and who wanted to reproduce in his new residence the architectural styles that had impressed him the most. In 1979 the mansion was transformed into the **Museo de Ciencias Naturales Sandalio de Noda** (natural history museum) named after Tranquilino Sandalio de Nodas, a well-known land surveyor in this region. The museum illustrates the natural and geological history of Pinar and has on display stuffed birds and animals, including the tiny Cuban *zunzún* hummingbird and a crocodile that is more than 4 m (12 ft) long, as well as rare plants and butterflies. In the inner courtyard are sculptures of prehistoric animals.

The **Museo Provincial de Historia** illustrates the history of the province from the Pre-Columbian period to today. On display is a major collection of 19th-century arms, colonial furniture, works by local painters, including a huge landscape by Domingo Ramos (1955), and mementos of the musician Enrique Jorrín, the father of the cha-cha-cha.

A Neo-Classical gem and the city's pride and joy, the **Teatro Milanés** is named after the romantic poet José Jacinto Milanés. It started out as the Lope de Vega theatre, which first opened in 1845 and was then bought in 1880 by one Félix del Pino Díaz. He totally renovated it, modelling it on the Teatro Sauto in Matanzas *(p170)*. Its name was changed in 1898. This simple but functional structure has a rectangular plan, a linear façade and a portico with tall columns. Its opulent, three-level, U-shaped wooden auditorium has a seating capacity of about 500.

Since 1892 the **Fábrica de Guayabita Casa Garay** has produced Guayabita del Pinar, a liqueur based on an ancient recipe. It is made by distilling brandy from the sugar of the *guayaba* (guava), which is grown in this area. Guided tours of the small factory finish up at the tasting area, where visitors can try the sweet and dry versions of this popular drink.

At the tiny **Fábrica de Tabacos Francisco Donatién** cigar factory, housed in a former 19th-century jail, visitors can watch the 70 or so workers making Trinidad cigars. These and other cigars are sold in the small shop. You can also visit the prestigious **Finca El Pinar San Luis** plantation, which is renowned among cigar connoisseurs.

Museo de Ciencias Naturales Sandalio de Noda

🌐 🅰 Calle Martí 202, esq Comandante Pinares 📞 (48) 779 483 🕘 9am–5pm Mon–Sat, 9am–noon Sun 🚫 1 Jan, 1 May, 26 Jul, 10 Oct, 25 Dec

Museo Provincial de Historia

🌐 🕘 🅰 Calle Martí 58 e/ Colón y Isabel Rubio 📞 (48) 754 300 🕘 8am–10pm Tue–Sat, 8am–5pm Sun 🚫 1 Jan, 1 May, 26 Jul, 10 Oct, 25 Dec

Teatro Milanés

🌐 🕘 🅰 Calle Martí y Colón 📞 (48) 753 871 🕘 Ticket office: 8am–5pm Tue–Sat, 8am–noon Sun; show: 9pm Wed–Sat

Fábrica de Guayabita Casa Garay

🕘 🅰 Calle Isabel Rubio 189 e/ Ceferino Fernández y Frank País 📞 (48) 752 966 🕘 9am–5pm Mon–Fri, 9am–noon Sat 🚫 1 Jan, 1 May, 26 Jul, 10 Oct, 25 Dec

Fábrica de Tabacos Francisco Donatién

🌐 🕘 🕘 🅰 Antonio Maceo 157 📞 (48) 773 069 🕘 Closed for restoration at time of writing; call to check

Finca El Pinar San Luis

🌐 🕘 🅰 Calle Isabel Rubio 📞 (48) 797 470 🕘 9am–5pm daily

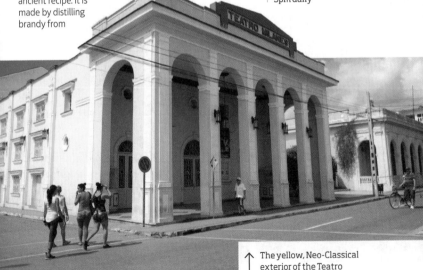

↑ The yellow, Neo-Classical exterior of the Teatro Milanés, Pinar del Río

A farmer working in a leafy tobacco field near Pinar del Río

The serene Iglesia del Sagrado Corazón de Jesus in the main square of Viñales ↑

❽
Viñales

Ⓐ B2 Ⓝ Pinar del Río 🚌

Under government protection so as to preserve this colonial settlement, the town of Viñales is full of amazing architecture. Founded in 1607, its name (vineyard) derived from the grape vines that were planted here by a settler from the Canary Islands and its economy has always been based on agriculture.

Viñales's main street is lined with myriad colonial houses and their characteristic arcades are useful shelters from the hot sun and any sudden tropical rainstorms. The street is named after Salvador Cisneros Betancourt, a 19th-century nationalist who is notable for being one of the signatories of the 1869 Cuban constitution.

The town's most important architecture can be seen around the main square, the Parque Martí, on which stand the Iglesia del Sagrado Corazón de Jesús – built in 1888 – and the former Colonia Española (the diplomatic headquarters of the Spanish gentry), which now serves as the town's Casa de la Cultura.

Viñales also contains a minor architectural gem, the **Casa de Don Tomás**, which was built in 1887–8 for Gerardo Miel y Sainz, a rich merchant and agent for a shipping line. The building was blown down in the 2008 hurricane, but then rebuilt true to the original.

Casa de Don Tomás
Ⓐ Salvador Cisnero, e/ Adela Azcuz y Carratera a Pinar del Río Ⓒ (48) 796 300

> Viñales's main street is lined with myriad colonial houses and their characteristic arcades are useful shelters from the hot sun and any sudden tropical rainstorms.

❾
Vuelta Abajo

Ⓐ B2 Ⓝ Pinar del Río

The small area between Pinar del Río, San Juan y Martínez and San Luís produces very high-quality tobacco. The good growing conditions here are the result of a series of factors – primarily the protection afforded by the Sierra del Rosario which shields the plants from heavy rainfall, and the fact that the

sandy red soil in which the tobacco plants grow is well drained and rich in nitrogen. This is a unique environment; in fact, the former land-owners who left Cuba in 1959 have tried in vain to reproduce the miracle in Nicaragua, Honduras, Santo Domingo and the US.

On the road from the provincial capital to San Juan y Martínez, the prestigious Hoyo de Monterrey plantations can be visited. Here plants are protected from the sun by cotton cloth to maintain the softness of the tobacco leaves. There are also curing houses, windowless storehouses where the leaves are left to dry on long poles.

Cayo Levisa

A B1 **A** Pinar del Río
A From Palma Rubia (1 hr), departures 9am & 10am, return 5pm & 6pm; excursions from Pinar del Río **A** Havanatur, Calle Osmani Arenado, esq Martí; (48) 778 494

This small island, with its white-sand beaches, an offshore coral reef and mangroves, is the most geared up for tourists in Los Colorados archipelago, and the only one with diving facilities. Despite this, it is still unspoiled and is home to several species of bird; the surrounding waters, too, have an abundance of fish.

Rancho La Guabina

A B2 **A** Carretera de Luis Lazo Km 9.5 (Pinar del Río) **A** (48) 757 616

For an authentic country experience, head to this ranch. Expropriated from wealthy landowner Antonio Ferro following the revolution, the 10 sq km (4 sq miles) of undulating, lake-studded countryside are located 10 km (6 miles) northwest of Pinar del Río town.

The farm – which is named after a species of fish that inhabits the lake – raises horses, rabbits and chickens. Watch the rodeo show, which takes place three times weekly, and take a tour by horse-drawn carriage or on horseback. You can also stay at the small boutique lodge that has an elegant restaurant.

STAY

Hotel Moka
The spacious rooms at this airy hilltop hotel overlooking Las Terrazas have a colonial feel.

A C1 **A** Las Terrazas **W** lasterrazas.cu

$ $ $

Hotel Los Jazmines
Although it does not make for the most luxurious stay, Hotel Los Jazmines' lofty location is unbeatable.

A B2 **A** Carretera de Viñales Km 25 **W** cubanacan.cu/en

$ $ $

Cubanacán Cayo Levisa
This state-run beachfront hotel offers three types of accommodation. Don't miss out on the hotel's extensive watersports programme.

A B1 **A** Cayo Levisa **W** cubanacan.cu/en

$ $ $

Casa Estudio del Arte Aliuska
Run by ecologically minded artists, this lovely *casa particular* offers rooms in a rustic thatched cottage.

A C1 **A** Carretera Soroa Km 8.5, Soroa **A** (48) 598 116

$ $ $

←
Bleached driftwood on one of Cayo Levisa's beaches

↑ Scuba diver admiring brain coral and other marine life in the waters off María La Gorda

 12

María La Gorda

🅰3 Pinar del Río
ℹ Hotel María La Gorda Diving Centre; (48) 778 131, 778 077

The best-known bathing spot on the southwestern coast owes its name to a sad legend. A few centuries ago, an overweight *(gorda)* girl named María was abducted by pirates on the Venezuelan coast, transported to Cuba, and then abandoned at this place. In order to survive, she was forced to sell herself to the many buccaneers who passed

---

GREAT VIEW
Road with a View

The 60-km- (37-mile-) long road from La Bajada, in the Parque Nacional Península de Guanahacabibes, to Cabo San Antonio is spectacularly scenic. The best section lies beyond Punta Holandés, where you emerge on a raised platform overlooking the azure sea.

---

by this coast, and this section of shoreline still bears her moniker – María the Fat.

The extraordinarily beautiful coral reefs are richly populated by marine life including sea turtles, reef sharks and a number of other rare species of tropical fish. This makes these 8 km (5 miles) of coastline, with fine white sand and a warm, translucent sea, a real tropical aquarium. The reefs are also incredibly easy to reach, lying just a short distance from the shore. This means that you can see vibrant fish swimming around the coral from the shore; you don't even need to get in the water.

From the jetty opposite the diving area, a twice-daily boat takes divers out to the various dive sites. Locations of particular interest include the so-called Black Coral Valley, which is a wall of coral over 100 m (328 ft) long, and the Salón de María, a sea cave which lies at a depth of 18 m (60 ft) and is the habitat of rare species of fish.

→ A beach in the Parque Nacional Península de Guanahacabibes

13

Parque Nacional Península de Guanahacabibes

🅰2 Pinar del Río
ℹ Estación Ecológica, La Bajada; (48) 750 366

Named after a Pre-Columbian ethnic group, this peninsula is a strip of land 100 km (62 miles) long and 6–34 km

(4–21 miles) wide. In 1985 it was declared a world biosphere reserve by UNESCO, to protect the flora and fauna, so access to the inner zone is limited. Permission to visit is granted by the park rangers at La Bajada, and visitors use their own vehicles to get here, then proceed on foot with a local guide.

The mixed deciduous and evergreen forest has some 600 species of plants and many animals, including deer, boar, reptiles and *jutías*, opossum-like rodents that live in trees. Birds include woodpeckers, parrots, hummingbirds, *cartacuba* and *tocororo*.

Cabo San Antonio, Cuba's western tip, is identifiable by the 23-m- (75-ft-) high Roncalli lighthouse, built in 1849 by the Spanish governor after whom it was named.

14
Cayo Largo

△E3 ⬠Isla de la Juventud

This 25-km- (15-mile-) long slender, low-lying wisp of an island is a wonderful holiday destination for those who love sun, sea and sand. Cayo Largo is semi-arid and lined along its southern shore by sand as white and fine as powdered sugar dissolving into shallow turquoise seas, perfect for snorkeling and wading. The most impressive beach is Playa Sirena, at the west end of the cay, while the few hotels on the island are concentrated along Playa Lindamar.

There are no inhabitants other than Cuban workers who live north of the airport in Combinado. Here you'll find the marina and tourist office, as well as the Granja de las Tortuga (Turtle Breeding Centre), where eggs laid in the sands by green and leather-back turtles are hatched for release. Scuba-diving and fly-fishing excursions are offered, and you can sail to nearby Cayo Iguana, which is named after the endemic iguanas that live here.

EAT

3J Tapas Bar
This hip bar-restaurant specializes in tapas, such as Spanish sausage and ravioli with spinach.

△B2 ⬠Cisneros 5, Viñales ☎(48) 793 334

$$⑤

Paladar Buena Vista
Enjoy sensational views over the valley from this rustic hilltop restaurant, serving *criolla* classics.

△B2 ⬠Carretera de Viñales Km 25, Viñales ☎(53) 364 434

$$⑤

Finca Agroecológico El Paraíso
Criolla dishes made with organic produce from the farm are on the menu at this hillside restaurant.

△B2 ⬠Carretera al Cementerio Km 1.5, Viñales ☎(58) 188 581

$$⑤

CENTRAL CUBA - WEST

The history of this area is punctuated by strife. In 1509, the Spanish navigator Sebastián Ocampo caught sight of a bay on Cuba's northern Atlantic coast, claimed the land from the Siboney Indians and assigned it to settlers from the Canary Islands. The indigenous people opposed this injustice so fiercely that the city of Matanzas, which was built in that bay in the 1600s, probably owes its name to the memory of a massacre *(matanza)* of Spaniards. The Jagua Indians were also wiped out when a bay on the south coast was "discovered" by Columbus in 1494, although Cienfuegos wasn't founded here until 1819. The city was settled by Roman Catholics from Haiti and Louisiana, who were granted this territory to counterbalance the massive presence of African slaves.

From the mid-1500s to the mid-1700s, both coasts in this region had to face the serious threat of pirate raids. As a result, in 1689, 20 families from the village of Remedios, not far from the sea, decided to move to the interior to be at a safe distance from the buccaneers' ships and cannons. As a result, Santa Clara was founded. The city holds a special place in Cuban hearts since it was the setting for heroic acts by Che Guevara and his rebel forces. On 28 December 1958, they captured the area after what was to be the last battle of the revolution before Batista fled.

CENTRAL
CUBA – WEST

Atlantic   Ocean

*Cayo Cruz
del Padre*

HAVANA
p56

Santa Cruz
del Norte

**CAMILO
CIENFUEGOS** ❼

VARADERO ❷

*Bahía de
Cárdenas*

Tapaste

Bainoa

MATANZAS ❶

Juan Gualberto
Gómez Airport ✈

❽ **CÁRDENAS**

San José
de Las Lajas

Aguacate

José Smith
Comas

Bejucal

MAYABEQUE

Madruga

**CUEVAS DE
BELLAMAR** ❾

Coliseo

Máximo
Gómez

San Felipe

Güines

Cabezas

**SAN MIGUEL
DE LOS BAÑOS** ❿

Jovellanos

Batabanó

Melena del Sur

Vegas

Nueva Paz

Unión
de Reyes

La Isabel

Colón

*Playa
Mayabeque*

*Playa
Rosario*

Playa del
Caimito

La Lanza

Pedro
Betancourt

MATANZAS

*Playa
Tasajera*

Torriente

**WESTERN
CUBA**
p142

*Ensenada
de la Broa*

Calimete

Jagüey Grande

Amarillas

Santo
Tomás

Australia

Boca de
Guamá

Maneadero

Llanura Central de Zapata

Aguada de
Pasajeros

El Maíz

Guamá

Playa Larga

PENÍNSULA DE ZAPATA ❸

*Bay
of
Pigs*

Bermejas

La Salina

*Cayos Blancos
del Sur*

Playa
Girón

Playa
Maceo

*Caribbean
Sea*

0 kilometres   30
0 miles   30

N
↑

CENTRAL CUBA – WEST

Must Sees
1. Matanzas
2. Varadero
3. Península de Zapata
4. Cienfuegos
5. Santa Clara
6. Jardín Botánico Soledad

Experience More
7. Camilo Cienfuegos
8. Cárdenas

9. Cuevas de Bellamar
10. San Miguel de los Baños
11. Circuito Sur
12. Lago Hanabanilla
13. El Nicho
14. Remedios
15. Caibarién

↑ A typical street in the centre of Matanzas

❶

MATANZAS

🅰E1 🏠Matanzas ✈Carretera a Regaliot Km 5.5; (45) 247 015 🚉Carretera de Cidra y 181; (45) 292 409 🚌Calzada de Estévez; (45) 291 473 🛈Havanatur, Calle Jovellanos, e/ Medio y Río; (45) 253 856

The capital of the province of the same name, Matanzas sits on the shores of a large bay. Since the 19th century, the city has been called the "Creole Venice" due to the many bridges linking the historic centre to Matanzas' suburban districts, and the artistic and cultural life of the city at that time, which outshone that of Havana.

 ①

Museo Provincial

🏠Calle Milanés, e/ Magdalena y Ayllon
📞(45) 243 195 🕘9am-4pm Mon-Sat

This museum occupies the two-storey Palacio del Junco, a bright blue porticoed building constructed in 1838 for the Del Junco family. The collection documents the history of the province. The section devoted to the colonial period, with documents on slavery and sugar cane farm tools, is of particular interest. Copies of Aurora, the most interesting Cuban periodical of the 19th century, are also on display.

 ②

Teatro Sauto

🏠Calle Magdalena, e/ Medio y Milanés
📞(45) 242 721

The pride and joy of the city, this theatre was designed by the Italian architect Daniele Dell'Aglio, who was also responsible for the church of San Pedro in the French-populated Versalles district of the city. On 6 April 1863 the auditorium was opened to the public as the Esteban Theatre, in honour of the provincial governor who had financed the construction. It was later renamed the Sauto Theatre because of the Matanceros'

affection for the local pharmacist, Ambrosio de la Concepción Sauto, a passionate theatregoer. Saunto famously cured Queen Isabella II of Spain of a skin disease, using a lotion he had himself prepared.

A solidly built Neo-Classical structure with several Greek-inspired statues made of Carrara marble, the theatre has various frescoes of Renaissance inspiration, executed by Daniele Dell' Aglio himself. The U-shaped

THE DANZÓN

In 1879 Miguel Failde, who was born in Mantanzas, composed *Las Alturas de Simpson*. This slow piece of music introduced a new musical genre to Cuba, the *danzón*. This Caribbean and Creole adaptation of European country dancing became the most popular dance on the island for about fifty years. It is still danced in Matanzas, in the Casa Amigos del Danzón, the house where Miguel Failde was born.

interior is almost entirely covered with salubrious wood-panelling.

Because of its exceptional acoustics, the versatile theatre has been the chosen venue for all kinds of shows and the great Cuban artists of the 19th and 20th centuries have appeared here. World-famous performers have included French actress Sarah Bernhardt (in Alexandre Dumas' play *Camille* in 1887), Russian ballet dancer Anna Pavlova and the guitarist Andrés Segovia.

---

③

Castillo de San Severino

🏠 **Carretera del Puerto**
📞 **(45) 283 259** 🕐 **Mon**

This imposing fortress, dating from 1745, guards the western entrance to Matanzas Bay. It has had a varied past, serving as a Spanish prison for Cuban nationalists during the 19th century. Recently restored, it now hosts the Museo de la Ruta del Esclavo (Slave Route Museum), with exhibits dedicated to the horrifying realities of slavery, as well as the roots of the Afro-Cuban Santería religion.

→

Posing in front of the statue of José Martí in Parque de la Libertad

④

Parque de la Libertad

A large square, Parque de la Libertad was built on the site of the Indian village of Yacayo. In the middle of the plaza is an impressive statue of José Martí, surrounded by some attractive buildings: the Liceo Artístico y Literario (1860); the Casino Español, built in the early 1900s; the Palacio del Gobierno; the Catedral de San Carlos, dating from the 17th century; and the Museo Farmacéutico de Matanzas.

---

⑤

Museo Farmacéutico de Matanzas

🏠 **Calle Milanés 4951, e/ Santa Teresa y Ayuntamiento** 📞 **(45) 243 179** 🕐 **10am–5pm daily**

This fine example of a 19th-century pharmacy, overlooking Parque de la Libertad, was founded on

1 January 1882 by Ernesto Triolet and Juan Fermín de Figueroa and turned into a museum in 1964.

On the old-fashioned wooden shelves stand the original French porcelain vases decorated by hand, as well as vessels imported from the US, and an incredible number of small bottles with herbs, syrups and elixirs. The museum also has a collection of three million old labels, mortars and stills, and advertising posters boasting the miraculous curative powers of Dr Triolet's remedies. It's a fascinating look at how the practice of medicine has changed over the centuries.

The shop also serves as a bureau of scientific information, with more than a million original formulae and rare books on botany, medicine, chemistry and pharmaceuticals, in several foreign languages.

Did You Know?

The city has also been called the "Athens of Cuba".

Valle de Yumurí 5 km (3 miles)

Iglesia de San Pedro Apóstol

Hershey Station

Castillo de San Severino 1.5 km (1 mile) ③

Puente Concordia

Biblioteca General y del Monte

Teatro Velasco

Parque de la Libertad ④

Museo Provincial ①

Palacio de Justicia

Teatro Sauto ②

Museo Farmacéutico de Mantanzas ⑤

Catedral de San Carlos

PLAZA DE LA VIGÍA

Puente Calixto García

Río San Juan

0 metres 300
0 yards 300
N

Railway Station 1.5 km (1 mile)

Bus Station 750 m (800 yards)

②

VARADERO

🅰E1 🏠Matanzas ✈(45) 247 015 🚌Autopista del Sur y 36; (45) 614 886 ℹInfotur, Calle 13 y Ave 1, (45) 662 966

Cuba's top resort, which occupies the 19-km- (12-mile-) long Península de Hicacos, is connected to the mainland by a drawbridge, a sign of Varadero's 19th-century exclusivity. After Castro took power in 1959, the area was opened up to everyone, and is now especially popular with visitors, drawn to the clear blue water.

①

Parque Retiro Josone

🏠Avenida Primera y Calle 56 📞(45) 667 228 ⊙Daily

This is a beautiful park, populated by elegant trees, tropical flowers and plants. It also has plenty of facilities including three restaurants and a small lake where birds gather and tourists hire rowing boats and pedalos. The park was established in 1942 by José Iturrioz, the owner of the Arrechabala Ronera, the rum factory just outside Cárdenas. He named the park Josone because it was a combination of the first syllable of his Christian name and that of his wife, Onelia.

The park is a hit with children, who will particularly love the boat rides on the lake.

②

Restaurante Las Américas (Mansión Xanadú)

🏠Avenida Las Américas Km 8.5 📞(45) 667 388 ⊙Daily

During the years from 1920 to 1950 an American millionaire, chemical engineer Alfred Irénée Dupont de Nemours, gambled a great deal of money by purchasing most of the beautiful Hicacos peninsula from the heirs of the Spanish landowners who first colonized it. At that time there were only a few villas and one hotel on the peninsula. Dupont then parcelled the land out to Cubans and Americans who, within a few years, transformed Varadero into a centre for gambling and

prostitution. Dupont made a healthy profit and the area became a haven for vice.

At the height of his vast property dealings, Dupont asked the two Cuban architects called Govantes and Cabarrocas, who had designed the Capitolio in Havana (*p88*), to design a salubrious villa for him on the rocky promontory of San Bernardino, the highest

WATERSPORTS

Most hotels in Varadero have watersport facilities and beach outlets rent out sea-kayaks, Hobie Cats, sailboards and kitesurfing equipment. Scuba diving is a popular option and can be arranged at hotels or at Barracuda Scuba Cuba (*Avenida 1ra & 2; (45) 613 481*). Sportfishing is also available from any of the peninsula's three marinas.

↑ Varadero's many resort hotels, surrounded by towering palm trees

point in Varadero. Dupont's sumptuous four-storey building, completed in 1929 and named Mansión Xanadú, was dressed with Italian marble and precious wood. Constructed using the latest building innovations, the villa's roof was covered with green ceramic tiles with thermal insulation. The same attention was paid to the grounds as to the house itself and it was surrounded by a huge garden planted with rare plants. In the grounds, you'll also find an iguana farm and a golf course. All in all, Dupont's extravagant construction cost $338,000, an enormous sum at the time.

In 1959, after the revolution, Dupont escaped from Cuba, leaving the villa to the Cuban government, which, in 1963, turned it into "Las Américas", the most elegant restaurant in Varadero. It specializes in French cuisine, but the building can be visited without any obligation to eat there if you're just curious to see Dupont's mansion. The dining room still has its original furniture and the top-floor bar, with its wide selection of drinks and cigars, is a favourite spot in the resort for sundowners.

Apart from the house and restaurant, the golf course offers 18 manicured holes and breathtaking views. Upon request, golf players can book accommodation in the few luxury bedrooms in the villa.

③
Punta Hicacos

For those interested in wildlife, the most fascinating part of Varadero is the area near Punta Hicacos, at the end of the peninsula, which has become a protected nature reserve. Here you can visit some quiet, secluded beaches, as well as several caves, including the Cueva de Ambrosio, with fossils, Pre-Columbian rock paintings.

The peninsula is also an attraction for scuba divers, who can choose from 23 dive sites, offering both deep and shallow dives.

Must See

EAT

Salsa Suárez
This classy *paladar* combines chic décor with superbly executed fusion cuisine.

🏠 Calle 31, 103 📞 (45) 612 009 🕐 Tue

$$⑤

Varadero 60
With an eclectic menu, attentive service and an outdoor terrace, this 1950s-themed *paladar* is an original dining choice. The best dishes are lobster and steak, and there are plenty of rum options here too.

🏠 Calle 60 y 3ra 📞 (45) 613 986

$$⑤

Restaurante Kike-Kcho
The chicest place in town, this gourmet restaurant, found on the tip of the peninsula, serves sumptuous seafood dishes.

🏠 Marina Gaviota 📞 (45) 664 115

$$$

↑ Huts made from royal palm in Guamá on the Península de Zapata

③

PENÍNSULA DE ZAPATA

🅰E2 **🌐Matanzas** **🚌 From Boca de Guamá to Guamá**
🛈 Cubanacán, Jagüey Grande, (45) 913 224; National Park office, (45) 987 249

As well as being the site of the infamous Bay of Pigs invasion, the Península de Zapata is synonymous with unspoiled nature and luxuriant tropical vegetation. It is a place where visitors can lie in a hammock in the shade of palm trees, observe birds with multicoloured plumage or row a boat on the Laguna del Tesoro.

①
Refugio de Fauna Bermejas

The top bird-watching site on the Zapata peninsula, the Refugio de Fauna Bermejas adjoins the eastern extent of the Parque Nacional Cienaga de Zapata (p176). While walking on this trail, visitors are virtually guaranteed to spot endemic bird species, including the patriotically coloured Cuban trogon. If you're lucky, you might also see the green flash of Cuban parrots flying overhead.

Book a tour with a specialist guide *(Armando Herrera; (45) 987 249)*.

> ### Did You Know?
> The peninsula is named after the landowner who was given the land by the Spanish in 1636.

②
Guamá

This unusual holiday village in the Laguna del Tesoro (Treasure Lake), measuring 16 sq km (6 sq miles), is named after Guamá, a Taíno warrior who resisted the Spanish conquistadors. Guamá was killed in 1533.

The village consists of 18 huts standing on stilts on several small islands in the lagoon. The only way to reach the village is by boat along the luxuriantly fringed canal from Boca de Guamá. Guamá is home to the Horizontes Villa

Guamá (p176), an unusual hotel that also includes a restaurant, a bar and a small museum. The Muestras Aborígenes displays finds from the Laguna del Tesoro area, dating back to the Taíno civilization (p50).

Also of interest is the reconstructed Taíno village of Aldea Taína, which occupies another island. It comprises four earth *bohíos* (typical Indian huts), a *caney* (a larger round building) and 25 life-size statues of natives by the well-known Cuban sculptress Rita Longa. The figures form the Batey Aborigen, or native Indian square, and represent the few people who lived in the village: a young girl named Dayamí; a crocodile hunter, Abey; Cajimo, hunter of *jutías* (a type of rodent); Manguanay, the mother who is preparing *casabe* (cassava) for her family; Yaima, a little girl who is playing; and the key figure, Guamá, the heroic Taíno warrior.

→ Vibrant green and red zunzuncito, or bee hummingbird, in flight

③

Playa Larga

At the end of the Bay of Pigs is one of the better beaches along this part of Caribbean coastline, where thick vegetation usually grows down as far as the shore. The coral reef found here offers magnificent dive sites and the beach's resorts offer diving, fishing and bird-watching excursions.

Near the car park, a small monument commemorates the landing of the anti-Castro troops in 1961, while along the road to Playa Girón there are numerous memorials to the Cuban defenders who died in the famous three-day battle.

Northeast of Playa Larga is an ornithological reserve.

> ⊙ HIDDEN GEM
> ## Casa de Zunzuncitos
>
> The zunzuncito is endemic to only a few regions of Cuba, but you're sure to see the world's smallest bird in this fragrant garden in Palpite, 5 km (3 miles) inland of Playa Larga. The owner only asks for tips from visitors.

TOP 5 FAUNA OF ZAPATA SWAMP

Cuban Crocodile
This species has been protected since the 1960s.

Manatees
The Caribbean species is over 4 m (13 ft) long and weighs about 600 kg (1,320 lbs).

Cuban Pygmy Owl
A small nocturnal raptor bird.

Grey Heron
Lives in the mangrove swamps and feeds on small fish and amphibia.

Zunzuncito
This bee hummingbird is multicoloured when male and black-green if female.

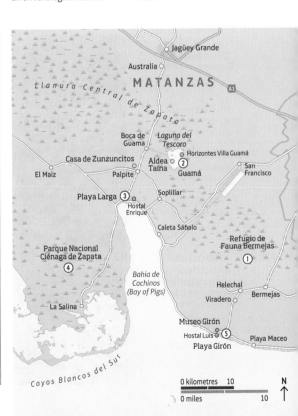

Jagüey Grande
Australia
MATANZAS
Llanura Central de Zapata
A1
Boca de Guama
Laguna del Tesoro
Horizontes Villa Guamá
Casa de Zunzuncitos
Aldea Taína ②
San Francisco
El Maiz
Palpite
Guamá
Playa Larga ③
Soplillar
Hostal Enrique
Caleta Sábalo
Parque Nacional Ciénaga de Zapata ④
Refugio de Fauna Bermejas ①
Bahía de Cochinos (Bay of Pigs)
Helechal
Bermejas
Viradero
La Salina
Museo Girón
Hostal Luis ⑤
Playa Maceo
Playa Girón
Cayos Blancos del Sur

0 kilometres 10
0 miles 10
N ↑

④

Parque Nacional Ciénaga de Zapata

⌖ 2 km (1.3 miles) W of Playa Larga

The Zapata Swamp National Park is Cuba's largest protected area and comprises the biggest wetlands in the Caribbean. The park's distinct ecosystems include mangrove forest, swamp forest and marsh grassland. The access gate is 2 km (1.3 miles) west of Playa Larga, and a guide is compulsory.

STAY

Horizontes Villa Guamá

A re-creation of an indigenous village, this state-run hotel is made up of thatched cabins on stilts. It occupies several islands in the Laguna del Tesoro.

⌖ Boca de Guamá
🌐 cubanacan.cu/en

$$$

Hostal Enrique

A superb *casa particular*, with nine rooms, Hotel Enrique is a stone's throw from the beach. Filling meals are served on the breeze-swept rooftop.

⌖ Playa Larga
📞 (52) 686 785

$$$

Hostal Luis

A delightful five-bedroom *casa particular* located a five-minute walk from the beach.

⌖ Playa Girón
📞 (45) 984 258

$$$

⑤

Playa Girón

This beach was named in the 1600s after a French pirate, Gilberto Girón, who found refuge here. It became famous three centuries later, when it was the site of the ill-fated, American-backed landing in 1961. A large sign at the entrance to Playa Girón reads: "Here North American imperialism suffered its first major defeat."

Situated on the eastern side of the Bay of Pigs, this is the last sandy beach in the area, ideal for fishing and diving and also equipped with good tourist facilities.

A must is a visit to the small **Museo Girón**, which covers the anti-Castro invasion using photos, documents, weapons, a tank and the wreckage of aeroplanes that took part in the last battle, as well as films taken during the invasion.

Museo Girón
⊗⊗ ⌖ Playa Girón, Península de Zapata 📞 (45) 984 122 🕘 9am–5pm daily

> A large sign at the entrance to Playa Girón reads: "Here North American imperialism suffered its first major defeat."

THE BAY OF PIGS INVASION

The long, narrow Bay of Pigs (Bahía de Cochinos) became known throughout the world in 1961. On 14 April of that year, at the height of the Cold War, a group of 1,400 Cuban exiles, trained by the CIA with the approval of President John F Kennedy, left Nicaragua for Cuba on six ships. The next day, six US B-26 aeroplanes attacked the island's three military air bases, their bombs killing seven people and wounding 53.

On 16 April the group of counter-revolutionaries landed on the main beaches along the bay, Playa Larga and Playa Girón. They were confronted by the Cuban armed forces *(right)*, headed by Fidel Castro himself, who were well prepared for the battle and had the support of the local population. The fighting lasted just three days and ended in the rapid defeat of the invaders. In order to avoid an international crisis, which could have escalated into an extremely serious situation, given the USSR's support of Cuba, the US suddenly withdrew its aerial support. The invading forces were later allowed to return to the US in exchange for supplies.

↑ Swimming at Playa Girón, where Castro's forces in the Bay of Pigs invasion are remembered *(inset)*

4

CIENFUEGOS

⚑F2 🏛Cienfuegos 🚌Ave 58 y Calle 4; (43) 525 495 🚍Calle 49, e/ Ave 56 y 58; (43) 518 114 ℹ️Ave 56 No 3117 e/ Calles 31 y 33, (43) 514 653; Cubatur, Calle 37 e/ 54 y 56, (43) 551 242

The maritime city of Cienfuegos has a well-preserved historic centre and one of the most captivating bays in the Caribbean Sea – hence its nickname, the "Pearl of the South". Originally occupied by Jagua Indians, the gulf was "discovered" by Columbus in 1494 and the town of Fernandina de Jagua, which became Cienfuegos, was founded here in 1819.

① Parque Martí

The "zero kilometre", the central point of Cienfuegos, is in the middle of Parque Martí, the former Plaza de Armas (parade ground). The vast square has been declared a national monument because of the surrounding buildings and its historic importance. It was here that the foundation of Cienfuegos was celebrated with a solemn ceremony in the shade of a hibiscus tree, chosen as a marker for laying out the city's first 25 blocks.

Lions on a marble pedestal flank a monument to José Martí, erected here in 1906. One side of the square is entirely occupied by the Antiguo Ayuntamiento, now the home of the provincial government assembly, supposedly modelled on the Capitolio in Havana.

②
Teatro Tomás Terry

🏛Ave 56 No 2703 y Calle 27 📞(43) 513 361 🕐9am–6pm daily

This theatre was built from 1886 to 1889 to fulfil the last will and testament of Tomás Terry Adams, an unscrupulous sugar factory owner who had become wealthy through the slave trade and held the position of mayor. World-famous figures such as Enrico Caruso and Sarah Bernhardt performed here in the early 1900s.

The Italian-style theatre was designed by Lino Sánchez Mármol, with a splendid two-tiered auditorium and a huge fresco by Camilo Salaya, a Philippine-Spanish painter who moved to Cuba in the late 1800s. The austere façade on the Parque Central has five arches corresponding to the number of entrances. The Byzantine mosaic murals on the pediment, made by the Salviati workshops in Venice, represent the muses.

③
Catedral de la Purísima Concepción

🏛Ave 56 No 2902 y Calle 29 📞(43) 525 297 🕐7am–noon Mon-Fri, 8am-noon Sat & Sun

The cathedral of Cienfuegos, constructed between 1833 and 1869, is one of the major buildings on the city's central square. Its distinguishing features are the Neo-Classical

> **Did You Know?**
>
> Cienfuegos was named after the first Cuban Governor General in 1829.

↑ The grand Antiguo Ayuntamiento in Parque Martí

façade with two bell towers of different heights, and its stained-glass windows.

Museo Provincial

🏛 Ave 54 No 2702 esq Calle 27 📞 (43) 519 722 🕐 10am-6pm Tue-Sat, 9am-1pm Sun 🚫 1 Jan, 1 May, 26 Jul, 25 Dec

Cienfuegos's Provincial Museum is located in the former Casino Español, an eclectic-style building first opened in 1896. The furniture, bronze and marble objects, and crystal and porcelain collections bear witness to the refined taste and wealth of 19th-century families in Cienfuegos.

___

⑤ Palacio Ferrer

🏛 Ave 54 esq Calle 25 📞 (43) 516 584 🕐 Open for cultural events

This palace, which houses the Casa Provincial de la Cultura, was built in the early 1900s by the sugar magnate José Ferrer Sirés. Famous tenor Enrico Caruso is said to have stayed here when he performed at the Teatro Tomás Terry.

The building stands on the western end of the plaza and is the most bizarre and eclectic in the square. It is distinguished by its cupola with blue mosaic decoration. It is worth climbing up the wrought-iron spiral staircase to enjoy the fine views over the city.

STAY

Hostal Bahía
This *casa particular* has bay views and a gourmet restaurant.

🏛 Avenida 20, 3502
📞 (43) 526 598

💲💲💲

Hotel Meliá Jagua
This 1950s hotel has heaps of retro charm.

🏛 Calle 37 e/ 0 y 2
🌐 meliacuba.com

💲💲💲

Hotel Meliá San Carlos
Opened in 2018, this downtown, historic hotel offers true luxury.

🏛 Avenida 56 e/ 33 y 35
🌐 meliacuba.com

💲💲💲

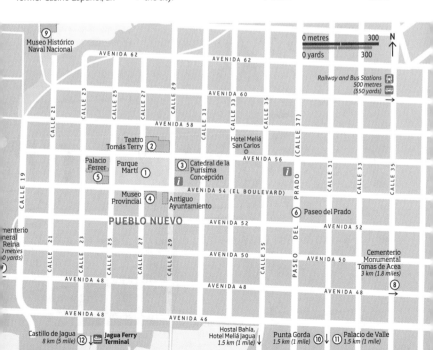

⑥
Paseo del Prado

The liveliest street in town is known for its elegant, well-preserved buildings and the monuments honouring leading local figures. It crosses the historic centre and goes south as far as Punta Gorda on the tip of the bay. It was laid out in 1922.

⑦
Cementerio General La Reina

🏠 Ave 50 y Calle 7, Reina
🕐 Daily

The municipal cemetery of La Reina is located at the western end of the city, and has been declared a national monument. It's not hard to see why – laid out in the 1830s, this is a beautiful Neo-Classical cemetery. Don't miss the famous funerary statue of La Bella Durmiente (Sleeping Beauty), leaning against a cross and cradling flowers.

⑧
Cementerio Monumental Tomás de Acea

🏠 Ave 5 de Septiembre
📞 (43) 525 257 🕐 7am-6pm daily

This monumental cemetery lies in the eastern suburb of Cienfuegos. Varied in stylistic influences, it was conceived as a large garden with paths and fruit trees. The entrance is a replica of Athens's Parthenon.

⑨
Museo Histórico Naval Nacional

🏠 Ave 60 y Calle 21, Cayo Loco 📞 (43) 516 617
🕐 10am-6pm Tue-Sat, 9:45am-noon Sun

Housed in the town's rose-pink naval barracks, on the Cayo Loco peninsula, is the most important naval museum in Cuba. It features a series of documents concerning the local anti-Batista insurrection of 5 September 1957, and an interesting display recording the history of the Cuban Navy.

⑩
Punta Gorda

At the southern tip of the bay of Cienfuegos lies Punta Gorda, the aristocratic quarter of the city in the early 1900s, which affords a lovely panoramic view of the bay. A short walk along the seafront takes you past many attractive villas and various brightly coloured wooden houses can be seen

← View over the bay from the balustrade of Castillo de Jagua

as you approach the tip of the peninsula. These buildings were modelled on the American prefabricated "balloon frame" homes that were so much in vogue in the early 20th century.

Palacio de Valle

🏠 Calle 37 e/ Ave O y 2, Punta Gorda 📞 (43) 551 003, ext 830 🕙 10am–10pm daily

The most original building in the Punta Gorda quarter, Palacio de Valle was designed by the Italian architect Alfredo Colli between 1913 and 1917. The architect was engaged by the sugar merchant Acisclo del Valle Blanco, one of the wealthiest men in Cuba in the 20th century.

The two-storey building, which is now a restaurant, is lavishly decorated with Gothic, Venetian and Neo-Moorish motifs, much in the Arab-Spanish style of the Alcázars in Granada and Seville. The façade has three towers of different designs symbolizing power, religion and love. The terrace is open to the public.

← A multitude of beautiful tombs in the Cemeterio General La Reina

⑫ Castillo de Jagua

🏠 Poblado Castillo de Jagua 📞 (43) 965 402 🕙 9am–5pm daily

Built by engineer José Tantete, following a design by Bruno Caballero, to protect the bay and the region from Jamaican pirates, the Castillo was the third most important fortress in Cuba in the 18th century and the only one in the central region of the island. The original moat and drawbridge are still intact.

According to legend, the citadel was haunted by a mysterious lady dressed in blue, who every night walked through the rooms and corridors, frightening the guards. It is said that one morning one of the guards was found in a state of shock while wringing a piece of blue cloth in anguish. The unfortunate man never got over this experience and ended up in an asylum.

At the foot of the Castillo is the fishing village of Perché, whose picturesque wooden houses are in striking contrast to the majestic military structure above. Most visitors arrive by ferry here from the dock in Cienfuegos.

BENNY MORÉ

A great source of pride to Cienfuegos is Maximiliano Bartolomé Moré, better known as Benny Moré, who was born at nearby Santa Isabel de las Lajas in 1919. Moré inspired many generations of Cubans with his unique voice, which enabled him to interpret a variety of musical genres. For this reason the artist was nicknamed *el bárbaro del ritmo* (the barbarian of rhythm). He was self-taught, and when still quite young performed with famous orchestras such as those led by the Matamoros brothers and Pérez Prado. He died in the early 1960s. For some time Cienfuegos – which he proclaimed to be "the city that I like the most" in his song about the city - has paid tribute to him with the Benny Moré International Festival.

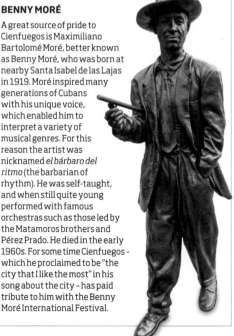

↑ Aerial view over the peaceful Parque Leoncio Vidal and the city centre

5

SANTA CLARA

🅰G2 🏠Villa Clara 🚉Luis Estévez 323 🚌Carretera Central Km 2.5 🛈Infotur, Calle Cuba 68 e/ Eduardo Machado y Maestra Nicolosa; (42) 227 557

Founded in 1689 when a group from Remedios moved away from the coast to escape from pirate raids, Santa Clara became famous in 1958 when it was the setting of the battle, led by Che Guevara, that marked the end of Batista's dictatorship. Santa Clara is now known as "the city of the heroic guerrilla".

① Parque Leoncio Vidal

The heart of the city, this charming square with its pristine flower beds, wrought-iron benches and period street lamps has retained its original 1925 atmosphere.

The obelisk which stands on the edge of the square was commissioned by the rich heiress Marta Abreu de Estévez in honour of two priests, Juan de Conyedo and Hurtado de Mendoza. As well as this monument, you will also find a bust of Leoncio Vidal, a colonel in the national independence army who died in battle in 1896, right in this very square.

Until 1894 the square was partly off limits to black people, who could only walk along certain areas of the pavement.

___

② Teatro La Caridad

🏠Parque Vidal 3 📞(42) 205 548 🕘9am–9pm daily

Built to a design by the engineer Herminio Leiva y Aguilera for the heiress Marta Abreu de Estévez, this theatre was inaugurated in 1885. At that time, the theatre offered many additional services – a barber shop, ballroom and gambling room, café and restaurant. The aim of all these enterprises was to raise money to be given to the city's poor (hence its name, Charity Theatre).

The building has a simple, linear façade, in contrast to the ornate interior, with its profusion of chandeliers and painted panels. The auditorium itself, which has three tiers of boxes with wrought-iron balusters, was the first theatre in Cuba to have folding seats in the stalls.

Perhaps the best feature of the theatre is the frescoed ceiling, executed by the Spanish-Philippine painter Camilo Salaya. Look up to see the artist's allegorical figures representing Genius, History and Fame.

↑ One of Camilo Salaya's frescoes on the ceiling of Teatro La Caridad

Museo de Artes Decorativas

🏠 Calle Marta Abreu, esq Luis Estévez 📞 (42) 205 368 🕓 9am-6pm Mon, Wed & Thu, 1-10pm Fri & Sat, 6-10pm Sun

The excellent Decorative Arts Museum, housed in a building dating from 1810, contains ornate furniture, from the 17th to 20th centuries, and paintings that once belonged to leading local families.

Among the objects on display here, those donated by the Cuban poetess Dulce María Loynaz are particularly elegant and delightful.

Tren Blindado Monument

🏠 Carretera Camajuaní, junction with railway line 📞 (42) 202 758 🕓 8:30am-5pm Tue-Sat, 9am-1pm Sun

On 28 December 1958, with the aid of only 300 men, Che Guevara succeeded in conquering Santa Clara. It was a brilliant victory for Guevara's troops considering the fact that the city had been fiercely defended by 3,000 of Batista's soldiers. The following day, Guevara handed the dictator another severe setback when he derailed an armoured train that was supposed to transport 408 soldiers and many weapons to eastern Cuba. If the train had successfully made it to its destination, it may have halted the advance of the rebels. The episode ended with the surrender of Batista's men.

Cuban sculptor José Delarra commemorated the halting of the train by creating a museum and monument on the spot where it took place, in the northeastern part of Santa Clara, on the line to Remedios. The sequence of events is re-created using original elements from the day such as four wagons from the armoured train, military plans and maps, photographs and weapons. Also on show is the D-6 Caterpillar bulldozer that was used by the guerrillas to remove rails and cause the derailment.

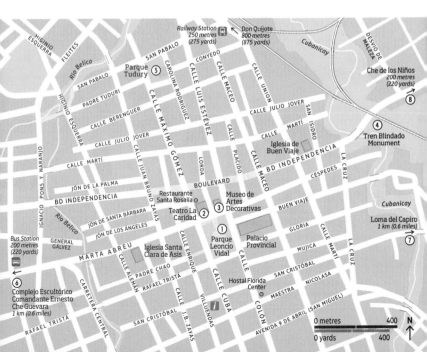

Parque Tudury

This square, in front of the Neo-Classical Iglesia de Nuestra Señora del Carmen – built in 1756 – is also known as Parque El Carmen. The most notable aspect of the square is a monument commemor- ating the foundation of Santa Clara. It was erected in 1951 around a tamarind tree, on the spot where, on 15 July 1689, the first Mass was celebrated in the new city. The monument consists of 18 columns on which are carved the names of the first families in Santa Clara, crowned by a cross.

Did You Know?

Alberto Korda's photograph of Che Guevara is the world's most replicated image.

⑥

Complejo Escultórico Comandante Ernesto Che Guevara

🏛 Avenida de los Desfiles, Santa Clara ☎ (42) 205 878
🕐 8:30am–5pm Tue–Sun

The monument which stands in Santa Clara's appropriately named Plaza de la Revolución was built to commemorate the 30th anniversary of the notorious battle of Santa Clara and its heroic leader – Ernesto "Che" Guevara. It was designed by the architect Jorge Cao Campos and the sculptor José Delarra, and was unveiled on 28 December 1988.

The complex comprises a museum, a memorial and Che Guevara's grave. Dominating the monument is an impres- sive bronze statue of Che, with his arm in plaster (he had broken it in a previous battle). Beneath, a bas-relief depicts scenes from the battle, on which are carved the historic words that Che wrote in his farewell letter before leaving

↑ The statue at the Complejo Escultórico Comandante Ernesto Che Guevara

for Bolivia: "…one thing I learned in the Guatemala of Arbenz was that if I would be a revolutionary doctor, or just a revolutionary, first there must be a revolution."

Under the monument (the entrance is at the back) is the museum, which was designed by the architect Blanca Hernández Guivernau.

↑ The monument in front of the Iglesia de Nuestra Señora del Carmen in Parque Tudury

→ Looking out over Santa Clara from Loma del Capiro hill

Inside, you'll find a fascinating chronological reconstruction of Che's life, which clearly reveals the evolution of his revolutionary ideas.

Some of Che's personal effects are also on display here, including his guerilla uniform, his pistol holder, watch, pipe and the iconic beret that the revolutionary is usually depicted wearing. The museum's collection of his belongings also includes the container from which he used to drink *mate* tea (an Argentinian caffeinated drink made from Yerba mate leaves) and the telephone he used during the campaign of Santa Clara, along with his binoculars, camera and radio.

The newest construction in the Complejo is the memorial containing the remains of Che and 38 other comrades, found in Bolivia 30 years after their death and transferred to Cuba in December 1998. The tomb is in the shape of a cave, perhaps to symbolize his Cueva de los Portales headquarters in the Parque Nacional la Güira *(p157)*. Inside, the walls are lined with niches holding gruesome ossuaries. There is also a central brazier where an eternal flame burns in memory of Che. Cubans flock to the tomb in order to pay their respects.

⑦

Loma del Capiro

🅐 Calle Ana Pegudo, 1 km SE of El Che de los Niños

At 177 m (579 ft) tall, Capiro's Hill is Santa Clara's highest point. The hill was famously used as a command post by Che Guevara during the Battle of Santa Clara. The peak is pinned by a monument, as well as the flags of both Cuba and the 26 July Movement.

⑧

Che de los Niños

🅐 Avenida Liberación y Calle F 🅒 (42) 205 878
🅓 9:30am–5pm Tue–Sun

"Che of the Children", a life-sized bronze statue of Guevara stands outside the Communist Party head-quarters, 400 m (450 yards) east of the Tren Blindado Monument. Designed by Basque artist Casto Solano Marroyo, it shows Che striding forth with a boy in his arms. Peer up close and you'll note that the sculpture is engraved with symbolic figures, inclu-ding a ram on his shoulders, a quixotic guerrilla-knight figure riding a mule and Che riding his motorcycle through South America.

ERNESTO CHE GUEVARA

When Argentinian Ernesto Guevara de la Serna was killed in Bolivia upon orders from the CIA, he was only 39 years old. In the summer of 1997 - while Cuba was celebrating the 30th anniversary of the death of the *guerrillero heroico* - his body was returned to the island. He was one of only two foreigners in history (the other is the Dominican general Máximo Gómez) to be proclaimed a Cuban citizen "by birth". Watching his coffin being lowered from the aeroplane to the sound of the *Suite de las Américas* reminded everyone that Che was not merely a 20th-century legend, emblazoned on posters and T-shirts, but a reality for millions of people who had shared his ideas. Che had many accomplish-ments - as well as being a revolutionary, he was also a qualified doctor, an economist, a skilled military theoretician, an ambassador, philosopher and a political agitator.

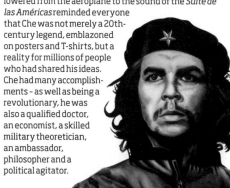

6 🛝 🏖 🛍

JARDÍN BOTÁNICO SOLEDAD

🅰F2 🏠 Calle Real 136, Pepito Tey (Cienfuegos) 📞 (43) 545 115 ⏰ 8am-6pm daily (last entry 4:30pm)

Starting life as a small sugar cane research centre, the Soledad botanical garden is now one of the largest in Latin America. With a surface area of 1 sq km (0.5 sq miles), the garden is home to more than 1,400 different species of plant, including 195 palms.

In 1901 Edwin Atkins, owner of the Soledad sugar works, transformed part of his estate into a specialized research centre, and filled the garden with a great number of tropical plants. In 1919 the University of Harvard bought the property and founded a botanical institute for the study of sugar cane and tropical flora. The botanical garden has been run by the Cuban government since 1961. Guided tours, made partly on foot and partly by car, reveal the exceptional diversification of the garden. Here, you'll find indigenous plants with healing properties, such as aloe vera, as well as over 50 varieties of fig – perhaps the most striking is a huge *Ficus benghalensis* or banyan tree. This species is unique for its huge aerial roots, which have a circumference of over 20 m (65 ft). The glasshouse, meanwhile, is home to many species of cactus. Grown after the serious damage inflicted by Hurricane Lilly in 1996, these are young specimens. The pool near the glasshouse is entirely covered with water lilies of different colours: bright pink, white, dark purple, violet, blue and yellow.

Photographing a petticoat palm *(inset)*, and relaxing in the Jardín Botánico Soledad ↑

TOP 5 PLANTS IN THE GARDEN

Aloe Vera
This plant is an effective treatment for sunburn.

Royal Palm
Roystonea regia is Cuba's national tree.

Banyan Tree
Its roots, trunk and branches form an impenetrable barrier.

Mimosa
With its deeply divided leaves, the mimosa makes a very attractive ornamental plant.

Bottle Palm
Also known as the *barrigona* (pregnant one), this palm's trunk swells in the middle.

↑ The romantic Hotel Hershey, surrounded by towering palms

EXPERIENCE MORE

7

Camilo Cienfuegos

🅐 D1 🚶 2 km (1.5 miles) inland of Santa Cruz del Norte (Matanzas) 🚃 From Matanzas or Casablanca

Before the revolution, the Pennsylvania-based Hershey chocolate company owned nearly 500 sq km (193 sq miles) of sugar cane fields around the then-modern *batey* (sugar-processing town) of Hershey. Following the revolution, the property was nationalized and the town, which lies midway between Havana and Matanzas, was renamed Camilo Cienfuegos, after one of Castro's top commanders. The mill closed down in 2002, but the American-colonial buildings, albeit weatherworn, are still standing and the railway station still bears its original "Hershey" sign. The most fun way to reach the town is to take the "Hershey Train".

THE HERSHEY TRAIN

The first stretch of the Hershey rail line, inaugurated in 1916, connected the Hershey sugar factory and the village of Canasí, both near the coast west of Matanzas. The electrical system was one of the first in Cuba. In 1924 there were 38 pairs of trains, though only four covered the full distance between Havana and Matanzas. Today, the Hershey train links Casablanca *(p131)* and Matanzas *(p170)* via beautiful scenery, covering 89 km (55 miles) in 3 hours 20 minutes, with frequent stops.

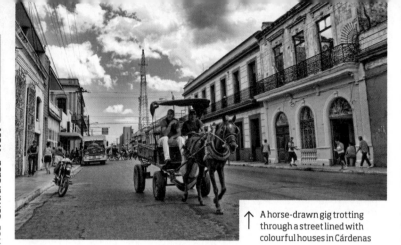

↑ A horse-drawn gig trotting through a street lined with colourful houses in Cárdenas

8

Cárdenas

🅰 E1 🏛 Matanzas

On arriving in the town of Cárdenas, where swarms of old-fashioned gigs and one-horse carriages circulate in the streets, visitors may feel as if they are entering another age.

The town, which is 50 km (31 miles) east of Matanzas and 18 km (11 miles) south of Varadero, was founded in 1828 as San Juan de Dios de Cárdenas, and in the 19th century it thrived thanks to the sugar industry. Today, however, except for a rum factory near the port, Cárdenas offers only two possible areas of employment to its inhabitants: work on a farm or get a job in Varadero's important tourist industry.

A closer look at the squares and monuments allows visitors to appreciate the little hidden gems in this town. Parque Colón, one of the two main squares, is dominated by the first statue of Christopher Columbus erected in Cuba, inaugurated in 1862 by Gertrudis Gómez de Avellaneda, the 19th-century Hispanic-Cuban author.

Next to the Iglesia de la Inmaculada Concepción (1846) is a very important monument: the Dominica building. In 1850, when it was the headquarters of the Spanish government in Cuba, Cuban nationalist troops, led by Narciso López, hoisted the Cuban flag here for the first time.

In the second major square, Parque Echevarría, is a fine Neo-Classical building, erected in 1862, which was once the city's district prison. It became the **Museo Municipal Oscar María de Rojas** in 1900, making it the oldest town museum in Cuba. It houses a collection of coins, arms, shells, butterflies, minerals and stuffed animals.

Cárdenas is also famous for being the birthplace, in 1932, of José Antonio Echevarría, the revolutionary who was president of the University Students' Federation in Havana. He waged an anti-Batista campaign and died in 1957. The house in which he was born is now the **Museo Casa Natal de José Antonio Echevarría**.

The town is also home to the **Museo a la Batalla de Ideas**. In 1999, five-year-old Elián González was shipwrecked off Miami in a failed escape attempt by his mother. After months of legal tussles between the US and Cuba and an international outcry, Elián was repatriated to his father in Cárdenas. The museum is dedicated to this incident.

Did You Know?

Student José Antonio Echevarría was only 25 years old when he was assassinated by the police.

→ Climbing the well-lit stairs on a tour of the Cuevas de Bellamar

Museo Municipal Oscar María de Rojas

⊘⊗ 🅰 Calle 13e/ Ave 4y Ave 6 📞 (45) 522 417 🕒 9am-6pm Tue & Fri, 8am-5pm Wed, Thu & Sat, 9am-1pm Sun

Museo Casa Natal de José Antonio Echevarría

⊘⊗ 🅰 Ave 4e/12y 13 📞 (45) 524 145 🕒 9am-noon & 1-5pm Tue-Sat, 9am-noon Sun 🕒 1 Jan, 1 May, 26 Jul, 25 Dec

Museo a la Batalla de Ideas

⊘⊗ 🅰 Ave 6 esq 12 📞 (45) 527 599 🕒 9am-noon & 1-5pm Tue-Sat, 8am-noon Sun

---

 🟑 ⊘ ⊗ 🍴 🖵 🛍

Cuevas de Bellamar

🅰 E1 🅰 Carretera de las Cuevas de Bellamar (Matanzas) 📞 (45) 261 683 🕒 Daily

Discovered by chance in 1861 by a slave who was surveying the terrain in search of water, the fascinating Bellamar caves lie just 5 km (3 miles) southeast of Matanzas.

Only the first 3 km (2 miles) of these extensive caves have been explored to date, and expert speleologists say there are still many surprises in store. Access to the public, with a specialist guide, is limited to the first 1,500 m (5,000 ft) of the caves but goes 26 m (85 ft) below sea level, and visitors can see marine fossils dating from 26 million years ago. This stretch includes caves and galleries covered with crystal formations in intriguing shapes. The temperature is a constant 26° C (79° F), thanks to the continuous seepage of the cave walls.

At Varadero (p172), guided tours of the Bellamar caves can be booked at the larger hotels.

🔟

San Miguel de los Baños

🅰 E1 🅰 25 km (16 miles) SW of Cárdenas (Matanzas)

A century ago, this atmospheric community set amid the rolling hills of Matanzas was considered the "Saratoga of Cuba", after the famous spa town of New York State. Visitors flocked here to partake of the soothing waters, and many wealthy Cubans built elaborate Neo-Classical and Beaux Arts mansions here. They also built the many clapboard bungalows that line the Avenida de Abril.

Today, although still inhabited, San Miguel de los Baños is a tumbledown time-capsule awaiting a long-touted restoration. The French-style Gran Hotel y Balneario, which opened in 1930, is a relic of the town's former grandeur. Famously, it was at this hotel that Che Guevara was treated for his asthma in 1961.

DRINK

The Beatles Bar
Live music from the "Fab Four" and other rock sounds are performed on the patio here.

🅰 E1 🅰 Avenida 1ra y Calle 59, Varadero 📞 (45) 668 167

El Mejunje
Lively LBGT-friendly bar, famous for its weekend drag-shows. It also hosts music from *trova* to rap.

🅰 G2 🅰 Calle Marta Abreu 107, Santa Clara 📞 (42) 282 572 🕒 Mon

---

Club Cienfuegos
With a fabulous harbourfront setting, this state-run bar has live-music on the patio and an English-style floor complete with a pool table.

🅰 F2 🅰 Calle 37 e/ 8 y 12, Cienfuegos 📞 (43) 526 510

⑪ Circuito Sur

🅰F2 🏘Cienfuegos

A scenic coastal highway, the Circuito Sur connects Cienfuegos to Trinidad and runs in the lee of the Sierra Escambray. Rivers scythe their way down from the mountains to the shoreline, where tiny rivermouth beaches draw the locals to bathe. One of these beaches is at Yaguanabo, which has a pleasant hotel, a riverside restaurant and some funky fishing boats tethered beneath the cliffs.

Hikers can follow the course of the Río Yaguanabo, which cuts through the Valle de Yaguanabo and flows onward to create a number of waterfalls and freshwater pools on its way.

Adventurous thrill-seekers can take a four-wheel-drive vehicle, with a guide, to the hamlet of El Colorado and then hike to the Cueva de Martín Infierno. A National Monument, this huge cave system contains masses of flower-like *flores de yeso* (gypsum formations) and

Did You Know?

Every spring, billions of land crabs migrate to the ocean to spawn, smothering the Circuito Sur.

other types of dripstones, including one of the world's largest stalactites, which is 67 m (220 ft) high.

Immediately to the east of Yaguanabo the road rises past Camaronera Yaguanabo, an enormous oceanside shrimp farm.

---

⑫ Lago Hanabanilla

🅰F2 🚗8 km (5 miles) S of Carretera Cumanayagua-Manicuraguac (Villa Clara)

Studding the Alturas de Santa Clara like a glittering jewel, this large 32-sq-km (12-sq-mile) man-made *embalse* (reservoir), home to the country's largest hydroelectric power station

→

El Nicho, Cuba's second highest waterfall, surrounded by forest

(completed in 1963), is a popular centre for both water-sports, including sailing, and shoreline activities, such as bird-watching. The serpentine southern shore curls and twists along the base of the rugged and heavily forested Sierra Escambray mountain range (officially called the Sierra de Guamuhaya).

The Soviet-style Hotel Hanabanilla sits beside the dam and its spillway, on the northern shore. This hotel makes a good base for exploring; it offers many guided excursions around the lake, including fly-fishing for bass and trout.

From the hotel, you can also make hiking excursions to El Nicho, the Cascada Arroyo Trinitario waterfall, and Casa del Campesino, a coffee farm offering a taste of traditional country life to its visitors.

Be aware that the hotel and its swimming pool are lively with boisterous Cuban families most weekends.

El Nicho

⚐F2 ⌖17 km (10 miles) SE of Cumanayagua (Cienfuegos) ☎(43) 433 351

One of the most spectacular waterfalls in Cuba, El Nicho is a picture-perfect cascade framed by ferns and subtropical rainforest on the northwestern slopes of the

Sierra Escambray. An outlier of Gran Parque Nacional Topes de Collantes, the waterfall is reached by following an unpaved track off the Cumanayaga-Manicuragua road.

From the entrance, the easy Sendero El Reino de las Aguas hike follows the course of the Río Hanabanillo to the cascade, which tumbles 20 m (66 ft) into a jade-coloured pool. It's chilling waters are the perfect place to cool off after the hike. After your dip, you can follow the trail more sharply uphill to a *mirador* (lookout), offering amazing views over the surrounding landscape. To cater to hungry hikers, there is a picturesque thatched trailside restaurant here that serves lunches.

Hotel Hanabanilla, on Lago Hanabanilla, offers guided hiking excursions to the falls, but for a unique experience, journey to El Nicho in an ex-Soviet army truck on a fun day-long excursion from Trinidad with Sunwing (*www.sunwing.ca*).

←

Blue boats moored on a pontoon on the tranquil waters of Lago Hanabanilla

EAT

Finca del Mar
A superb bayfront restaurant.

⚐F2 ⌖Calle 35 e/ 18 y 20, Cienfuegos ☎(43) 526 598

―――――――

El Lagarto
The set menus here feature traditional *criolla* favourites.

⚐F2 ⌖Calle 35, 4B, Cienfuegos ☎(43) 519 966

―――――――

Los Laureles
Suckling pig that has been roasted in the open air is the highlight at the Hotel Meliá Jagua's garden-restaurant.

⚐F2 ⌖Calle 37 e/ 0 y 2, Cienfuegos ☎(43) 551 003

―――――――

Paladar La Mallorca
A hilltop *paladar* serving *criolla* dishes.

⚐E1 ⌖Calle 334, 7705, Matanzas ☎(45) 283 282

⑭

Remedios

🅰 G2 🅰 Villa Clara 🚆🚌
ℹ Infotur, Calle Pi y
Margall; (42) 397 227

Founded in 1515 by Vasco
Porcallo de Figueroa and
named Santa Cruz de la
Sabana, the town became
San Juan de los Remedios
del Cayo after a fire in 1578.

A peaceful place, it has a
small, well-preserved colonial
centre in the area around
Plaza Martí, where the Iglesia
de San Juan Bautista is considered one of Cuba's most
important churches. It was
restored in the 20th century
thanks to the rich landowner
Eutimio Falla Bonet, who
revived its original Baroque
splendour without touching
the Neo-Classical bell tower.
Most striking are the lavish
Baroque altar and magnificent
decorative ceiling.

Behind the cathedral is the
**House of Alejandro García
Caturla**. Here, the musical
instruments, photographs
and some personal
belongings of this talented
20th-century personality
are on display. García Caturla
was a composer, pianist,

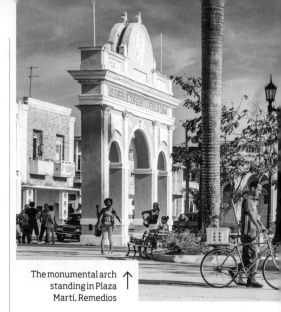

The monumental arch ↑
standing in Plaza
Martí, Remedios

saxophonist, percussionist,
violinist and singer, as well as
a fine tennis player and rower,
journalist and art critic.

Also in the square is the
Hotel Mascotte. This was the
site of an important meeting
between Generalíssimo
Máximo Gómez, the Major
General in Cuba's Ten Years'
War against Spain, and a
US delegation in 1899. Other
notable sights on the square

include the former Casino
Español, now Casa de la
Cultura, and the El Louvre
café, founded in 1866.

However, Remedios is most
famous for the Parrandas, the
lively local December festival
that is documented in the
fascinating **Museo de las
Parrandas Remedianas**.
Here, photographs, musical
instruments, costumes,
sketches, carriages and

PARRANDAS DE REMEDIOS

In 1829 the parish priest of Remedios,
Francisco Virgil de Quiñones, had the
idea of getting some boys to bang on
sheets of tin in order to get lazier
church members out for the night-
time Advent Masses, which take place
from 16 to 24 December. In time this
strange concert developed into a fully
fledged festival, now starting on 4
December and lasting until Christmas
Eve. Featuring music, dances, parades
with floats and huge wooden
contraptions (trabajos de plaza), it is a
sort of cross between Mardi Gras and
the Italian Palio horse race, based
on the competition between the San
Salvador and Carmen quarters of
Remedios. The most endearing aspect
of the Parrandas, enlivened by songs,
polkas and rumbas, is that all the
inhabitants, of all ages, take part.

trabajos de plaza – decorated wooden structures – bring to life Parrandas celebrations past and present.

House of Alejandro García Caturla

📷 🕐 📍 Calle Camilo Cienfuegos 5 📞 (42) 396 851 🚫 Closed for restoration

Museo de las Parrandas Remedianas

📷 🕐 📍 Alejandro del Río 74 e/ Máximo Gómez y Enrique Malaret 📞 (42) 396 818 🕐 1-5pm Mon, 8am-noon & 1-5pm Tue-Sat 🚫 1 Jan, 1 May, 26 Jul, 25 Dec

🔟⑤ Caibarién

📍 G2 📍 8 km (5 miles) NE of Remedios, Villa Clara

Although badly battered by Hurricane Irma in 2017, this coastal city exudes quirky charm with its weathered colonial mansions, simple clapboard homes and bandstand where music is played twice a week.

The Museo María Escobar Laredo tells the town's history, but Imprenta Villagraf – a print shop still using antique Linotype printers – is more interesting. The Paseo de Martí boulevard is pinned by the Carrara marble Monumento José Martí. A 19th-century fortified tower and a huge stone crab guard the town's southern entrance.

Located on the southwest outskirts of the town, the **Museo de Agroindustria Azucarera** (Museum of Sugar) is set in the defunct Central Marcelo Salado sugar-processing factory. Inside, you'll find many exhibits detailing the history of the sugar industry in Cuba, including a fascinating collection of antique steam trains. It's a great way to learn about how "the white stuff" has affected the fortunes of the island over the years.

Museo de Agroindustria Azucarera

📷 🕐 📍 Carretera Caibarién-Remedios Km 3.5 📞 (42) 353 864 🕐 9am-4pm Mon-Sat

STAY

Hotel E Barcelona

Overlooking Remedios' plaza, this charming boutique hotel is furnished with antiques.

📍 G2 📍 Calle José Peña 67, Remedios 📞 (42) 395 144

$⑤$⑤

Hostal Florida Center

Antique-filled *casa particular,* where gracious hosts serve the best meals in town.

📍 G2 📍 Calle Maestra Nicolasa 56, Santa Clara 🌐 hostalflorida center.com

$⑤$⑤

Hotel E Velasco

With 17 rooms, this lovely historic hotel is located on Matanzas' main square.

📍 E1 📍 Calle Contreras e/ Santa Teresa y Ayuntamiento, Matanzas 🌐 cubanacan.cu/en

$⑤$⑤

Meliá Marina Varadero

You'll find ten restaurants on site at this stylish hotel overlooking the marina.

📍 E1 📍 Autopista del Sur y Final, Varadero 🌐 melia-marina varadero.com

$⑤$⑤

←
The bandstand in Caibarién's Parque de la Libertad, in the centre of town

CENTRAL CUBA - EAST

The cities of Trinidad, Camagüey and Sancti Spíritus were founded in the 16th century by a small group of Spaniards led by Diego Velázquez. In the 17th and 18th centuries great landowners, rich from the sugar grown in the surrounding countryside, resided in luxurious mansions in these three cities, but this wealth attracted state-sanctioned pirates. Camagüey (then Puerto Príncipe) was famously raided by the Welsh privateer Henry Morgan in 1666.

In the second half of the 19th century, a period of crisis began with the advent of new technology, for which there was no skilled labour. Slave revolts became increasingly frequent and violent. In the late 19th century the major landowners left the cities and as time went on they gradually ceded their sugar factories to American businessmen, who converted them into one large sugar-producing business. Camagüey turned to raising livestock, while Trinidad engaged in handicrafts and cigar-making. The region remained isolated from the rest of Cuba for a long time, since the railway was not extended to Trinidad until 1919 and the road to Cienfuegos and Sancti Spíritus was only laid out in the 1950s. One result of this isolation, however, is that the historic centres of Trinidad and Sancti Spíritus have preserved their colonial atmosphere.

Atlantic   Ocean

*Playa
Uvero*

Sagua
la Grande

*Cayos
del Pajonal*

VILLA CLARA

*Cayo
Fragoso*

Cifuentes

Cayos de Villa Clara

Encrucijada

*Cayo
Guillermo*

**JARDINES
DEL REY**

CAYO COCO ③   ⑩

**Abel Santamaría
International
Airport**

Camajuaní

*Bahía de
Buena Vista*

**Jardines del Rey
International
Airport**

Santa Clara

**CENTRAL
CUBA – WEST**
p166

YAGUAJAY
⑦

Meneses

*Bahía de
Perros*

San Rafael

*Laguna de
la Leche*

*Playa
Cumagua*

Potrerillo

Báez

Mayajigua

Sierra de Jatibonico

Jarahueca

Chambas

Manicaragua

Fomento

Venegas

La Rana

**Máximo Gómez
International
Airport**

⑨ **MORÓN**

*Embalse
Hanabanilla*

Cabaiguán

San
Felipe

Ciro Redondo

**CIEGO
DE ÁVILA**

*Miraflores
Nuevo*

Guayos

SANCTI SPÍRITUS

Sierra del Escambray

**VALLE DE
LOS INGENIOS**
⑥

**SANCTI
SPÍRITUS** ②

Jatibonico

Majagua

Santo Tomas

TRINIDAD
①

Casilda

Banao

*Presa
Zaza*

La Ferrolana

CIEGO DE ÁVILA ⑧

Colorado

Llanura de Júcaro-Morón

**PENÍNSULA
DE ANCÓN**
⑤

San Pedro

La Unión

Venezuela

Limpio
Abarcas

Limones
Palmero

Baraguá

*Carlos Manuel
de Céspedes*

Tunas de Zaza

Júcaro

Embarcadero
Baraguá

*Cayos
Ana María*

Llanura Meridional

*Golfo de
Ana María*

*Playa
Los Caneyes*

Jagüe

*Caribbean
Sea*

*Cayo
Caballones*

⑭
**JARDINES DE
LA REINA**

0 kilometres   30

0 miles   30

N
↑

CENTRAL CUBA – EAST

Must Sees

1. Trinidad
2. Sancti Spíritus
3. Cayo Coco
4. Camagüey

Experience More

5. Península de Ancón
6. Valle de los Ingenios
7. Yaguajay
8. Ciego de Ávila
9. Morón
10. Jardines del Rey
11. Sierra de Cubitas
12. Sierra del Chorrillo
13. Playa Santa Lucía
14. Jardines de la Reina
15. Las Tunas
16. Puerto Padre

←

1 Relaxing on Playa Ancón.

2 Climbing the bell tower of the Iglesia y Convento de San Francisco.

3 A tour on horseback.

4 Flowers in Plaza Mayor.

3 DAYS
In Trinidad

Day 1

Morning Rise with the dawn and watch, while other visitors are asleep, as Trinidad comes alive before your eyes. Make your way to Plaza Mayor to visit the Museo Romántico in Palacio Brunet *(p203)*, Iglesia Parroquial de la Santísima Trinidad *(p201)* or the Museo de Arquitectura Colonial *(p202)*. Then, head towards the distinctive yellow-and-blue tower of the Iglesia y Convento de San Francisco. Although the inside is interesting, the real reason to visit the church is to climb the bell tower, which has stupendous views over the city *(p205)*.

Afternoon Enjoy lunch at Sol Ananda *(p203)* on Plaza Mayor, then walk downhill 50 m (164 ft) to explore the Palacio Cantero (Museo Histórico Municipal; *p204*). Return to Plaza Mayor to visit the Casa Templo de Santería Yemayá *(Calle Real del Jigüe)* for an insight into Santería. The rest of the afternoon is yours to explore the lovely Plazuela del Jigüe *(p204)* and humble Plaza de los Tres Cruces *(p205)*.

Evening Enjoy a buffet dinner at Vista Gourmet *(p203)*, then head downhill into Plaza Seguarte for ebullient traditional *son* at the historic Casa de la Trova *(p204)*. It'll be a night to remember.

Day 2

Morning Take a guided horseback ride into the countryside with Julio Muñoz *(www. trinidadphoto.com/riding)*. Rides typically last three hours, providing plenty of time to soak up the rural lifestyle of Cuba.

Afternoon Back in Trinidad, head to Bar-Restaurante Guitarra Mía for lunch *(www. restaurantguitarramia.com)*, then hop onto the Trinidad Bus Tour, operated by Transtur *(p272)*, to Playa Ancón *(p214)*. Here you can rent a sunlounger and relax on the gorgeous sands, hire a sea kayak or even opt for a scuba-diving excursion.

Evening Back in the city, La Redacción Cuba *(www.laredaccioncuba.com)* is a good choice for dinner. After selecting from the menu of traditional Cuban dishes, which changes every day, dance an Afro-Cuban rumba at Palenque de los Congos Reales *(Echerri y Av Jesus Menendez)*.

Day 3

Morning Drive, or take a guided excursion with Ecotur *(www.ecoturcuba.tur.cu)*, into the scenic Valle de los Ingenios *(p214)*. This dramatic area earned its name because it is studded with historic sugar mills *(ingenios)*. The must-visit sites here include Hacienda Manaca Iznaga, with its soaring tower, and the Sitio Histórico Guáimiro, which has fabulous murals and a *guarapería* serving freshly squeezed sugar cane juice. You'll probably have lunch included in your tour.

Afternoon Return to Trinidad in the late afternoon and visit Casa-Estudio Lázaro Niebla *(p201)* to see the unique portraits.

Evening After a full-on day, dine in a *casa particular* – we love Casa Colonial Muñoz *(p215)* – before heading to Disco Ayala. This party in a cave is the ultimate end to your trip to Trinidad.

The colourful centre of Trinidad, surrounded by verdant mountains →

❶

TRINIDAD

🅰G3 🏛Sancti Spíritus 🚌Calle Piro Guinart 224, e/ Maceo y Izquierdo, (41) 994 448 🚉Ave Simón Bolívar 422, (41) 993 348 🛈Cubatur, Calle Antonio Maceo esq Francisco Javier Zerquera, (41) 996 314; Infotur, Calle Gustavo Izquierdo, (41) 998 258

Trinidad was founded by Diego Velázquez in 1514, but its perfectly preserved cobblestone streets and pastel-coloured houses are more a reflection of the landscape of the city in colonial times. From the 17th to 19th centuries, Trinidad was a major player in the sugar trade, and the buildings around the Plaza Mayor bear witness to the wealth of the landowners of the time.

① Iglesia Parroquial de la Santísima Trinidad

🅰Plaza Mayor ⏰10:30am-1pm Mon-Sat, 11:30am-1pm Sun

Completed in 1892, this austere church, with a Neo-Classical façade, has an elegant four-aisle interior. The church's real attraction, however, is an 18th-century wooden statue made in Spain, the *Señor de la Vera Cruz* (Lord of the True Cross), which is associated with a curious story. The sculpture, made for one of the churches in Vera Cruz, Mexico, left the port of Barcelona in 1731, but three times in succession the ship was driven by strong winds to the port of Casilda, 6 km (4 miles) from the city of Trinidad. While preparing to make a fourth attempt to reach Mexico, the ship's captain decided to leave behind part of the cargo, which included the huge chest containing the statue of Christ. The locals regarded the arrival of the sacred image as a sign from Heaven, and from that time on the *Señor de la Vera Cruz* became an object of fervent worship in Cuba.

← ⑬ *Plaza de los Tres Cruces (500m)*

← ⑫ *Cabildo de los Congos Reales de San Antonio (500m)*

Taberna La Canchánchera (p204), a typical casa de infusiones housed in an 18th-century building, is known for its namesake cocktail. Live music is played here.

SHOP

Casa-Estudio Lázaro Niebla

A highly respected contemporary artist, Niebla creates stunning wooden portraits of senior Trinidadians. These tributes are carved on colonial doors and window panels throughout the city.

🏠 Calle Real del Jigüey 452 🌐 lazaroniebla.com

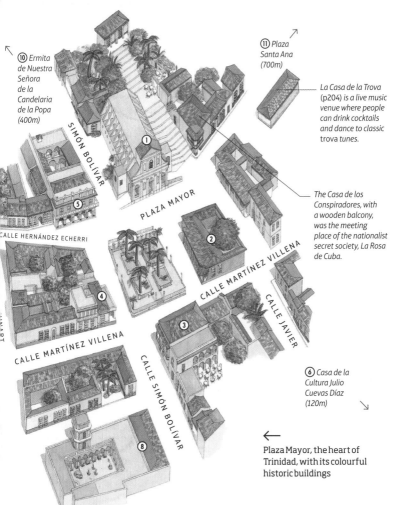

⑩ *Ermita de Nuestra Señora de la Candelaria de la Popa (400m)*

⑪ *Plaza Santa Ana (700m)*

La Casa de la Trova (p204) is a live music venue where people can drink cocktails and dance to classic trova tunes.

The Casa de los Conspiradores, with a wooden balcony, was the meeting place of the nationalist secret society, La Rosa de Cuba.

SIMÓN BOLÍVAR

PLAZA MAYOR

CALLE HERNÁNDEZ ECHERRI

CALLE MARTÍNEZ VILLENA

CALLE JAVIER

CALLE MARTÍNEZ VILLENA

CALLE SIMÓN BOLÍVAR

⑥ *Casa de la Cultura Julio Cuevas Díaz (120m)*

Plaza Mayor, the heart of Trinidad, with its colourful historic buildings

THE ARCHITECTURE OF TRINIDAD

The historic centre of Trinidad has an extraordinarily dense concentration of Spanish colonial houses, many still inhabited by the descendants of old local families. The oldest single-storey buildings have two corridors and a porch parallel to the street, with a courtyard at the back. In the late 1700s another corridor was introduced to the layout. In the 19th century, the houses formed a square around an open central courtyard. In general, the entrance consists of a large living room that gives way to a dining room, either through an archway or a *mampara* – a half-height double door.

Museo de Arquitectura Colonial

🏛 Calle Ripalda 83, e/ Hernández Echerri y Martínez Villena, Plaza Mayor 📞 (41) 993 208 🕒 9am-5pm Sat-Tue

The front of the 18th-century mansion, which is now home to the Museum of Colonial Architecture, features a lovely portico with slim columns, a wrought-iron balustrade and wooden beams. Originally, the building consisted of two separate houses, both of which belonged to sugar magnate Saturnino Sánchez Iznaga. The houses were joined during the 19th century.

The museum, the only one of its kind in Cuba, covers Trinidad's architecture and illustrates the building techniques used during the colonial period. There is a collection of various locks, latches, doors, hinges, windows and grilles, as well as parts of walls and tiles.

In one of the bathrooms facing the inner courtyard is a fine example of a 19th-century shower, with a complicated network of pipes supplying hot and cold water.

Universal Benito Ortiz Galería de Arte

🏛 Calle Rubén Martínez Villena y Bolívar, Plaza Mayor 📞 (41) 994 432 🕒 9am-5pm Mon-Sat

This beautiful mansion with a long wooden balcony is evocative of the city's golden age. It was built in 1809 for Ortiz de Zúñiga, a former slave trader who later became the mayor of Trinidad. The house currently serves as an art gallery.

The first floor has paintings on display (and for sale) by contemporary Cuban artists, including Antonio Herr, Juan Oliva, Benito Ortiz, Antonio Zerquera and David Gutiérrez. Once you have admired the artworks on display, head out onto the wooden balcony for a fine view over the entire Plaza Mayor.

← Porcelain exhibit in the Museo de Arquitectura Colonial

Museo de Arqueología Guamuhaya

🏛 Calle Simón Bolívar 457, e/ Fernando Hernández Echerri y Rubén Martínez Villena, Plaza Mayor 📞 (41) 993 420 🕒 9am-5pm Tue-Sun

The building that is now the home of the Archaeological Museum was constructed in the 18th century and was purchased in the 1800s by the wealthy Don Antonio Padrón, who added a portico with brick columns and Ionic capitals.

The Guamuhaya (the native Indian name for the Sierra Escambray area) collection includes Pre-Columbian archaeological finds as well as objects associated with the Spanish conquest of the island and Cuba's history of slavery. As well as cultural artifacts, the museum also houses a fascinating collection of stuffed animals, including the *manjuari*, an ancient species of fish that still lives in the Parque Nacional Ciénaga de Zapata swamp.

In the museum's courtyard, there is a bronze bust commemorating the German geographer and naturalist Alexander von Humboldt, who stayed here as Padrón's guest in 1801, during his travels in the New World.

(5)

Palacio Brunet (Museo Romántico)

⌂ Calle Hernández Echerri 52, esq Simón Bolívar, Plaza Mayor ☎ (41) 994 363 🚫 Closed for restoration

Built in 1812 as the residence of the wealthy Borrell family, Palacio Brunet now contains the Museo Romántico. Most of the objects on display here once belonged to Mariano Borrell, the family's founder. They were inherited by Borrell's daughter, the wife of Count Nicolás de la Cruz y Brunet (hence the name Palacio Brunet), in 1830.

The museum's 14 rooms all face the courtyard gallery with its elegant balustrade.

The spacious living room has a Carrara marble floor and a coffered ceiling, furnished with Sèvres vases and Bohemian crystalware. There are also English-made spittoons, which reveal that the 19th-century aristocratic landowners were partial to smoking cigars.

Other rooms of interest are the countess's bedroom, with a bronze baldachin over the bed, and the kitchen, which is still decorated with its original painted earthenware tiles.

---

(6)

Casa de la Cultura Julio Cuevas Díaz

⌂ Calle Zerquera 406 ☎ (41) 994 308 🕘 9:45am-noon & 3-7pm Mon-Fri, 9:45am-noon Sat

During the day, the vestibule of this building is used as exhibition space by local artists (some of whom also have their studios here). In the evening, performances – theatre, dance, concerts and shows for children – are held in the rear courtyard.

↓ The bright exterior of the Palacio Brunet (Museo Romántico)

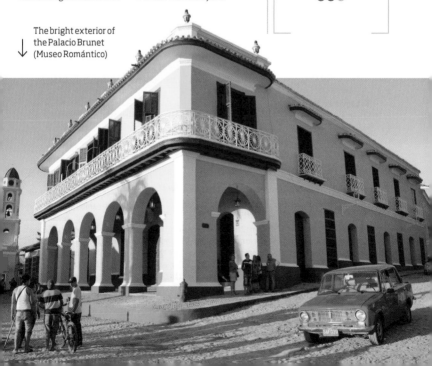

↑ El Jigüe, a beautiful tiled restaurant on Plazuela del Jigüe

DRINK

Taberna La Canchánchera
Enjoy the rum, honey and lemon cocktail here.

⌂ Calle Rubén Martínez y Ciro Redondo
☎ (41) 996 231

Taberna La Botija
Cuban beers on tap.

⌂ Calle José Mendoza 71B ☎ (52) 830 147

Casa de la Música
Come here for salsa.

⌂ Off Plaza Mayor
☎ (41) 993 414

Casa de la Trova
Locals love this place for its live music.

⌂ Calle Echerrí 29
☎ (41) 996 445

---

⑦

Plazuela del Jigüe

This peaceful little square is rich in history. It was here that Father Bartolomé de Las Casa celebrated the first Mass in Trinidad in 1514. El Jigüe restaurant, housed in a lovely porticoed building decorated with panels of painted tiles, is the perfect place for lunch on the square.

---

⑧

Palacio Cantero (Museo Histórico Municipal)

⌂ Calle Bolívar 423 ☎ (41) 994 460 ◷ 9am–5:30pm Mon–Thu, Sat, alternate Sun

This 1830s mansion, which belonged originally to Don Borrell y Padrón – one of the major figures in local sugar production – was purchased in 1841 by María de Monserrate Fernández, the widow of a sugar magnate. A year later

Did You Know?

Plazuela del Jigüe is named after the acacia tree *(jigüe)* which once stood here.

she married the landowner Cantero, renaming the mansion and transforming it into a sumptuous Neo-Classical residence. The building is now the Museo Histórico Municipal.

In rooms ranging from the grand entrance hall to the servants' quarters, the history of Trinidad can be traced through exhibits, maps, and monuments relating to different themes: the Cantero family, piracy, the plantations in the Valle de los Ingenios, the slave trade and the wars of independence. The tower has a viewing platform and a rickety staircase that climbs past fresco-covered walls.

Iglesia y Convento de San Francisco

📍 Calle Hernández Echerri, esq Guinart 📞 (41) 994 121 🕐 5:30pm-8:30pm Mon, 9am-8:30pm Tue-Sun

This elegant church has had a tumultuous history. The striking yellow structure was built in 1813 by Franciscan monks, but it was taken from them in 1848 in order for it to be used as a parish church. In 1895 the authorities transformed the building into a garrison for the Spanish army. Then in 1922, because of the lamentable state of the place, the garrison and part of the church were demolished. Only the bell tower was salvaged, along with adjacent buildings, which were used as a school until 1984, when the complex became the Museo de la Lucha contra Bandidos.

The museum illustrates with documents, photographs and exhibits the struggle against the "bandits", the counter-revolutionaries who fled to the Sierra del Escambray after 1959. Fragments of a U2 plane, a boat, a militia truck and weapons are displayed in the building's cloister.

⑩ Ermita de Nuestra Señora de la Candelaria de la Popa

This small 18th-century church is connected to Plaza Mayor by a narrow, steep street. The striking three-arch bell tower loggia was added in 1812, when work was carried out on the church to repair the damage done by a violent cyclone. The complex is being converted into a hotel.

---

⑪ Plaza Santa Ana

In the eastern part of the city, this square is dominated by the 18th-century Iglesia de Santa Ana, which was partly rebuilt in 1812. The now decaying church is flanked by a royal poinciana tree.

The square is a popular place to gather, and is a favourite with children who come here to play ball games.

⑫ Cabildo de los Congos Reales de San Antonio

📍 Calle Isidro Armenteros 168

In the 1800s Cuba witnessed the rise of many *cabildos*, cultural centres aiming to preserve the spiritual and musical heritage of the slaves. This Cabildo was founded in 1859 and is dedicated to Oggún – a warrior god worshipped by followers of the Palo Monte religion

---

⑬ Plaza de los Tres Cruces

This broad, unpaved plaza in a picturesque working-class quarter is named for the three wooden crosses that mark the end point of Trinidad's Vía Cruz Easter procession.

→ Taking a photograph *(inset)* from the Iglesia y Convento de San Francisco

↑ Colourful buildings around the spacious Parque Serafín Sánchez

❷
SANCTI SPÍRITUS

 G3 Sancti Spíritus Carretera Central, Km 2 Avenida Jesús Menéndez Calle Máximo Gómez 7; (41) 328 518

The political, economic and military centre of Central Cuba, Sancti Spíritus was embellished with elegant mansions throughout the 17th and 18th centuries. Today, its small, attractive colonial centre receives few visitors, despite its "national monument" status.

---

①
Museo de Arte Colonial

Calle Plácido 74
(41) 325 455 9:30am-5pm Tue-Thu, 9:30am-1:30pm & 7-10pm Fri & Sat, 8am-noon Sun

This fine structure was built in 1720 and belonged to the affluent Iznaga family – the owners of the vast Manaca Iznaga Estate in the Valle de los Ingenios (p214). The house is now an outstanding museum of decorative art from around the world, dating from the 17th to 18th centuries, with a fine collection of porcelain, furniture and paintings.

---

②
Parroquial Mayor del Espíritu Santo

Calle Agramonte Oeste 58 (41) 324 855
9:30am-6pm Mon-Sat, 8:30am-6pm Sun

Using money donated by Don Ignacio de Valdivia, the local mayor, the present bright blue church was built of stone in 1680. It was constructed on top of the original 16th-century wooden church after it had been destroyed by pirates. Despite this later reconstruction, it is still one of Cuba's oldest churches. The simple and solid building is reminiscent of the parish

---

> 💬 **INSIDER TIP**
> **Get Shirty**
>
> Cuba's iconic guayabera was first created in Sancti Spíritus. The Casa de la Guayabera displays more than 200 of these short-sleeved shirts that have been worn by everyone from Fidel Castro to Colombian novelist Gabriel García Márquez. A tailor's workshop here produces and sells the shirts (Calle El Llano y Padre Quintero; (41) 322 205).

churches of Spain's Andalusia region, and, inside, it still has its original, exquisitely worked wooden ceilings. The 30-m (100-ft) bell tower, with three levels, was added in the 18th century, and the octagonal Cristo de la Humildad y la Paciencia chapel, built next to the church in the 19th century, has a remarkable half-dome.

The most atmospheric time of day to visit the church is during Mass, which is said at 8pm on Tuesday and Thursday, 5pm Wednesday and Friday and 10am on Sunday. Everyone is welcome to attend the service.

③
Parque Serafín Sánchez

The heart of Sancti Spíritus consists of a tranquil square with trees and a charming *glorieta* (gazebo), surrounded by Neo-Classical buildings. A national monument, the park is dedicated to Serafín Sánchez, a local hero in the wars of independence, whose house is open to the public in the nearby Calle de Céspedes. In the evenings, the park and its square are a popular gathering place.

The most notable buildings around the square are the Centro de Patrimonio, with its characteristic broad stained-glass windows and Seville mosaics, the large Biblioteca (library) and the Hotel Perla de Cuba. This was one of the most exclusive hotels in Cuba in the early 1900s but it is now a shopping centre.

In the evening, the most popular place on the square is the Hotel Plaza. The beautiful colonial building has a terrific bar, with seating on the colonaded terrace.

↑ The romantic terracotta arches of the Yayabo Bridge

④
Yayabo Bridge

Built in 1831, its medieval appearance and large terracotta arches make this bridge unique in Cuba, and for this reason it has been declared a national monument. According to one bizarre local legend, in order to make the bridge more robust the workmen mixed cement with goat's milk.

The Yayabo Bridge is an important part of the city's street network: it is the only route into town from Trinidad.

EAT

Taberna Yayabo
This riverside eatery serves tapas, as well as classic *criolla* dishes. Accompany your meal with a glass of wine from Taberna Yayabo's excellent list.

🏠 Calle Jesús Menéndez 306 ☎ (41) 837 552

$ $ $

Hostel E del Rijo
Enjoy lovely plaza views at this romantic patio restaurant. It is attached to the historic hotel, which is housed in a charming colonial building painted blue.

🏠 Plaza del Honorato ☎ (41) 328 588

$ $ $

Mesón de la Plaza
This rustic Spanish bodega is known for its *garbanzos* (chickpeas). Mesón de la Plaza is a good choice for a hearty lunch.

🏠 Calle Máximo Gómez 34 ☎ (41) 328 546

$ $ $

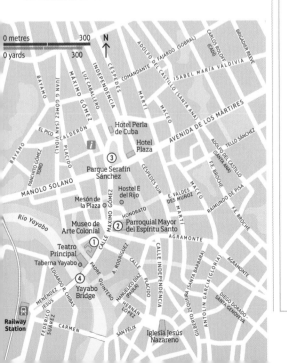

Did You Know?

The colony of iguanas on Cayo Coco floated here on coconut husks.

People relaxing on Playa las Colorades, one of Cayo Coco's three main beaches ↑

③

CAYO COCO

🅰B4 🏠Ciego de Ávila 🚗Cayo Coco; (33) 309 165 ⛴Marina Marlin, Cayo Guillermo; (33) 301 515 ℹInfotur, Aeropuerto Jardines del Rey, Cayo Coco; (33) 309 109

With 22 km (14 miles) of white sandy beaches and 370 sq km (143 sq miles) of partly marshy land abounding in mangroves and coconut palms, Cayo Coco is an important natural reserve for marine birds.

The name of the island derives from the rare species of bird that lives here: the white ibis, known to Cubans as the "coco," and flamingos may be spotted in the lagoon areas near the coast. The island is peaceful, and tourist amenities have been built and organized with environmental concerns in mind. The beaches are lovely, with fine sand washed by clear turquoise water. The warm, shallow water makes Cayo Coco particularly suitable for families with children, but the island is also popular among diving and watersports enthusiasts, who can take advantage of the modern sports facilities here.

> HIDDEN GEM
> ### Rocarena Climbing Center
> Rising 13 m (47 ft) over the sands of Cayo Coco, this climbing circuit is a fun aerial adventure for all ages. Here, you can climb walls, navigate a rope circuit, bungee jump or ride the zipline. Call (53) 156 628 to book.

STAY

Pullman Cayo Coco
This all-inclusive resort offers its guests eight restaurants. The chic rooms are divided into a family section and an adult-only section.

🏠Playa Las Coloradas, Cayo Coco
🌐pullmanhotels.com/gb

$$$

Iberostar Playa Pilar
With watersports facilities, five restaurants, a spa and a kids' club, this resort will not disappoint.

🏠Playa Pilar, Cayo Guillermo 🌐iberostar.com/en

$$$

↑ The pool at Iberostar Playa Pilar, named after Ernest Hemingway's yacht

↑ Pink flamingos paddling in the warm waters of Cayo Coco

④

CAMAGÜEY

🅰C5 **🏠Camagüey** **✈Ignacio Agramonte; (32) 261 010**
🚌Ave Avellaneda y Finlay; (32) 292 633 **🚍Carretera**
Central Km 3; (32) 270 396 **ℹInfotur, Calle Ignacio**
Agramonte 426; (32) 256 794

This city, declared a UNESCO World Heritage Site in
2008, lies in the middle of a vast area of pastureland.
It is nicknamed "the Legendary" for its traditions of
heroism and patriotism as well as for its Neo-Classical
architecture. The irregular, intricate street network
that distinguishes Camagüey from other Cuban cities
resulted from the need to protect itself from raids.

①

Parque Ignacio Agramonte

The former Plaza de Armas is
dominated by an equestrian
statue of Agramonte, a Cuban
independence hero, sculpted
by the Italian artist Salvatore
Boemi and inaugurated by
Amalia Simoni, Agramonte's
wife, in 1912. At the four corners
of the square stand royal
palms, planted in memory of a
group of nationalists executed
here in 1851. The palms are
symbolic monuments to the
rebels, as the Spanish would
never have allowed real
monuments to be built.

Buildings of interest on the
square include the Casa de la
Trova Patricio Ballagas – an
18th-century building with a
courtyard – the Biblioteca
Julio Antonio Mella and the
cathedral. With its benches
and shade from the palm
trees, the square is a natural
gathering point for the people
of Camagüey. It is also a popular spot to see the town's
famous *tinajones* (clay pots).

②

Catedral de Nuestra Señora de la Candelaria

**🏠Calle Cisneros 168, Parque
Agramonte** **☎(32) 294 965**
**🕐2:30–6pm Mon, Tue, Thu
& Fri, 8–11:45am & 2:30–
6pm Wed, 2:30–4pm Sat,
8–11:45am Sun**

Camagüey's cathedral,
dedicated to Our Lady of
Candelaria, who is also the
patron saint of the city, was
designed by Manuel Saldaña
and built in 1735. In 1777
a bell tower was added,
but it collapsed a year later.
Since then, the church has
been through phases of
reconstruction, taking on its
present appearance in 1864.
It now has a monumental

Did You Know?

Camellos - Camagüey's
articulated buses -
are called "camels" for
their sunken hump.

↑ The bustling Plaza de los Trabajadores square in the centre of Camagüey

façade surmounted by a pediment, and a bell tower crowned by a statue of Christ.

③ ⊛ ⊛

Casa Natal de Ignacio Agramonte

⌂ Calle Ignacio Agramonte 459, e/ Independencia y Cisneros ☎ (32) 297 116
🕒 9am–4:30pm Mon-Sat, 9am–noon Sun 🚫 1 May

Near Plaza de los Trabajadores, where a large ceiba tree marks

↑ The nave of the Catedral de Nuestra Señora de la Candelaria

the middle of the old town, is the former home of Ignacio Agramonte, the famous local patriot who died in battle in 1873 at the age of 31. His two-storey house dates from 1750 and has a beautiful inner courtyard with old *tinajones*.

Inside Agramonte's former home, the museum displays documents concerning the war of independence, the hero's personal belongings, such as his 36-calibre Colt revolver from 1851, and family furniture, including the piano of his wife, Amalia Simoni. Simoni was reputed to be one of the richest, most virtuous women in the city at the time.

A short walk away, you'll find another famous home. At Calle Hermanos Aguero 58 is the Casa Natal de Nicolás Guillén, birthplace of Cuba's poet laureate who was influenced by *son* and died in 1989.

THE TINAJONES

These romantic symbols of Camagüey can be seen everywhere you look – in parks and gardens and especially in the courtyards of the beautiful colonial houses that characterize the city. *Tinajones* are large jars, which may be as much as 2 m (6 ft) tall, made of clay from the nearby Sierra de Cubitas mountain range. The jars were introduced to the city by Catalonian immigrants in the early 1700s, and are still used today to collect rainwater and to store food.

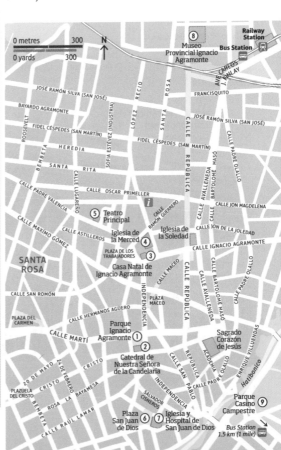

④
Iglesia de la Merced

 Plaza de los Trabajadores 4 🕐 8-11am & 4-5:30pm Mon-Fri, 8-11am Sat, 8-10am & 5-7pm Sun

The Iglesia de la Merced was built in 1601, but it was rebuilt from 1748 to 1756. It now has a Baroque façade with a central bell tower. Inside are striking, almost Art Nouveau-style murals. Most famous, however, is the Holy Sepulchre with an 18th-century statue of Christ by Mexican sculptor Juan Benítez Alfonso. It was cast from 23,000 silver coins collected from the faithful by Manuel Agüero, a citizen who, after his wife's death in 1726, became a monk and devoted himself to restoring the church.

⑤
Teatro Principal

 Calle Pedro Valencia 64 📞 (32) 293 048

First opened in 1850 and rebuilt in 1926 after a

 PICTURE PERFECT
Statue Subjects

Take a selfie with one of Martha Jiménez's lifesize bronze figures, which are scattered around the city. The artist's studio on Plaza del Carmen (*www.martha-jimenez.es*) overlooks Jiménez's frieze of three seated women, entitled *Chismosas* (The Gossipers). Sit in the empty fourth chair and pose with the statue.

---

devastating fire, this theatre is famous as the home of the Camagüey Ballet. Founded in 1967, it is one of the most highly regarded dance companies in Latin America.

⑥
Plaza San Juan de Dios

Laid out in 1732, this square is also known as Plaza del Padre Olallo, in honour of a priest who was beatified in 2008

---

because he dedicated his life to caring for the sick in the city's hospital.

Today, the square is a quiet, picturesque spot, but also a gem of colonial architecture. Around it are 18th-century pastel buildings, several of which have been converted into restaurants.

---

⑦ 🖋 🅜
Iglesia y Hospital de San Juan de Dios

Plaza San Juan de Dios 🕐 7-11am & 2:30-4pm Mon-Sat 🕐 1 Jan, 1 May, 26 Jul, 25 Dec

A church and an old hospital in the Plaza San Juan de Dios are now the home of the Dirección Provincial de Patrimonio and the Oficina del Historiador de la Ciudad, a body that takes care of the province's cultural heritage.

Despite its small size, the Iglesia de San Juan de Dios is one of the most interesting churches in Camagüey. It still has its original floors, ceiling and wooden choir, and, most

---

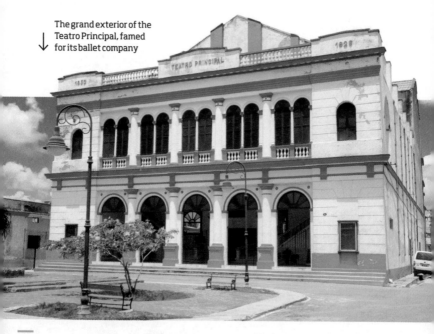

The grand exterior of the Teatro Principal, famed for its ballet company

Pastel-coloured houses looking over a shopping street in the centre of Camagüey ↑

importantly, the high altar with the Holy Trinity and an anthropomorphic representation of the Holy Ghost, the only one in Cuba. The church façade is simple and rigorously symmetrical.

The old hospital has had many roles in city life, including as a military infirmary, and, most recently, as the Instituto Tecnológico de la Salud (Technological Institute of Health). The square plan with two inner courtyards (clearly of *mudéjar* influence) was modelled on Baroque monasteries. The enclosure walls are thick and plain; in contrast the window grilles and wooden balustrades in the galleries are elegant and elaborate.

Museo Provincial Ignacio Agramonte

Avenida de los Mártires 2, esq Ignacio Sánchez (32) 282 425 9am–4:30pm Mon-Sat, 9am-noon Sun

The only military building in town was the headquarters of the Spanish army cavalry in the 19th century. In 1905 it

became a hotel, and since 1948 it has housed a large museum of the history, natural history and art of the city and province of Camagüey. The prestigious small art collection is second in the country only to that in the Museo de Bellas Artes in Havana, with three works by the famous Cuban artist Fidelio Ponce. Ponce's works were unique at their time, depicting poverty and sadness in Batista's Cuba in the 1930s. There is also a fine collection of books, including some manuscripts by the Canaries writer Silvestre de Balboa, author of *Espejo de Paciencia*, a 1608 poem regarded as the first literary work in Cuba.

Parque Casino Campestre

The largest natural park in any Cuban city, the Casino was for a long time used for agricultural fairs, but it became a public park in the 19th century. Besides the many statues of patriots and illustrious figures from Camagüey and the rest of Cuba, the park also has a monument to the Seville pilots Barberán and Collar, who on 10 June 1933 made a historic transatlantic flight from Seville to Camagüey in 19 hours 11 minutes. The Hatibonico river flows through the park.

→

Cycling past the central fountain in the Parque Casino Campestre

EXPERIENCE MORE

 5

Península de Ancón

⬛G3 ⬛Sancti Spíritus

About 14 km (9 miles) south of Trinidad, this was one of the first coastal areas in Cuba to be developed for tourism, and foreign visitors have been coming since 1980. It has fine white sand and turquoise water (though not as clear here as along the north coast), with a handful of hotels, bars, restaurants and watersports facilities. Cubans head mainly

---

SUGAR PRODUCTION

Sugar cane, introduced to Cuba in 1512 by Spanish settlers, has long been the mainstay of the economy. The cane is first washed, then pressed, treated chemically, filtered and evaporated to get a concentrated syrup. This is then heated to produce crystals of sucrose, which go into a centrifuge to be separated into different byproducts, including molasses.

---

for La Boca, 4 km (2.5 miles) from Trinidad, near the neck of the peninsula.

Playa Ancón, in the southern part of the peninsula, has 14 km (9 miles) of white sand, comfortable hotels, a splendid beach and a diving school. From the beach by Hotel Ancón, boats take divers and snorkellers out on the coral reef.

Cayo Blanco, 8 km (5 miles) off the coast, promises some fascinating diving. At its western tip is the largest of the black coral reefs found in Cuba, where divers can choose from a number of dive sites. On the rocky coasts near María Aguilar, on the other hand, there are pools where swimmers only need a mask to easily spot a great variety of tropical fish. A few small restaurants and bars are open here in the summer.

Instead of driving along the peninsula, hire a bicycle to get around.

Opposite the peninsula, across the bay, is the old port of Casilda, 6 km (4 miles) from Trinidad, where in 1519 Hernán Cortés recruited the troops that went on to conquer Mexico. Once a prosperous port, thanks to the sugar trade, Casilda has long since

declined, and is now above all a place to visit on the way to local beaches.

 6

Valle de los Ingenios

⬛G3 ⬛Sancti Spíritus ⬛ ⬛Excursions from Trinidad ⬛At railway station, (41) 993 348; Cubatur, Calle Antonio Maceo, esq Francisco J Zerquera, (41) 996 314

Leaving Trinidad and heading northeast, along the road to Sancti Spíritus, the beauty of the fertile plain is all around, with the green hills of the Sierra del Escambray forming a backdrop as you descend dramatically into the Valle de los Ingenios. Only 12 km (7 miles) separate Trinidad from the valley, whose name

Did You Know?

Slavery was abolished in Cuba in 1866 by royal decree.

← Shady parasols on the white sands of Playa Ancón, Península Ancón

derives from the sugar mills *(ingenios)* built here in the late 18th century, which gave the city its wealth. Most of the cane fields are long gone, replaced by barren patches and motley agricultural plots, interrupted only by towering royal palms.

The valley is rich in history with ruins providing evidence of the time when the sugar industry was at its peak and an insight into the social structure of the plantations. The whole zone, which covers 419 sq km (162 sq miles), includes the ruins of 56 *ingenios*. UNESCO has declared the valley a World Heritage Site. At the crest of the hill 6 km (4 miles) east of Trinidad is Mirador de la Loma del Puerto Del Valle de los Ingenios. Situated 92 m (630 ft) above sea level, this observation point offers a great view of the whole valley.

A good way to visit the area is to take the train that, when running, departs

from Trinidad and covers the entire valley. It stops at the impressive Hacienda Manaca Iznaga sugar plantation, where about 350 slaves lived in the early 1800s. The landowner's house survives and has been converted into a bar and restaurant. Also still standing are the *barracones* (slaves' huts) and a monumental seven-level tower 45 m (147 ft) high. Built in 1830, it symbolizes an assertion of authority over the valley by Alejo Iznaga, a rival to his brother Pedro, also a major sugar producer. The tower also functioned as a lookout for supervising the slaves. Reached via a steep wooden stairway, the top offers lovely, wide-ranging views. At the foot is the bell that once tolled the work hours on the plantation. Today, local women sell their traditional lacework here.

Nearby, Sitio Histórico San Isidro de los Estiladores also has a three-storey bell tower, as well as owner Jesús Nazareño's *hacienda*, *barracones* and other buildings. A nearly complete restoration has turned the once-ruined *batey* into the principal museum on

the colonial sugar industry and slave era. Further towards Sancti Spíritus, south of Caracusey, is the restored Guaimaro, built in 1859. Owner José Mariano Borrel y Lemus commissioned Italian painter Daniele Dell'Aglio, who also designed Teatro Sauto in Matanzas, to decorate the walls of the hacienda with European scenes.

STAY

Casa Colonial Muñoz
This friendly *casa particular* runs tours.

 G3 📍 Calle Martí 401, Trinidad 🖥 casa. trinidadphoto.com

⑤⑤⑤

Casa Colonial El Patio
A gorgeous colonial home with a leafy patio.

📍 G3 📍 Calle Ciro Redondo 274, Trinidad 📞 5359 2371

⑤⑤⑤

Iberostar Gran Hotel Trinidad
One of the island's finest hotels.

📍 G3 📍 Calle Martí y Lino Pérez, Trinidad 🖥 iberostar.com/en

⑤⑤⑤

Hotel E del Rijo
This colonial hotel has modern touches.

 G3 📍 Plaza Honorato, Sancti Spíritus 🖥 islazul.cu/en

⑤⑤⑤

← Lacework for sale in front of the tower at Hacienda Manaca Iznaga

← The opening of a cave in the Parque Nacional Caguanes, near Yaguajay

 8

Ciego de Ávila

 B5 Ciego de Ávila
Infotur, Calle Honorato del Castillo, esq Libertad; (33) 209 109

When Ciego de Ávila was founded in 1538 by the conquistador Jácome de Ávila, it was just a large farm in the middle of a *ciego* (wood). It only became a city in 1840 and occupies an expansive plain where sugar cane and pineapples – the city's symbol – are farmed. Although it is the provincial capital, Ciego de

EAT

Restaurante Blanco y Negro
Filling traditional *criolla* staples are on the menu at this homey family-run *paladar*.

B5 Calle Independencia 388, Ciego de Ávila
(33) 207 744

$$$

Restaurante Maité de Qaba
Excellent *paladar* serving delicious paellas, pastas and Cuban dishes.

B4 Calle Luz Caballero 40B, Morón
(33) 504 181

$$$

Restaurant 1800
Choose from Restaurant 1800's huge buffet and then dine on the cobbled plaza.

C5 Plaza San Juan de Díos, Camagüey
(32) 283 619

$$$

7

Yaguajay

A4 60 km (37 miles) NE of Sancti Spíritus (Sancti Spíritus)

An unassuming town on the Circuito Norte coast road, Yaguajay saw a decisive battle in 1958 between Batista's military and the Rebel Army led by Comandante Camilo Cienfuegos – the story of which is told at the **Complejo Histórico Comandante Camilo Cienfuegos**. On 28 October, the anniversary of his death, flowers are thrown into a moat.

To the northeast, Parque Nacional Caguanes protects colonies of flamingos and wintering sandhill cranes. Caves here preserve Pre-Columbian pictographs and are populated by mariposa ("butterfly") bats – the world's smallest bat species. The park is accessed via Mayijagua and local agencies offer tours.

Complejo Histórico Comandante Camilo Cienfuegos
Calle Eladio Carlata
(41) 552 689 8am-4pm Mon-Sat, 9am-1pm Sun

Did You Know?

Comandante Camilo Cienfuegos died in a mysterious plane crash in 1959.

→ Bicycles in the colourful centre of Ciego de Ávila

Ávila is still very much a rural town with two-storey houses fronted with Neo-Classical columns, and streets filled with one-horse carriages.

The centre is worth a stop to visit Parque Martí, the main square. Here, the Museo de Artes Decorativas displays a splendid array of colonial furnishings in a beautifully restored centenary mansion. To the south of Parque Martí, you'll find the Teatro Principal (dating from 1927), while the Museo Histórico Provincial sits in the former Spanish military garrison northwest of the square. The museum's four rooms hold documents and photographs as well as models of Sitio Arqueológico Los Buchillones – a Taíno village being excavated near Morón – and La Trocha. This 17-tower line of defence was built by the Spanish during the Ten Years' War (1868–78) to block the advance of the Cuban nationalists (mambises). Surviving towers include Fortín de la Trocha, on Plaza Máximo Gómez, four blocks west of Parque Martí. In the plaza stands a monument to General Máximo Gómez, who led the independence army.

↑ The Neo-Classical facade of Morón's Museo Municipal

Despite its relatively small size, Ciego de Ávila's baseball team, Los Tigres, has for several years dominated the national championship.

⑨
Morón

🅰B4 🏛Ciego de Ávila
🚌 🚹Cubanacán, Hotel Morón, Avda de Tarafa; (33) 504 720

Morón lies on the road north from Ciego de Ávila, a road known for its occupation in 1896 by nationalist rebels after they had breached the Spanish defence. It retains a small, well-preserved colonial centre, and the **Museo Municipal** has archaeological finds, including the famous Idolillo de Barro – a clay idol.

Only 3 km (2 miles) to the southeast of Morón is the former batey of Patria and Central Patri o Muerte sugar-processing mill. It is now converted into the **Museo de la Industria Azúcarera Avileña** (Museum of the Sugar Industry), where guided tours include an optional ride on a steam train.

Museo Municipal
🎨🕐 🏛Calle Martí 374 e/ Antuña y Cervantes 📞(33) 504 501 🕐9am–5pm Tue–Fri, 9am–1pm Sat 🚫1 Jan, 1 May, 26 Jul, 25 Dec

Museo de la Industria Azúcarera Avileña
🎨🕐 🏛Central Abel Santamaría Calle 1ra, 19, Batey 📞(33) 505 5111 🕐9am–6pm Tue–Sat, 9am–1pm Sun

---

THE COCKEREL OF MORÓN

"Be careful not to end up like the cockerel of Morón, which lost its feathers as well as its crest." This Spanish saying dates back to the 1500s, when the governor of Morón de la Frontera in Andalucia, dubbed "cockerel" for his arrogance, was thrashed and thrown out of town. To mark the event, a statue of a rooster was set up in the town. When the villagers emigrated to Cuba in the 1700s, they called their new home Morón and erected a statue of the rooster, replaced in 1981 by a bronze sculpture.

Jardines del Rey

A4-C5 Ciego de Ávila (Camagüey)

In the Atlantic Ocean, north of the province of Ciego de Ávila, the Sabana and Camagüey archipelagoes, known collectively as "Jardines del Rey", include about 400 small islands, most uninhabited.

They were discovered in 1522 by the conquistador Diego Velázquez, who was so struck by them that he dedicated them to the king *(rey)*, Carlos V. They became a hiding place for pirates and, after the official abolition of slavery, a clandestine landing point for slaves.

A causeway 27 km (17 miles) long, built in 1988 as a link between the archipelago and mainland Cuba, makes it easy for visitors to get to the lovely beaches, the coral reef and the beach resorts which are currently concentrated on Cayo Coco *(p208)* and Cayo Guillermo. Visitors must present their passport at a tollgate on the causeway.

Cayo Coco connects to Cayo Paredón Grande, which, at 6 km (4 miles) long, is the largest island in the Jardines. It is worth visiting for the lovely beaches and fine dive sites. An unpaved road leads to the distinctive black-and-yellow Faro Diego Velázquez, a lighthouse built by Chinese immigrants in 1859.

To the west are the gorgeous Cayos de Villa Clara, ringed by unbelievably white beaches and turquoise waters, and home to mangrove-fringed jade lagoons. To the east, Cayo Romano has a marshy coastline inhabited by flamingos and manatees. Cayo Sabinal, the easternmost of the cays is uninhabited except for deer and wild pigs.

HIDDEN GEM
In the Pink

The largest breeding flock of flamingos in the Caribbean inhabits the Refugio de Fauna Silvestre Río Máximo – the coastal wetlands and lagoons of the Bahía de la Gloria, southeast of Cayo Romano.

Sierra de Cubitas

C5 Camagüey

The range of hills that lies 40 km (25 miles) north of Camagüey forms the largest local reserve of flora and fauna, with over 300 plant species. To date, however, this area has no tourist facilities on any scale.

The main attractions are caverns such as Hoyo de Bonet, the largest karst depression in Cuba, and the Pichardo and María Teresa grottoes, where cave drawings have been discovered. Expert speleologists, on the other hand, can visit the Cueva de Rolando, a cave 132 m (435 ft) long with a subterranean lake 50 m (165 ft) across, the bottom of which has not yet been explored.

In the neighbouring Valle del Río Máximo is the Paso de los Paredones, a long, deep ravine with holes caused by

water erosion, some as much as 100 m (328 ft) deep and up to 1 km (0.6 mile) wide. The thick vegetation, through which sunlight penetrates for only a few hours, is home to a variety of native birds (*tocororo* and *cartacuba*), migratory birds, harmless reptiles and rodents.

Sierra del Chorrillo

🔼C6 🔼3 km (2 miles) SE of Najasa (Camagüey)

A limestone upland area about 50 km (30 miles) southeast of Camagüey city, the heavily forested Sierra del Chorrillo comprises

↑ A colourful Cuban trogon, the national bird of Cuba

semi-deciduous woodland and tropical montane forest ecosystems. The region is protected and is a popular bird-watching site where the Cuban parrot and the national bird, the Cuban trogon or *tocororo*, are easily spotted.

Visitors arrive at Finca La Belén, formerly a breeding centre for antelope, zebra and other imported species that were once hunted in this farm by the Communist elite. Today, Finca La Belén no longer breeds these exotic

animals and instead runs guided hiking, horseback riding and bird-watching tours. It also offers a lovely motel for those wishing to make an overnight visit. The dirt road that passes the entrance to the farm continues eastward to Bosque Fósiles de Najas, Cuba's only fossil forest, with petrified trees dating back 3 million years.

← Playa Pilar on Cayo Guillermo and the Faro Diego Velázquez *(inset)* in the Jardines del Rey

DRINK

Cabaret Cueva
A cave may seem like a strange location for a Tropicana-style cabaret, but the show and disco here are suitably glitzy and attract a young crowd.

🔼B4 🔼Laguna de la Leche, 6 km (4 miles) N of Morón 🕓Mon-Wed

Casa de la Trova
Traditional *son* fills the air in this beautiful colonial building.

🔼C5 🔼Calle Cisneros 171, Camagüey 📞(32) 291 357

El Cambio
This colourful offbeat dive bar on Parque Agramonte serves draft beer.

🔼C5 🔼Calles Independencia y Martí, Camagüey 📞(32) 286 240

Taberna Yayabo
Order a *cunyaga* - the sublime house cocktail made from lemon drops, sugar cane, honey and aged rum - at this riverside bar.

🔼G3 🔼Calle Jesús Menéndez 116, Sancti Spíritus 📞(41) 837 552

Flamingos reflected in a lagoon in the Jardines del Rey

⑬
Playa Santa Lucía

🅐D5 🅒Camagüey
🅘Cubatur, Ave Turística,
Playa Santa Lucía, (32) 336
291 or (32) 365 303

The most famous beach resort in the province offers 21 km (13 miles) of fine white sand lapped by turquoise waves. The large coral reef only 3 km (2 miles) from the shore is good for scuba divers. It shelters the coast from the currents of the Canal Viejo de Bahamas, thus safeguarding calm swimming conditions, as well as creating a good area for watersports.

There are more than 30 dive sites along the reef. One of the best spots is Shark's Point which offers dives full of romance. You'll explore the wrecks of pirate and Spanish vessels. For the brave there is also the chance to observe the bull shark (*Carcharinus leucas*) at close range from February to March and from July to September.

At the Boca de Nuevitas, 6 km (4 miles) west of Santa Lucía, near the tiny seashore village of La Boca, is Playa Los Cocos. This lovely unspoiled beach has fine white sand and clear water, and is a must for visitors to Santa Lucía.

↑ A catamaran on the sand of Playa Santa Lucía

Did You Know?

A family of bull sharks lives in the Boca de Nuevitas, near Playa Santa Lucía.

⑭
Jardines de la Reina

🅐A6-B6 🅒Ciego de Ávila
(Camagüey) 🚢Júcaro,
Embarcadero Avalón

This beautiful archipelago was discovered by Christopher Columbus and called Jardines de la Reina in honour of the queen (*reina*), Isabel of Castile. Established as a National Park in 1996, it is one of Cuba's largest protected areas, and its islands can be reached by boat from Júcaro.

The great number of unspoiled *cayos*, mangroves and palm groves are rich with fauna including crocodiles, iguanas, turtles, hutias and tropical birds, and the 200-km (124-mile) coral reef which runs the entire length of the archipelago is a paradise for divers.

Near Cayo Anclita, only about 100 m (328 ft) from the coast, is La Tortuga, a floating hotel reserved for sea anglers, divers and photographers. The waters abound with groupers, snappers, barracudas and Caribbean reef and silky sharks, among many other fish. Tours, diving trips and live-aboard accommodation can be booked via Avalon (*7204 7422*).

⑮
Las Tunas

🅐D6 🅒Las Tunas ✈🚌🚃
🅘Hotel Las Tunas, Ave 2 de
diciembre, (31) 345 014;
Ecotur, (31) 372 073

Las Tunas was just one of the cities in the old Provincia de Oriente until administrative reform made it the capital of an autonomous province in 1975. The town was founded on the site of two native villages that were razed to the ground by the conquistador Alonso de Ojeda in the early 1500s, but Las Tunas only really began to develop three centuries later. It progressively took on the character of a frontier town between central and eastern Cuba.

← Bluestripe snapper shoal swimming among the coral in the Jardines de la Reina

The historic centre has some colonial buildings, dating from the 16th to 19th centuries, but no major monuments of note. There are some artists' studios to explore.

The Museo Histórico Provincial, in the town hall, has archaeological finds and documents relating to the history of the province. The Museo Memorial Mártires de Barbados commemorates a terrorist act against Cuba carried out in 1976: a bomb placed by Cuban-Americans Orlando Bosch and Luis Posada Carriles exploded on a Cubana plane headed for Havana, killing 73 passengers and the entire crew.

Every year Las Tunas springs to life on the occasion of the Jornada Nacional Cucalambeana, a festival dedicated to Juan Cristóbal Nápoles Fajardo, known as El Cucalambé, a farmer and poet born here in 1829. Local and other Cuban artists, as well as foreign scholars, take part in a calendar of music and folk events.

Puerto Padre

D5 **Las Tunas**

This small and peaceful city, 30 km (18 miles) north of Las Tunas, is explored by few visitors. Once a significant player in the export of sugar, the port was the scene of many battles for independence. The Fuerte de la Loma, a small fortress at the southern approach to town, recalls its former importance.

White-sand beaches unfurl northeast of town and Playa La Herradura and Playa La Boca are the best spots.

→ The blue façade of the Museo Histórico Provincial, Las Tunas

A LONG WALK
TOPES DE COLLANTES

Distance 8 km (5 miles) **Time** 5 hours
Difficulty Starts uphill through tropical forest, then levels out **Nearest city** 30-minute drive north of Trinidad

The unspoiled landscape of the Sierra del Escambray (p191), where pine and eucalyptus grow alongside exuberant trees, ferns and tropical plants, offers extraordinarily beautiful scenery that can best be seen by hiking from Topes de Collantes. You start by walking through the tropical forest as far as the Caburní falls, before the terrain becomes easier and less tiring, with a detour to the Batata cave.

CENTRAL CUBA – EAST

Topes de Collantes

Locator Map
For more detail see p196

At 800 m (2,625 ft) above sea level and with clean air, **Topes de Collantes** was chosen as the location for a sanitarium for lung diseases in the 1950s.

After a 2-hour walk you will come to a plunging waterfall – **Salto del Caburní**. You can bathe in the pool here.

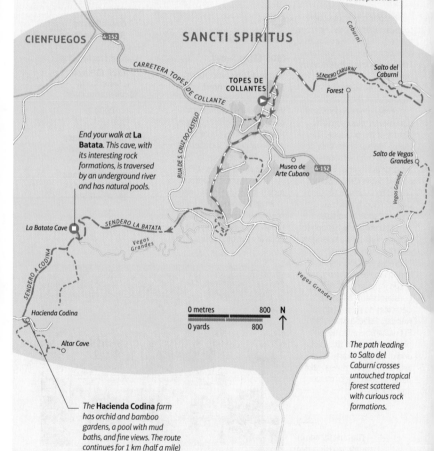

CIENFUEGOS

SANCTI SPIRITUS

CARRETERA TOPES DE COLLANTE

TOPES DE COLLANTES

Caburní

SENDERO CABURNÍ

Salto del Caburní

Forest

RUA DE S. CRUZ DO CASTELO

Museo de Arte Cubano

4-152

Salto de Vegas Grandes

End your walk at **La Batata**. This cave, with its interesting rock formations, is traversed by an underground river and has natural pools.

La Batata Cave

SENDERO LA BATATA

Vegas Grandes

Vegas Grandes

SENDERO A CODINA

Hacienda Codina

Altar Cave

| 0 metres | 800 |
| 0 yards | 800 |

N ↑

The path leading to Salto del Caburní crosses untouched tropical forest scattered with curious rock formations.

The **Hacienda Codina** farm has orchid and bamboo gardens, a pool with mud baths, and fine views. The route continues for 1 km (half a mile) among medicinal plants.

Did You Know?

The Salto del Caburní is 62 m (200 ft) high.

↑ Hikers traversing the trail to Salto del Caburní, past limestone cliffs

EASTERN CUBA

Cubans refer to the eastern part of Cuba as the Oriente, giving it an exotic, magical appeal. From the 17th to the 19th centuries, thousands of slaves were brought to Cuba from Africa and gave rise to the multi-ethnic nature of Eastern Cuba today: part African, but also part Spanish, part French and part Chinese. In this cultural melting pot, African and European, Roman Catholic and pagan traditions are blended, sometimes inextricably. This is no more apparent than in Santiago de Cuba's riotous annual carnival.

The area is full of contradictions: it is combative, rebellious and indomitable; and yet laid-back and full of music. The people of Eastern Cuba have always fought with great fervour. In the 16th century, the Indian chief Hatuey was burned at the stake here for organizing resistance against the Spanish, while in the 19th century, local nationalists led the wars of independence. The citizens of Bayamo even burned down their town rather than hand it over to the enemy. Then, in the 20th century, there were the *rebeldes* (many of whom were from Eastern Cuba, including the Castros themselves), who launched the struggle against Batista's dictatorship by attacking the Moncada Barracks in Santiago de Cuba.

227

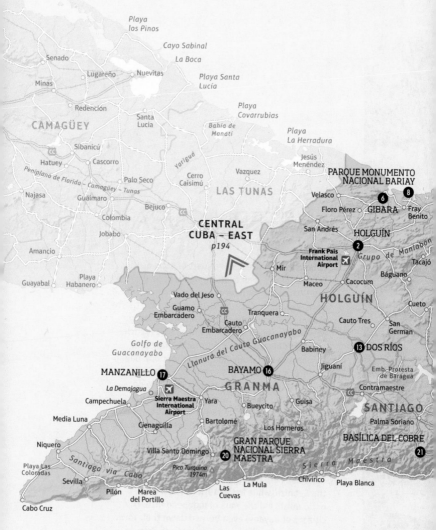

EASTERN CUBA

Atlantic Ocean

Playa los Pinos

Cayo Sabinal

La Boca

Nuevitas

Senado

Lugareño

Minas

Playa Santa Lucía

Redención

Santa Lucía

Playa Covarrubias

Bahía de Manatí

Playa La Herradura

CAMAGÜEY

Síbanicú

Cascorro

Hatuey

Peniplano de Florida – Camagüey – Tunas

Palo Seco

Najasa

Guáimaro

Bejuco

Colombia

Jobabo

Amancio

Cerro Caisimú

Yariguá

Vazquez

Jesús Menéndez

PARQUE MONUMENTO NACIONAL BARIAY

Velasco

6

8

LAS TUNAS

Floro Pérez

GIBARA

Fray Benito

San Andrés

HOLGUÍN

CENTRAL CUBA – EAST
p194

Mir

Frank País International Airport

2

Grupo de Maniabón

Tacajó

Maceo

Cacocum

Báguano

Guayabal

Playa Habanero

Vado del Jeso

Guamo Embarcadero

Cauto Embarcadero

Tranquera

HOLGUÍN

Cueto

San German

Cauto Tres

Golfo de Guacanayabo

Llanura del Cauto Guacanayabo

Babiney

13

DOS RÍOS

MANZANILLO

17

BAYAMO

16

Jiguaní

Emb. Presa de Baraguá

La Demajagua

GRANMA

Contramaestre

Campechuela

Sierra Maestra International Airport

Yara

Bueycito

Guisa

SANTIAGO

Media Luna

Cienaguilla

Bartolomé

Los Horneros

Palma Soriano

Niquero

Villa Santo Domingo

GRAN PARQUE NACIONAL SIERRA MAESTRA

BASÍLICA DEL COBRE

Playa Las Coloradas

Santiago vía Cabo

20

Pico Turquino 1974m

Sierra Maestra

21

Sevilla

Pilón

Marea del Portillo

Las Cuevas

La Mula

Chivirico

Playa Blanca

Cabo Cruz

EASTERN CUBA

Must Sees

1. Santiago de Cuba
2. Holguín
3. Castillo del Morro
4. Parque Baconao
5. Baracoa

Experience More

6. Gibara
7. Guardalavaca
8. Parque Monumento Nacional Bariay
9. El Chorro de Maíta
10. Banes
11. Museo Conjunto Histórico Birán
12. Pinares de Mayarí
13. Dos Ríos
14. Cayo Saetía
15. Mayarí Arriba
16. Bayamo
17. Manzanillo
18. La Farola
19. Parque Natural Duaba y El Yunque
20. Gran Parque Nacional Sierra Maestra
21. Basílica del Cobre
22. Guantánamo
23. Costa Sur
24. Parque Nacional Río Toa
25. Parque Nacional Alejandro de Humboldt
26. Boca de Yumurí
27. Punta Maisí

←

1 The majestic Catedral de la Nuestra Señora de la Asunción.

2 Museo del Carnaval exhibit.

3 Castillo del Morro.

4 Musicians playing in the Casa de la Trova.

2 DAYS

In Santiago de Cuba

Day 1

Morning Begin your exploration in Parque Céspedes (p240), the city's lively main square, with a cappuccino at Hotel Iberostar Casa Granda's café (p234). Then, head across the plaza to Casa de Don Diego Velázquez (p233) for a guided tour of Cuba's oldest building. Nip into the Catedral de la Nuestra Señora de la Asunción (p232) to admire its impressive interior, then check out Maqueta de la Ciudad (p236) – a scale model of the entire city. Climb the Escalinata Padre Pico (p236) and learn about the 1950s underground revolutionary movement at the Museo de la Lucha Clandestina (p235). Roy's Terrace Inn (p237) is a great choice for lunch.

Afternoon Follow Calle Heredia to the Museo del Carnaval, which tells the story of the city's sensational annual festivities (p235). A stone's throw away, don't miss the Museo Emilio Bacardí, a fascinating trove of eclectic displays (p234). To the east, Vista Alegre (p239) is full of architectural gems and tiny museums.

Evening For dinner, return to Hotel Iberostar Casa Granda (p239), but this time visit the romantic rooftop restaurant which is blessed with an impressive menu and a fabulous panoramic view over casco histórico – the city's colonial quarter. Plus, you're just one block from the city's Casa de la Trova (p234), considered the epicentre of traditional son music.

Day 2

Morning After a hearty breakfast, head to Museo Histórico 26 de Julio – Cuartel Moncada (p238), where the revolution was launched on 26 July 1953. A guided tour is a must. Next, walk east on Avenida Manduley, which is lined with eclectic mansions and quirky sites. From here, Calle 11 leads to the hilltop Parque Histórico Loma de San Juan (p239). The hill is studded with memorials recalling the battle that was fought here in 1898. Paladar La Canasta (p237) is a fun place to lunch on garlic shrimp or succulent ropa vieja – the quintessential Cuban dish.

Afternoon Pay homage to José Martí and Fidel Castro, whose graves lie side by side in the remarkable Cementerio de Santa Ifigenia (p237), among other notable Cuban figures. Don't leave before witnessing the half-hourly changing of the guard. Now, walk along the waterfront Avenida Jesús Menéndez, with its fascinating revolutionary murals, to enjoy a refreshing beer at the Cervecería Puerto del Rey (p234).

Evening End your sightseeing at the Castillo del Morro (p244), arriving in time to explore the castle before witnessing the sunset cañonazo (cannon firing). Back in the city, have dinner at the terrific St. Pauli (p237), followed by cocktails and music at the Iris Jazz Club (Calle Paraiso y Calle Aguilera).

↑ The twin towers of the Catedral de Nuestra Señora de la Asunción

❶

SANTIAGO DE CUBA

🅰 E7 **🏠 Santiago de Cuba** **✈ 7 km (4 miles) S of town** **🚌 Ave Jesús Menéndez, esq Hechevarría** **🚍 Ave de los Libertadores, esq Yarayó; (22) 628 484** **🛈 Infotur & Cubatur, Ave Garzón e/ 3ra y 4ta; (22) 652 560**

This is perhaps the most African, the most musical and the most passionate city in Cuba. Santiago de Cuba is a lively, exciting place where festivities are celebrated with fervour, never more so than during July's carnival.

①

Catedral de Nuestra Señora de la Asunción

🏠 Calle Heredia, e/ Lacret y Félix Peña **☎ (22) 628 502** **🕐 9:30am–12:30pm & 5–7:30pm Tue–Sat, 8–10am & 5–6:30pm Sun**

The cathedral of Santiago de Cuba, which was extensively restored in 2014, has a typical basilica layout, with a central nave and four aisles, an apse and a narthex or vestibule at the back. The church was originally built in 1522, but in the 17th century a series of pirate raids caused so much damage that the church had to be built from scratch in 1674 – only to then be tragically destroyed by an earthquake in 1766.

The existing church, rebuilt again in 1818, displays a mixture of styles, the result of a series of changes made by the architect Carlos Segrera Fernández in 1922. He added the bell towers, had the interior painted and also reworked the façade. A marble angel was set over the main entrance and statues of Christopher Columbus and Bartolomé de las Casas were placed in side niches at Fernández's command.

The cathedral also houses the Museo Eclesiástico, a museum of sacred art. The collection includes frescoes by the Dominican friar Luis Desangles, liturgical objects, statues and an important collection of ecclesiastical music scores.

Did You Know?

Santiago de Cuba is called the "Cradle of the Revolution".

SHOP

Galería René Valdés Cedeño

This well-lit modern gallery displays striking contemporary art pieces, including sculptures, jewellery, clothing and multimedia works.

🅐 Avenida Manduley 304 🄲 (22) 668 328

El Quitrín

Hand-sewn and embroidered white cotton guayaberas, blouses, shawls and dresses are made on site at El Quitrín.

🅐 Calle Hechavarría 477 🄲 (22) 622 528 🅓 Sat & Sun

Casa de la Cerámica

This ceramic workshop sells handmade vases, plates, sculptures and other ceramics.

🅐 Avenida Manduley 102 🄲 (22) 667 211

---

② ⊛ ⊛

Casa de Diego Velázquez (Museo Ambiente Histórico Cubano)

🅐 Calle Félix Pena 612, e/ Heredia y Aguilera 🄲 (22) 652 652 🕘 9am–4:30pm Mon–Thu, 1:30–4:30pm Fri, 9am–2:30pm Sun

This building, constructed in 1516–30 as a residence for the governor Diego Velázquez, is the oldest home in Cuba, according to architect Francisco Prat Puig, who restored the house in 1965. Other scholars have disputed this assertion, however. Whatever the truth, this splendid residence is still a fascinating place to visit.

The former House of Transactions (the ground floor still has an old furnace in which gold ingots were made) is a fine example of the *mudéjar* (Moorish) style. The upstairs gallery is closed off by a wooden blind, to screen residents from the eyes of strangers. Some of the original *alfarje* ceilings survive.

The building now houses the Museo Ambiente Histórico Cubano, covering the history of furniture in Cuba. It contains superb examples from

↑ The *mudéjar*-style upstairs gallery in the Casa de Diego Velázquez

all of Cuba's colonial periods. Among the mostly austere Creole furniture, dating from the 16th and 17th centuries, are a splendid priest's high-backed chair and a finely wrought coffer.

The basement has unique 18th-century "Luis Las Casas" furniture, a style peculiar to Cuba which combines English influences and French Rococo motifs. The 19th-century section includes a dining room with stained-glass windows and French furniture, including rocking chairs and a console table.

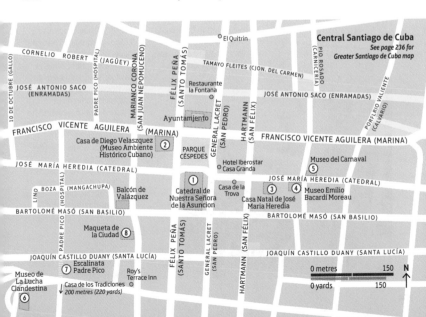

Central Santiago de Cuba
See page 236 for Greater Santiago de Cuba map

DRINK

Hotel Iberostar Casa Granda

There's no better spot for watching city life than this patio bar.

🏠 Calle Heredia 201
🌐 iberostar.com/en

Cervecería Puerto del Rey

Pulsating with live music, this huge brewpub, set in a former seafront warehouse, is always packed with groups of locals.

🏠 Avenida Jesús Menéndez at Aduana
☎ (22) 686 048

Casa de la Trova

Cuba's top "Trova House" is acclaimed for its *son* and often hosts famous musicians.

🏠 Calle Heredia 208
☎ (22) 652 689

La Casa de los Tradiciones

Looking for a more off-beat venue? This lively bar is always fun.

🏠 Calle Rabí 154
☎ (22) 653 892

The *comparsas* are the people wearing masks or costumes, dancing the conga and carrying streamers and *farolas* (brightly coloured paper lamps) in the carnival.

Casa Natal de José María Heredia

🏠 Calle Heredia 260, e/ Hartmann (San Félix) y Pío Rosado (Carniceria) ☎ (22) 625 350 🕐 9am–7pm Mon–Sat, 9am–4pm Sun

This is the modest but elegant 18th-century house where the nationalist poet José María Heredia (1803–39) was born. Heredia, who was very highly regarded for his odes to nature, should not be confused with his cousin, a French Parnassian poet, who was also born in Cuba but spent practically all his life in Europe.

The well-preserved house contains period furniture and objects, wooden ceilings and tiled floors, and is well worth a visit. From the large entrance hall, with a coffered ceiling and paintings of the poet's ancestors on the walls, a large arch leads into the central peristyled courtyard. Here there are wooden columns, an old stone well and abundant vegetation.

Other rooms in the house include Heredia's bedroom with its impressive mahogany bed and elegant lamps.

Cultural events and poetry readings are often held in the museum's large porticoes. In addition, every year literary seminars and workshops are held here as part of the Fiesta del Caribe, or Fiesta del Fuego. This summer cultural event takes over the entire city of Santiago de Cuba.

Museo Emilio Bacardí Moreau

🏠 Calle Pío Rosado (Carnicería), esq Aguilera ☎ (22) 628 402 🕐 9am–4:30pm Mon–Fri, 9am–6:30pm Sat, 9am–2:30pm Sun

The Museo Emilio Bacardí Moreau is the oldest museum in Cuba. It was founded in 1828 and is a rich source of relics dating from the Spanish conquest to the wars of independence. The objects were collected and organized in the late 1800s and early 1900s by Emilio Bacardí, founder of the famous rum distillery. Bacardí was also a famous patriot and the first mayor of Santiago when Cuba became a republic. His aim was to display the origin and development of the Cuban nationalist movement from a cultural point of view, and he asked the architect Segrera to design a building for the objects and works of art he had collected.

The museum is housed in an eclectic building with a broad staircase and an atrium dominated by large statues of

A model of a man shaping oak for rum barrels at the Museo Emilio Bacardí Moreau

CARNIVAL IN SANTIAGO DE CUBA

The roots of the carnival in Santiago de Cuba are religious: since the end of the 17th century there have been processions and festivities from 24 June to 26 July in honour of the city's patron saint, Santiago Apóstolo. At the end of the parade, slaves who were members of the *cabildos* - societies that kept alive African languages, traditions and beliefs - were allowed to go out into the streets, where they sang to the accompaniment of drums, rattles and other instruments. These were the forerunners of the *comparsas*, the soul of carnival. The *comparsas* are the people wearing masks or costumes, dancing the conga and carrying streamers, banners and *farolas* (brightly coloured paper lamps) during the carnival. In the second half of July the whole of Santiago de Cuba hosts a celebratory carnival, with every district taking part in the parades, each with at least one *comparsa*.

Minerva and Liberty. On the ground floor is a collection of arms used by nationalist heroes such as Antonio Maceo, Máximo Gómez and José Martí. There is also a collection of works by great 19th-century Cuban painters, including Felipe López González, Juan Emilio Hernández Giro, José Joaquín Tejada Revilla and Buenaventura Martínez. Twentieth-century artists represented here are Wifredo Lam and René Portocarrero. The archaeology section includes the only Egyptian mummy in the country.

 PICTURE PERFECT
Parque Life

The sweeping view over the centre of Santiago de Cuba from the rooftop terrace of the Hotel Iberostar Casa Granda is truly inspiring. A wide-angle, or panoramic, lens will capture the square, with the Sierra Maestra beyond. Visit at sunset or at night, when the plaza is illuminated by moonlight.

---

⑤

Museo del Carnaval

🏛 Calle Heredia 303, esq Pío Rosado (Carniceria) 📞 (22) 626 955 ⏰ 4–5pm Mon, 9am–5pm Tue–Fri, 9am–9pm Sat, 9am–1pm Sun

A lovely late 18th-century building, this structure was converted into an elementary school in the mid-1900s, then into an office building, but it eventually became the offices of the Carnival Commission. In 1983, it became the home of the Museo del Carnaval. The six rooms contain vibrant photographs of the festivities, with some explanatory captions in Spanish (there are none in English), chronologies, banners, musical instruments, costumes and papier mâché masks. The collection is a complete survey of the carnival festivities held in Santiago every summer. Carnival in Cuba differs from the traditional Spanish model as it combines many African and Franco-Haitian elements.

The best day to visit the museum is Monday. At 4pm every week, performers, such as traditional music ensemble La Peña Folklórica Raices, play in the museum's courtyard.

---

⑥

Museo de la Lucha Clandestina

🏛 Calle Rabí 1, e/ San Carlos y Santa Rita 📞 (22) 624 689 ⏰ 9am–5pm Tue–Sun

The Museum of the Clandestine Struggle overlooks a pleasant square in the district of Tivolí, which was first inhabited by French settlers, southwest of Parque Céspedes. The building was the headquarters of Batista's police from 1951 to 1956. On 30 November 1956 it was burnt down by revolutionaries.

Nowadays, the four rooms in the restored building commemorate the activities of the Movimiento 26 de Julio. This clandestine movement to overthrow Batista was headed in Santiago de Cuba by Frank País, who was born in the city *(p237)*. País met a tragic end in 30 July 1957, when the young rebel leader was assassinated by the police.

⑦

Escalinata Padre Pico

🏠 Calle Padre Pico e/ Duany y Santa Rita

This staircase, at the southern end of Calle Padre Pico, has 52 steps with 12 landings. Although it is not particularly long, Escalinata Padre Pico is significant because it was here, on 30 November 1956, the three members of the Movimiento 26 de Julio were killed while assaulting the police station. Today, the former police station houses the Museo de la Lucha Clandestina (p235).

⑧

Maqueta de la Ciudad

🏠 Calle Mariano Corona e/ Masó y Duany 📞 (22) 652 095 🕐 Mon

For an overview of the entire city, check out this amazingly detailed 1:1,000 scale model. It displays every building in Santiago de Cuba, as well as the city's every contour, extending as far south as the Castillo del Morro.

↑ Strolling down the street from the Escalinata Padre Pico

⑨

Casa Natal de Antonio Maceo

🏠 Calle Los Maceo 207, e/ Corona y Rastro 📞 (22) 623 750 🕐 9am–4:30pm Mon–Sat

The house where the great independence general Antonio Maceo was born on 14 June 1845 is a modest place. Visitors can see some of the Ten Years' War hero's personal belongings and family photographs, including one of his brother José, who was also a general, and his mother.

⑩

Museo Memorial Vilma Espín

🏠 Calle Hechaverría 473 📞 (22) 622 295 🕐 Sun

This 19th-century townhouse was the home of revolutionary combatant Vilma Espín from 1938 to 1958. This guerrilla fighter married Raúl Castro and later founded the Cuban Women's Federation. The building, which famously served as a secret meeting place for the Movimiento 26 de Julio, now houses a collection of artifacts that tell the story of Espín's life.

⑪

Museo Hermanos País

🏠 Calle Banderas 266 📞 (22) 652 710 🕐 Sun

Brothers Frank and Josué País were born and raised in this home. Frank famously became the leader of the Movimiento 26 de Julio and was assassinated by police on 30 July 1957, one month after Josué, a fellow revolutionary, was murdered.

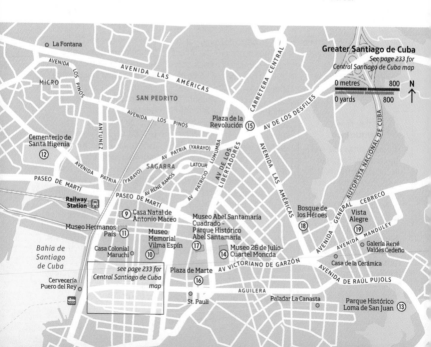

See page 233 for Central Santiago de Cuba map

Greater Santiago de Cuba

0 metres 800
0 yards 800
N

↑ Fidel Castro's simple grave in the Cementerio de Santa Ifigenia

Cementerio de Santa Ifigenia

 Avenida Crombet 🕻 (22) 632 723 ⏰ 8am–5pm daily

This monumental cemetery (1868) is the second most important in Cuba after the Necrópolis de Colón cemetery in Havana (p116). It was originally laid out with a Latin cross plan and divided into courtyards, the most important of which were reserved for those of higher social status. A visit to the Santa Ifigenia cemetery evokes two centuries of Cuban history, past the tombs of such illustrious 19th-century figures as José Martí, Carlos Manuel de Céspedes, Emilio Bacardí and the mother of Antonio Maceo, as well as the 20th-century revolutionaries of the Movimiento 26 de Julio such as Frank País. The cemetery's most famous resident by far, however, is Fidel Castro whose resting place is marked with a boulder reading "Fidel". Significantly, this rock, which represents a kernel of corn, was taken from the Gran Parque Nacional Sierra Maestra (p258), the stronghold of the guerilla fighters during the revolution.

The funerary monuments themselves are fascinating. The Neo-Classical tombs nearest the entrance are the oldest, followed by the eclectic and then Modernist tombs. The Rationalist tombs built from the mid-20th-century on include Martí's large octagonal mausoleum.

Parque Histórico Loma de San Juan

📍 Avenida Pujol y Calle 13

San Juan Hill was the site of the seminal land battle of the Spanish-American War of 1898, when Teddy Roosevelt's "Rough Riders" and Cuban *mambises* (independence fighters) stormed the Spanish forces on the hill. The park is now home to several monuments to the battle.

STAY

Casa Colonial Maruchi
Stuffed with antiques, this *casa particular* has three rooms.

📍 Calle San Félix 357
🕻 (22) 620 767

$$$

Hotel Iberostar Casa Granda
Don't miss the excellent rooftop restaurant at this upmarket hotel.

📍 Calle Heredia 201
🖥 iberostar.com/en

$$$

Hotel Meliá Santiago
This contemporary hotel offers its own cabaret show.

📍 Avenida de las Américas y Calle M
🖥 meliacuba.com

$$$

→

Imposing statue of General Maceo in the Plaza de la Revolucíon

EAT

Roy's Terrace Inn

Dine on excellent traditional Cuban fare on the shaded rooftop terrace at Roy's Terrace Inn.

🏠 Calle Diego Palacios 177 📞 (22) 620 522

$$$

Paladar La Canasta

A former professional basketball player runs this beautiful garden *paladar*. The menu here features succulent seafood, as well as classic Cuban dishes.

🏠 Calle Fernando Marcané 51 📞 (22) 642 964

$$$

St. Pauli

Hidden off Plaza de Marte, this cubbyhole *paladar* serves a great *ropa vieja* (shredded beef and vegetables).

🏠 Calle Saco 605 📞 (22) 652 292

$$$

Restaurante La Fontana

You'll find this stylish open-air restaurant at the deluxe Hotel Meliá Santiago. The restaurant serves Italian dishes.

🏠 Avenida de las Américas y Calle M 🌐 meliacuba.com

$$$

---

⑭

Museo 26 de Julio – Cuartel Moncada

🏠 Calle General Portuondo (Trinidad), e/ Moncada y Ave de los Libertadores 📞 (22) 661 1575 🕐 9am–12:30pm Mon & Sun, 9am–4:30pm Tue–Sat

On 26 July 1953, at the height of the carnival festivities, the rebels staged a coordinated sting in Santiago de Cuba. Fidel Castro, wanting to secure a large stock of weapons, led the attack on the Moncada Barracks. Although this bold attempt failed, the attack did increase public awareness of the revolutionaries' activities and ideals.

Since 1959 the barracks, which still bears bullet holes, has housed the Ciudad Escolar 26 de Julio school, as well as the Museo 26 de Julio, which tells the story of the attack.

---

⑮

Plaza de la Revolución

In the northeastern part of Santiago is Plaza de la Revolución, a large, rather soulless square at a cross-roads of three major avenues. The square is dominated by a vast monument executed in the early 1990s by the Santiago sculptor, Alberto Lezcay, representing Antonio Maceo, a general in the Ten Years' War (p52) on horseback.

---

⑯

Plaza de Marte

East of Plaza Dolores is the third largest square in Santiago de Cuba, which was laid out in the 19th century. It is of great historic importance as it was here that capital punishment was meted out

both in the colonial period and under General Machado. At its centre is a 20-m (65-ft) column (1902) celebrating Cuban independence.

Museo Abel Santamaría Cuadrado - Parque Histórico Abel Santamaría

📍 Calle General Portuondo (Trinidad), e/ Calle Nueva y Ave de los Libertadores
📞 (22) 624 119 🕐 9am–5pm Mon–Sat

The Moncada Barracks, former Saturnino Lora hospital and law court buildings form part of the Parque Histórico Abel Santamaría. In the 1953 raid, the former hospital was the target of a group of rebels led by Abel Santamaría, who was captured and killed by the police after the failed attempt. The remaining buildings now house a museum with documents relating to the trial of Fidel Castro and other rebels, which was held a few days after the attack.

Besides photographs of the difficult economic conditions in Cuba during the 1950s, there is the manuscript of Castro's landmark self-defence in court, later entitled "History Will Absolve Me" (p153).

Bosque de los Héroes

East of the centre lies a small, unobtrusive hill. A white marble monument was erected on the site in 1973 to honour Che Guevara and the comrades-in-arms who died with him in Bolivia. Their names are engraved here.

Vista Alegre

As well as eclectic buildings, dating from the 1920s and 1930s, this quarter of the city also has two important institutions. The Centro Cultural Africano Fernando Ortíz displays a comprehensive collection of African masks, statues and musical instruments, while the Casa del Caribe is an archive, library, alfresco music venue and centre for conferences, workshops and events. During the Fiesta del Caribe, the Casa del Caribe stages Yoruba, Congo and voodoo rites.

A SHORT WALK
PARQUE CÉSPEDES

Distance 1 km (0.5 mile) **Time** 15 minutes
Nearest bus station Ave de los Libertadores

The former Plaza de Armas in Santiago is the heart of the city, both geographically and spiritually, making it the perfect place to take a stroll. Renamed Parque Céspedes in honour of the nation's founding father – Carlos Manuel de Céspedes – this square is a place for socializing, relaxing, chatting and celebrating. At all hours of the day and night, the benches are filled with people: young, old, women, children and visitors. Everyone sooner or later gets involved in a conversation or entertainment of some kind, because this square's other role is as an open-air venue where music – live, recorded or improvized – takes the leading role. Finish your walk at the Balcón de Velázquez, admiring the magnificent view.

↑ A musician performing in Santiago de Cuba's famous Casa de la Trova

Music is performed daily at the Casa de la Trova (p234).

CALLE GENERAL L.

CALLE HARTMANN

The Casa Natal de José María Heredia, where the poet was born, is a fine 18th-century building with a leafy courtyard (p234).

CALLE HEREDIA

Housed in an elegant Neo-Classical building, the Museo Emilio Bacardí Moreau (p234) is not only the oldest museum in Cuba but the most eclectic. Items on display include an Egyptian mummy, mementos of the wars of independence and works by living artists.

CALLE AGUILERA

Did You Know?

José Maria Heredia is known as "El Cantor del Niagra" or "the Singer of Niagra".

One of Cuba's historic hotels, Hotel Casa Granda opened in 1920. Graham Greene (p90) described it in Our Man in Havana as a hotel frequented by spies. Its terrace overlooks the park.

| 0 metres | 50 | N |
| 0 yards | 50 | ↑ |

The **Catedral de Nuestra Señora la Asunción**'s (p232) façade may be Neo-Classical, but the original church is four centuries old. It is believed that the Spanish painter Diego Velázquez is buried somewhere beneath the building, but there is no proof.

Locator Map
For more detail see p233

SANTIAGO DE CUBA

Parque Céspedes

FINISH

The **Balcón de Velázquez** is a spacious viewing terrace built over the site of a Spanish fortress. It offers a magnificent view of the picturesque quarter of Tivolí, as well as the port and the bay of Santiago.

CALLE BARTOLOMÉ MASÓ

CALLE FÉLIX PEÑA

CALLE HEREDIA

CALLE MARIANO CORONA

Built in 1516–30, the **Casa de Diego Velázquez**, the residence of the Spanish conquistador Diego Velázquez is considered by some to be the oldest building in Cuba. Restoration was carried out in 1965 and 2013, and it is now the home of the Museo Ambiente Histórico Cubano (p233).

START

The **Ayuntamiento** (town hall), a symbol of the city, was built in 1950 according to 18th-century designs found in the Indies Archive. It was from this building's central balcony that Fidel Castro made his first speech to the Cuban people, on 1 January 1959.

PARQUE CÉSPEDES

The **Casa de la Cultura Miguel Matamoros**, an eclectic building (1919) housing the sumptuous Salón de los Espejos, is a venue for artistic and cultural events.

→
The grand exterior of the infamous Hotel Casa Granda

↑ A gazebo in leafy Parque Peralta, overlooked by Catedral de San Isidoro

❷
HOLGUÍN

🅰 E6 🏠 Holguín ✈ 13 km (8 miles) S of town 🚌 Calle V Pita; (24) 468 559 🚍 Carretera Central y Independencia; (24) 422 111 🅸 Infotur, Calle Libertad, esq Martí; (24) 425 013

Called the city of parks because of its many leafy squares, Holguín is a colonial town situated between two hills. Holguín is famed for the active part it played in the wars of independence under the leadership of Calixto García, the famous general who liberated the city from the Spanish in 1872.

①

La Periquera (Museo Provincial de Holguín)

🏠 Calle Frexes 198, e/ Libertad y Maceo 📞 (24) 463 395 🕐 9am–noon & 12:30–5pm Tue–Sat, 8am–noon Sun 🔒 1 Jan, 1 May, 26 Jul, 10 Oct, 25 Dec

This large Neo-Classical building was built in 1860 as the private home of Spanish merchant Francisco Roldán y Rodríguez. In 1868, at the beginning of the Ten Years' War, the building was occupied by the Spanish army and converted into barracks. Hence the building's nickname, La Periquera, which translates as "parrot cage", a reference to the brightly coloured uniforms of the Spanish army.

Today, the building is the home of the Museo Provincial de Holguín, where five rooms illustrate the cultural development of the town. Also on display are archaeological relics of the Taíno Indians, who lived here from the 8th to the 15th centuries. The most famous item in the collection is the Hacha de Holguín, a stone axe head carved as a human figure, which has become the symbol of the city.

②

Museo de Historia Natural Carlos de la Torre

🏠 Calle Maceo 129, e/ Martí y Luz Caballero 📞 (24) 423 935 🕐 9am–noon & 12:30–5pm Tue–Sat, 9am–noon Sun

Holguín's museum of natural history is housed in a brightly

 GREAT VIEW
Loma de la Cruz

There are marvellous far-reaching vistas from the top of the Loma de la Cruz (Hill of the Cross). Although the 458 steps to the top were only added in 1927, this hill was used to plan the orginal grid layout of the town. Every year on 3 May, Christian pilgrims climb up the hill for the Romerías de Mayo.

painted building with a handsome portico and Spanish tiling throughout. An interesting collection of birds and shells, including Polymita snails from Baracoa is on display, along with a 50-million-year-old fossil fish, found in the Sierra Maestra.

③
Catedral de San Isidoro

◽ Calle Manduley, e/ Luz Caballero y Aricochea, Parque Peralta ☎ (24) 422107 🕐 5:30-6:45pm Mon, 7am-noon & 3-5:30pm Tue & Fri, 7am-noon & 3-6:45pm Wed & Thu, 7am-noon & 7-8:45pm Sat & Sun

Consecrated as a cathedral in 1979, San Isidoro was built in 1720 on Parque Peralta, named after Julio Grave de Peralta (1834–72), who led an uprising against Spain in Holguín in October 1868. The square is also known as Parque de Flores because a flower market used to be held here.
The church contains a copy of the popular Madonna of Caridad, the original of which is in the Basilica del Cobre near Santiago de Cuba (p259). On 4 April there is a celebration in honour of the Virgin.

④
Bazar de Artesanía

Two blocks north of Parque Calixto García is Bazar de Artesanía, a charming indoor market selling a range of handmade accessories, carved wooden ornaments and seed and resin jewellery. The pedestrianized street outside the market is a peaceful spot to sit.

⑤
Plaza de la Revolución

Situated east of the city centre, this square contains a monument to the heroes of Cuban independence, the mausoleum of Calixto García and a small monument to García's mother. The square is the main venue for popular festivities in Holguín.

EAT & DRINK

Restaurante Los Almendros
Replicating a traditional farmstead, with cowhide seats, this downtown *paladar* serves the expected meat-based *criolla* staples, as well as delicious lobster and shrimp dishes.

◽ Calle José Cardet 68 ☎ (24) 429 652

⑤⑤⑤

Taberna Pancho
Attached to the Hotel Pernik, this bodega offers bargain-priced *criolla* dishes, including shrimp enchilada, which is best washed down with one of the draft beers on the extensive drinks menu here.

◽ Avenida Dimitrov ☎ (24) 481 868

⑤⑤⑤

Casa de la Trova "El Guayabero"
This is the place in town to listen to traditional *danzón*, *son* and *trova*. It's the perfect place to dance the night away, partying with the ebullient locals.

◽ Calle Maceo 174 ☎ (24) 453 104

Taberna Mayabe
Taberna Mayabe is a cosy Spanish bodega-style "pub" serving local Mayabe draft beer.

◽ Calle Libertad y Aguilera ☎ (24) 461 543

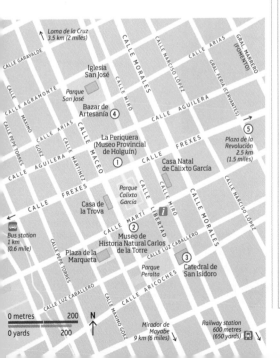

3 🏛️ 🏛️

CASTILLO DEL MORRO

📍E7 🏠 Carretera del Morro, Km 7.5, Santiago de Cuba
📞(22) 691 569 🕐8am–5pm daily

At the entrance to the Bay of Santiago, 10 km (6 miles) southwest of the city centre, stands an imposing castle – the Castillo del Morro San Pedro de la Roca – which was declared a World Heritage Site by UNESCO in 1997.

Combining medieval elements with a modern sense of space, the Castillo del Morro adheres to classical Renaissance principles of geometric forms and symmetry. The fortress was designed in 1638 by engineer Giovanni Bautista Antonelli for the governor Pedro de la Roca, who wanted to defend the city against pirate raids. Three separate main structures, built on five different levels, form the skeleton of the castle. This unusual construction is a result of the uneven terrain of the headland. Large enough to house 400 soldiers when it was built, the castle was converted into a prison in 1775, becoming a fortress once again in 1898 during the wars of independence, when the US fleet attacked the city. Today it houses a naval and piracy museum, and has excellent views over the bay from the fortress walls.

Artillery area

Underground passageways link the various parts of the castle.

The stone stairway on the side of the castle leads to the upper levels.

Plataforma de la Punta (morrillo, or bluff)

① The castle is reached by passing over a wooden bridge over a dry moat. The bridge used to be raised to protect Castillo del Morro from intruders.

② Central Square was the nerve centre of the castle, used as an area for organizing daily activities.

③ Baluarte de Santa Bárbara is the setting for the nightly firing of an 18th-century cannon.

Central square

Museo de la Piratéria

In the casemates a display of prints illustrates the history of Santiago's forts.

The Triangular Lunette was the main protection for the fortress gate.

This well-preserved bridge passes over a dry moat and has its original winch.

Dry moat

Baluarte de Santa Bárbara, site of the nightly cañonazo

↑ The fortified Castillo del Morro, with its well-preserved balustrades

THE BAY OF SANTIAGO

About 8 km (5 miles) southwest of the centre of Santiago de Cuba is the Marina Punta Gorda. From here ferries cross over to Cayo Granma, a small island in the middle of the bay, home to a picturesque fishing village made up of multicoloured huts and small houses. This island is a peaceful place with a few places to eat. You can see the Cayo Grande from the Castillo del Morro *(right)*.

4

PARQUE BACONAO

F7 ◻ Santiago de Cuba ◻ Cubatur, Ave de las Américas y Calle M; (22) 68 7040

The largest and most original park in Cuba (800 sq km/ 309 sq miles) has it all, from mountains and beaches to coffee plantations and a dinosaur museum.

Lying between the Caribbean Sea and the eastern fringes of the Sierra Maestra, and straddling the provinces of Santiago de Cuba and Guantánamo, Parque Baconao has been declared a biosphere reserve by UNESCO. The park was developed in the 1980s thanks to the voluntary work of students and labourers, and has been updated periodically. Unfortunately, the park received a severe battering from Hurricane Sandy in 2012 and has still not entirely recovered. It is possible to explore the area by car or taxi in a day, although accommodation is available. Most of the attractions are suitable for families and can be reached by car, but the peak of the Gran Piedra, which is surrounded by old coffee plantations, and the easternmost beaches are only accessible on foot.

THE ORIGINS OF COFFEE GROWING IN CUBA

Coffee was introduced to Cuba at the end of the 18th century, by which time it had been a fashionable drink among the European aristocracy and bourgeoisie for some time. With both water and shade, the Parque Baconoa boasts ideal coffee growing conditions, located as it is in the hills around Santiago de Cuba. Coffee from this area was an immediate success, and demand increased. The number of coffee trees planted on the island increased from 100,000 coffee trees in 1803 to four million in 1807.

↑ A boat anchored off the coast in Parque Baconao

Must See

STAY

Casa de Enrique y Rosa
Located in the Comunidad Artística Los Marmoncillas artists' community in the park, this one-bedroom *casa particular* is charming.

⌂ Carretera de Baconao Km 17.5 ☎ (22) 625 760

$ $ $

Villa Gran Piedra
High atop the mountain, this state-run hotel has modest cabins and a restaurant with stupendous views.

⌂ Carretera de Gran Piedra Km 14
☎ (22) 686 147

$ $ $

1 The Prado de las Esculturas sculpture garden, laid out in the 1980s, has 20 works by Cuban and foreign artists. Following the damage caused by Hurricane Sandy, the park was restored and reopened in 2015.

2 The Valle de la Prehistoria children's park features huge sculptures of dinosaurs and there is also a Natural History Museum.

3 Playa Siboney is a favourite with the citizens of Santiago. Only 19 km (12 miles) from town, it can be reached by regular bus service or taxi.

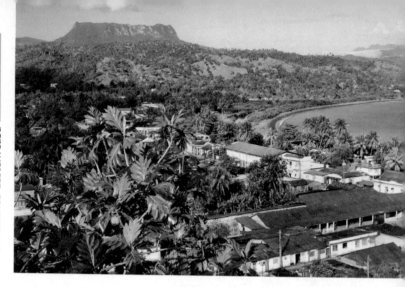

BARACOA

⊞ G6 ⊞ Guantánamo ⊞ 4 km (2 miles) W of town,
(21) 645 376 ⊞ Ave Los Mártires, esq Martí; (21) 643 880
⊞ Cubatur, Calle Maceo 149 esq Pelayo Cuervo, (21) 645
306; Ecotur, Hotel 1511, Calle Ciro Frías esq Rubert López,
(21) 642 478; Infotur, Calle Maceo 129-A, (21) 641 781

The oldest city in Cuba lies at the far eastern tip of
the island. Aptly, its name in the Arauaca language,
spoken by the former inhabitants of the area, means
"the presence of the sea". After a brief reign as the
political and ecclesiastical capital of Cuba, Baracoa
has long been the island's most isolated city.

Parque Independencia

In Baracoa's main square,
overlooked by the cathedral,
is a famous bust of the Indian
leader Hatuey (p254). Nearby
are both the Fondo de Bienes
Culturales, which exhibits
works by local painters, sculptors and craftsmen, and the
Casa de la Cultura, an eclectic
building with colonial elements
that hosts evening performances and events.

At No 123 Calle Maceo is
the Casa del Chocolate, which
serves excellent hot chocolate.
Baracoa cocoa is famous
throughout Cuba.

Catedral de Nuestra Señora de la Asunción

⊞ Calle Maceo 152 ⊞ (21)
643 352 ⊞ 8-11am & 4-7pm
Tue-Fri, 8-11am & 5-9pm
Sat, 8am-noon Sun

This modest cathedral, built in
1807, is most famous as the
home of the Cruz de la Parra,
a wooden cross that is said
to be the oldest symbol of
Christianity in the New World.
According to legend, the
cross was brought to Cuba
by Columbus, and in 1492 it
was placed here. It earned
its name because the cross
disappeared one day and was

then found under a climbing
vine (parra). The tips of the
cross are covered with metal
sheets, because worshippers
used to pull off splinters and
keep them as relics. Scientific
analysis proves the cross is
some 500 years old, but the
discovery that it is made from
indigenous Cuban wood
disproves the legendary
connection to Columbus.

Fuerte Matachín (Museo Municipal)

⊞ Calle Martí y Malecón
⊞ (21) 642 122 ⊞ 8am-
noon & 2-6pm Mon-Sat,
8am-noon Sun

This small museum, which
provides an interesting

GREAT VIEW
Va-Va-View

The best view of the
town is seen from the
terrace of the Hotel
el Castillo, which
occupies an 18th-
century fortress. From
here you can see all of
the bay of Baracoa,
dominated to the west
by El Yunque mountain.

↑ Baracoa Bay, overlooked by the distinctive El Yunque mountain

Did You Know?

Three hurricanes – Ike (2008), Sandy (2012), Mathew (2016) – have struck Baracoa in the past decade.

overview of local history, is housed in a military fortress built during the colonial period to defend the city from pirates in the 18th and 19th centuries.

The displays start with archaeological finds of the Pre-Columbian era, and are followed by documents, maps, paintings and prints related to Spanish domination, pirates, slaves and the plantations.

The museum is also a historical and geographical research centre and fosters initiatives to preserve and develop local culture; city tours are available from here.

④
Malecón

The ideal place for a gentle afternoon stroll, the Malecón is the seafront that connects the two 18th-century forts in

Baracoa: Fuerte Matachín to the east, and Fuerte de la Punta to the west.

On Saturdays a bustling food market takes over the Malecón in the morning, and in the evening the road is prepared for the lively *noche baracoesa* – "Baracoan night". During this lively folk festival, people gather here to eat, drink and dance along the seafront.

⑤
Museo Arqueológico de las Cuevas del Paraíso

📍 Loma Paraíso 🕐 8am–5pm daily

The Pre-Columbian history of Baracoa is best explored in this fascinating museum set in a series of caves. The Taíno Indians once used these caves for ceremonies and as funeral chambers. Some of the original archaeological finds are on display, including 3,000-year-old petroglyphs, skeletons and *esferolitas*. These burial rite stones, which are carved into spheres, were used to indicate a person's age and social standing. Replicas of relics and models complete the display. The caves are hidden in the lush vegetation of Loma Paraíso. This hill is also known for its views of the town and the bay.

DRINK

El Ranchón
This open-air hilltop disco-bar, reached via a long staircase, is a hotspot for salsa.

📍 Calle Coroneles Grajales 📞 (21) 642 364

Casa de la Trova
Come here for traditional music, such as *nengón* and *kiribá*.

📍 Calle Maceo 149A

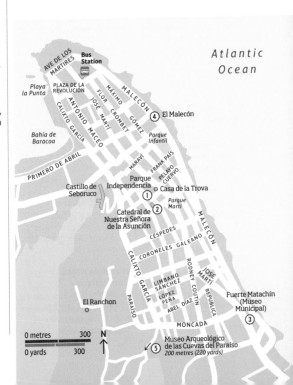

EXPERIENCE MORE

Gibara

◫E6 ♠Holguín

South of the bay that Columbus named Río de Mares (River of Seas) is the picturesque town of Gibara, famous for an extensive network of caves on the edge of town, perfect for exploring. In the 19th century, Gibara was the main port on the northern coast of the province of Oriente, and has the most important colonial architecture in the area.

COLUMBUS IN CUBA

On 28 October 1492, when he first set foot on Cuban land, Christopher Columbus wrote in his journal: "I have never seen a more beautiful place. Along the banks of the river were trees I have never seen at home, with flowers and fruit of the most diverse kinds, among the branches of which one heard the delightful chirping of birds. There were a great number of palms."

The shady Malecón (seafront) has a statue of Columbus shown gazing at the horizon, a restored garrison and views of the small fishing harbour. From here, narrow streets lead to the main square, which is overlooked by the Iglesia de San Fulgencio (1854), and an old theatre.

The **Museo de Artes Decorativas** (Decorative Arts Museum) is housed in a 19th-century manor. A staircase bordered by marble columns and fine stained-glass windows represents the region's best ensemble of 19th- and 20th-century furniture and objects.

About 2 km (1 mile) from the centre of Gibara are the **Cavernas de Panaderos**, a complex cave system etched with fascinatinh ancient pictographs and home to a huge population of bats. Be sure to explore the caves with a guide as there are no signs in the dark depths. Adventurous visitors can also go cave diving in the Cavernas de Panaderos' underground lake with an instructor.

Museo de Artes Decorativas

⊛⊛ ♠Calle Independencia 19 ☎(24) 844 687 ◷8:30am–noon & 1–4pm Mon–Fri, 8:30am–noon Sat

Cavernas de Panaderos

♠Oficina de Monumentos Technicos, Calle Sartorio 7 ☎(24) 845 107

Guardalavaca

◫E6 ♠Holguín

Converted in the mid-1980s into a holiday resort, the beaches of Guardalavaca are among Cuba's most popular holiday destinations. Although the resort is within easy reach of Holguín, which lies 58 km (35 miles) to the southwest along a road through curious conical hills, the location still feels remote.

The 4-km (2-mile) crescent-shaped main beach, enclosed at either end by rocks, is backed by abundant vegetation. The sea is crystal-clear, the sand is fine and there is a coral reef quite close to the shore. To the west are several developed beaches.

The name "Guardalavaca" (watch the cow) derives from the Spanish word for the cattle egret, a bird which is common throughout Cuba, and especially in this area.

West of the beach is Bahía de Naranjo, a natural park that comprises 32 km (20 miles)

Customers waiting outside a colourful bakery in Gibara

of coastline and 10 sq km (3.9 sq miles) of woods, with karst hills covered with thick vegetation. There are three small islands out in the bay; on one, Cayo Naranjo, there is an aquarium. Boat tours, diving and fishing trips are also organized from this well-equipped island.

Parque Monumento Nacional Bariay

E6 **Holguín**

East of Gibara is a bay with a spit of land in the middle called Cayo de Bariay. Most historians agree that Columbus first landed here in 1492. With its abundance of flowers and trees heavily laden with fruit, it looked like a paradise to the famous explorer.

In 1992, on the 500th anniversary of Columbus's landing in Cuba, a monument was erected here. It was called Encuentro (Encounter), and was dedicated to the indigenous Taíno people Columbus met when he landed, but "took fright and fled" at the sight of him. The site is relatively remote if travelling by car, but boat trips can be arranged from Guardalavaca. To the east of Cayo de Bariay is the beautiful Playa Don Lino, a long white-sand beach.

El Chorro de Maíta

E6 **Cerro de Yaguajay, Banes (Holguín)** **(24) 430 201** **9am-5pm Tue-Sat, 9am-1pm Sun**

Near the coast, just 5 km (3 miles) to the south of Guardalavaca, El Chorro de Maíta is the largest aboriginal necropolis in Cuba and the Antilles, a highly important discovery, and now a national monument. El Chorro de Maíta is an unmissable site, where archaeologists have found 108 skeletons and a number of clay objects, bone amulets, funerary offerings and decorated shells, offering insights into the lives of some of Cuba's earliest inhabitants.

All this material can be seen from a boardwalk inside the museum. Across the road is an *aldea taína*, a reconstruction of a Pre-Columbian rural village. It was built primarily to entertain, but it is nevertheless historically accurate. Visitors can view the huts, buy souvenirs and sample the kind of food that the Amerindians used to eat. In front of the huts are life-size statues of the villagers.

↑ Models of indigenous people at El Chorro de Maíta

EAT

Restaurante La Cueva
Order delicious lobster, shrimp or other seafood dishes at this *paladar*.

E6 **Calle 2da 131, Gibara** **(24) 845 333**

$ $ $

Restaurant La Maison
In a superb hilltop site with ocean views, this *paladar* serves seafood.

E6 **200 m (210 yd) W of Playa Mayor, Guardalavaca** **(24) 480 839**

$ $ $

Restaurante Calalú
Filling *criolla* meals and dishes unique to Baracoa, such as tiny *tetí* fish, are served here.

G6 **Calle Calixto García 151, Baracoa** **(53) 104 810**

$ $ $

Encuentro monument in the Parque Monumento Nacional Bariay

10
Banes

 E6 ⬧ 32 km (20 miles) SW of Holguín, Holguín

This country town is in a vast and rich excavation zone – Holguín province has yielded a third of Cuba's archaeological finds. The **Museo Indocubano Bani**, Cuba's most important archaeological museum outside Havana, displays over 1,000 objects, including axes, terracotta vases, flint knives and, most notably, a gold 4-cm- (2-in-) high figure, Ídolo de Oro. Found near Banes, it dates from the 13th century.

Museo Indocubano Bani
Calle General Barrero 305, e/ Martí y Céspedes (24) 802 487 9am-5pm Tue-Sat, 8am-noon Sun

11
Museo Conjunto Histórico Birán

E6 ⬧ Birán, 60 km (37 miles) SE of Holguín, Holguín (24) 286 114

Many visitors are surprised to discover that the birthplace of

Did You Know?

Raúl Castro and Vilma Espín fell in love when they were both guerrilla fighters in the Sierra Cristal.

Fidel and Raúl Castro was a rural hamlet surrounded by sugar cane fields at the base of the Altiplanicie de Nipe Mountains. Their father, Ángel Castro y Argiz, was a wealthy landowner and the patriarch of the region.

Today, the family estate is a museum run by the Ministry of Interior. Guided tours of the site include their parents' grave, the schoolroom (with Fidel's desk at the front) and the two-storey home, where displays include Fidel's hunting rifle and childhood baseball paraphernalia.

It was in this hamlet that the Castro brothers witnessed, and became radicalized by, their neighbours' destitution at the hands of the United Fruit Company, which owned most of the surrounding land for miles around.

12
Pinares de Mayarí

 E6 ⬧ Holguín

A perfect alpine escape from the heat of the lowlands, this cool upland region of mist-shrouded pine forest is reached via a deteriorated road from the town of Mayarí. The road ends up at Loma de Mensura, at a height of 995 m (3,264 ft). Visitors can stay at **Villa Pinares de Mayarí**, a rustic lodge that's a good base for bird-watching and hiking. The region is within the Parque Nacional La Mensura, although the eastern slopes have been mined. There's plenty to see, including **Orquideario La Mensura** – an orchid farm with trails – and Salto El Guayabo, Cuba's highest waterfall which tumbles 260 m (853 ft). A *mirador* offers splendid views over the falls and trails lead to its base.

Villa Pinares de Mayarí
Loma de Mensura gaviotahotels.com

Orquideario La Mensura
Loma de Mensura 8am-5pm daily

← Portraits of Fidel and Raúl Castro in the Museo Conjunto Histórico Birán

STAY

Hotel E La Caballeriza
This charming boutique hotel is set in a restored 19th-century mansion.

E6 Calle Miró 203, Holguín
cubanacan.cu/en

$$$

Hotel E Ordoño
Don't miss the rooftop bar at this elegant hotel.

E6 Calle Peralta e/ Mármol y Independencia, Gibara
cubanaca.cu/en

$$$

Villa Paradiso
A superb hillside B&B close to downtown.

G6 Calle Moncada 92B, Baracoa
villaparadiso baracoa.com

$$$

Hotel El Castillo
Enjoy the views from this hotel's pool.

G6 Loma del Paraíso, Baracoa
gaviotahotels.com/en

$$$

 Dos Ríos

E6 Jiguaní, 26 km (16 miles) E of Bayamo, Granma

Punctuating the semi-arid plains of eastern Granma is the Monumento Martí, marking the place where José Martí (p101) was killed during the War of Independence. Despite being ordered by General Máximo Gómez, the leader of the independence army, to stay at the rear, Martí charged forward on his white horse and was shot. A bas-relief at the entrance to the monument reads "When my fall comes, all the sorrow of life will seem like sun and honey."

The simple 10-m- (33-ft-) tall obelisk of whitewashed concrete bears the words "He died in this place on 19 May, 1895" and is surrounded by white roses – an allusion to his poem *Cultivo Una Rosa Blanca* – and royal palms. On 19 May, a tribute to the national hero is held here.

 Cayo Saetía

F6 Holguín

Lying at the mouth of the Bay of Nipe, this small island covering 42 sq km (16 sq miles), with stunning coves, is connected to the mainland by a drawbridge. Cayo Saetía was formerly a private hunting reserve, and in the woods and meadows, antelopes and zebra still live side by side with species native to Cuba. On safaris, led by expert guides, visitors travelling on horseback or in jeeps can observe and photograph the animals. The few tourist facilities here are for paying

↑ One of the lovely coves on Cayo Saetía, an ecological treasure

guests only and were designed with every care for the natural environment. A boat trip to Cayo Saetía from Guardalavaca is a highlight.

 Mayarí Arriba

F6 Santiago de Cuba

During the "Armed Struggle" to overthrow Fulgencio Batista, Raúl Castro set up his headquarters in this small town at the base of the Sierra Cristal when he opened the second guerrilla front in 1958. The **Complejo Histórico de Museos del Segundo Frente** (Second Front Museums Historic Complex) details the socialist administration he set up. A palm-lined boulevard leads to the Mausoleo del Segundo Frente, a monument to fallen revolutionaries and the grave of Vilma Espín, on which Raúl's name is already engraved.

Complejo Histórico de Museos del Segundo Frente
Ave de los Mártires
9am-5pm Mon-Sat
(22) 425749

16

Bayamo

🅐D7 🚉Granma ✈Carlos Manuel de Céspedes 🚌Saco y Línea; (23) 423 034 🚍Carretera Central y Jesús Rabí; (23) 424 036 🛈Infotur, Plaza del Himno; (23) 423 468

The second oldest town in Cuba after Baracoa, Bayamo was founded in 1513 by Diego Velázquez and in 1975 it became the capital of Granma province. It has been home to nationalists and the cradle of political revolts and struggles.

In 1869, rather than surrender their town to Spain, the citizens burned it down, hence Bayamo's relatively modern centre. Parque Céspedes is the main square, dominated by a statue of local plantation owner and war of independence hero Carlos Manuel de Céspedes (1955). The square contains almost all the important buildings.

Adjacent to the main square is Plaza del Himno (Square of the Hymn), named after *La Bayamesa* (the Cuban national anthem) which was first played in the church here on 20 October 1868. A sculpture that includes a bronze plaque engraved with the words and music by Perucho Figueredo

marks the event. A bust of the composer stands by the nationalists' flag. In the smaller Parque Maceo Osorio, north of Parque Céspedes is the Casa de la Trova Olimpio La O, one of the town's few 18th-century buildings. Local groups give concerts in the courtyard.

Facing Parque Céspedes is the birthplace, on 18 April 1819, of the leading figure in the first war against Spain in the 19th century. **Casa Natal de Carlos Manuel de Céspedes** is a handsome, two-storey colonial building, architecturally the most important in the city. The ground floor contains the main collection: Céspedes's documents and personal items, including his sword. Upstairs are several rooms with colonial furniture, and a gallery leads to the old kitchen, which still has its original ceramic oven.

Next door, the Museo Provincial portrays the

city's history and occupies the birthplace of Manuel Muñoz Cedeño, composer of the national anthem.

When the nationalists of Bayamo chose to burn down their town, they put the holy images kept in the **Parroquial Mayor de San Salvador** (the Cathedral) into safekeeping. Unfortunately, the only things from the early-17th building to be spared by the fire were the font and the Capilla de los Dolores, a chapel built in 1740, which contained an image of the Virgin Mary and a Baroque altarpiece of gilded wood. The altarpiece has a particularly fine frame decorated with tropical motifs and representations of local fruit and animals, an unusual and very Cuban element in the art of the 18th century.

In 1916, Bishop Guerra commissioned the reconstruction of the church and the large three-aisle church opened on 9 October 1919. Above the marble altar, you'll see a mural by the Dominican artist

---

BAYAMO "THE REBELLIOUS"

Bayamo has a long tradition of rebellion. In the early 1500s, the native people fiercely resisted the Spanish here, for which their leader, Hatuey, was burned at the stake. A few years later an African slave killed the pirate Gilberto Girón, displaying his head in the central plaza. But the most dramatic episode in its history concerns the struggles for independence, during which, on 10 October 1868, a group of local nationalists, including Carlos Manuel de Céspedes *(right)*, organized an anti-Spanish revolt. They entered the town on 20 October, and declared it the capital of the Republic in Arms.

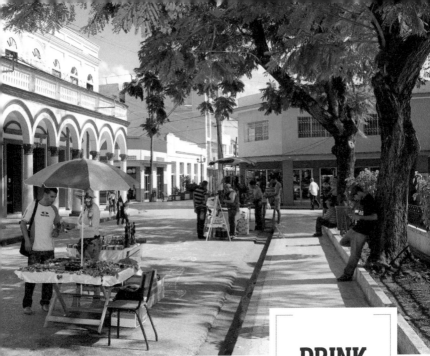

Street vendors in Bayamo's colourful Plaza de la Revolución ↑

Luis Desangles showing the blessing of the flag in 1896. The church was elevated to the status of cathedral by Pope John Paul II in 1995.

The five traffic-free blocks to the south of the Parque Céspedes, El Bulevár, are a delight to stroll, with their funky art installations. Stop at the Museo de Cera (No 253), a wax museum, and La Maqueta (No 254), which displays a scale model of the city.

The **Parque Museo Ñico López**, in the town's former medieval style army barracks, is named for the revolutionary

> In 1869, rather than surrender their town to Spain, the citizens burned it down, hence Bayamo's relatively modern centre.

leader who led an assault on 26 July 1953, to coincide with the attack on Moncada (p238).

The vast concrete Plaza de la Patria (Fatherland) was laid out after the revolution for political rallies. A huge bas-relief marble tableau depicts the city's history here.

Bayamo is known as the "City of Carriages" and many one-horse carriages, made locally, ply the streets.

Casa Natal de Carlos Manuel de Céspedes
♨♨ ♿ 🏠 Calle Maceo 57, e/ Marmol y Palma 📞 (23) 423 864 🕐 9am–5pm Tue–Fri, 9am–2pm & 8–10pm Sat, 10am–1:30pm Sun

Parroquial Mayor de San Salvador
🏠 Plaza del Himno, esq José Joaquín Palma 📞 (23) 422 514 🕐 9am–noon & 2:30–5pm Mon–Fri, 9–10:30am Sun

Parque Museo Ñico López
🏠 General García y Amado Estévez 📞 (23) 42 3742 🚫 Mon

DRINK

Casa de la Trova
This traditional *trova* pays tribute to Bayamo's local singer and composer Pablo Milanes.

🅰 D7 🏠 Calle Martí y Maceo, Bayamo 📞 (23) 425 673 🚫 Mon

La Ruina
It's not hard to see why this *bodega*-style beer hall, housed in the shell of a colonial building, is so popular.

🅰 F7 🏠 Calle Galixto García y Gulo, Guantánamo 📞 (21) 929 565

Casa de Changüí
Casa de Changüí is the place to hear *changüí-son* – Guantánamo's native sound.

🅰 F7 🏠 Calle Serafín Sánchez 710, Guantánamo 📞 (21) 324 178 🚫 Mon

↑ Manzanillo's intricately decorated Glorieta Morisca, where local bands play

17

Manzanillo

 D7 🏛 Granma ✈ "Sierra Maestra", 8 km (5 miles) S 🚌 🚐 From Bayamo, Yara, Camagüey, Havana, Pilón

Built along the Caribbean Bay of Guacanayabo, Manzanillo is a charming seaside town. It was founded as Puerto Real in 1784, and reached its apogee in the second half of the 19th century, thanks to sugar and the slave trade.

The town is closely associated with the local heroine Celía Sánchez, who ran the secret supply network to Fidel's Rebel Army in the Sierra Maestra. She later

---

GREAT VIEW
Skip the Hike

Only a few hardy souls make the arduous trek to Pico Turquino - Cuba's highest summit. Instead, take the road into the Sierra Maestra from Bartolomé Masó for jaw-dropping panoramas without the hike.

---

became a guerrilla fighter and, after the revolution, was Castro's secretary. Sánchez is honoured by the striking Monumento Celía Sánchez, a pedestrian staircase adorned on each side by bas-relief ceramics of white doves and sunflowers – symbols of the woman called "the most beautiful flower of the revolution".

In Parque Céspedes, the central square, a brickwork bandstand for concerts by local bands dates from 1924. The so-called Glorieta Morisca gained its name for its Arab-influenced decoration, designed by José Martín del Castillo, from Granada. Other notable buildings, all near the Parque Céspedes, include the Neo-Classical Iglesia de la Purísima Concepción, built in the 1920s; the atmospheric Café 1906; the 19th-century Asamblea Municipal del Poder Popular; and the 1935 Colonia Española, a social club for

Spanish immigrants, which has an Andalusian courtyard and a panel of painted tiles representing Columbus's landing in Cuba.

Located just 10 km (6 miles) south of Manzanillo town are the remains of La Demajagua, the estate belonging to Carlos Manuel de Céspedes. On 10 October 1868, he freed

→ Baracoa Bay, overlooked by the distinctive El Yunque

all his slaves and urged them to join him in fighting the Spanish settlers.

Yara, 24 km (15 miles) east of Manzanillo, is where Céspedes proclaimed Cuban independence, and where the Taíno hero Hatuey was burned at the stake. There is a small museum in the central square, Plaza Grito de Yara.

La Farola

G7 **Guantánamo**

Cajobabo marks the start of La Farola, a spectacular 49-km (30-mile) road that wends its way from the coast over the mountains to Baracoa.

In 1947 engineers initiated the Vía Mulata to link Baracoa, then accessible only by sea, to Guantánamo, excavating sections of mountainside in the Sierra del Purial to create a kind of "flying highway". The road, which was completed in 1964, acquired its name (meaning beacon) because in some stretches it looks like a beam, suspended in air. It is regarded as one of the great engineering feats of recent Cuban history.

This road and the periodic viewpoints offer incredible views of the peaks of the Sierra Maestra, lush valleys, tropical forests, pine groves, banana plantations, rivers, waterfalls and royal palm trees. The vegetation seems to swallow up the road in places. Along the way, people sell local produce such as coffee, red bananas, chocolate and *cucurucho* – coconut and sugar, wrapped in a cone shaped palm leaf.

Parque Natural Duaba y El Yunque

G6 **Guantánamo**
Ecotur, Calle Ciro Frías, Baracoa, (21) 642 478

A limestone formation 575 m (1,885 ft) high and covered with thick vegetation, El Yunque was a sacred site for the Taíno for many centuries. Later it became a natural landmark for navigators aiming for the port of Baracoa. Its shape has led to local misapprehension that this was the rock that Columbus described as "a square mountain that looks like an island" in 1492. He was referring to a similar rock at Bariay near Gibara (*p250*).

The mountain has been declared a biosphere reserve by UNESCO for its botanical rarities, including carnivorous plants and *Podocarpus*, one of the world's oldest species.

El Yunque is also home to endangered species of bird, the smallest amphibian in the world, the *Sminthillus limbatus*, less than 1 cm (0.4 inch) long, and the Cuban solenodon, a rare mammal similar to a rat.

The Duaba river flows into the Playa Duaba, where, on 1 April 1895, General Antonio Maceo landed to renew the independence struggle. A roadside bust and cannon commemorate his cause, while a more substantial grey marble monument stands on the eastern headland of Playa Duaba. Upriver, Finca Duaba is a fruit farm and cacao plantation, where guided tours provide an insight into chocolate production.

Did You Know?

The Spanish called it "El Yunque" (the anvil) because of its unmistakeable outline.

A hiker surveys the mist-shrouded Gran Parque Nacional Sierra Maestra ↑

Gran Parque Nacional Sierra Maestra

🅐D7 🄰Granma, Santiago de Cuba 🄸Ecotur, Hotel Sierra Maestra, Bayamo, (23) 487 006 ext 639; Flora y Fauna, Santo Domingo, 5356 5349; Villa Santo Domingo, (23) 565 568

This national park, which covers an area of 380 sq km (147 sq miles), spans the provinces of Granma and Santiago de Cuba. This is where the major peaks of the island are found, including Pico Turquino (at 1,974 m/ 6,390 ft, the highest in Cuba), as well as sites made famous by the guerrilla war waged by Fidel Castro and the *barbudos*.

The main starting point for exploring the Sierra Maestra mountain range is Villa Santo Domingo, located about 35 km (22 miles) south of the Bayamo–Manzanillo road (there is comfortable accommodation in Santo Domingo).

From Santo Domingo, you can make the challenging 5-km (3-mile) journey – on foot or in a good off-road vehicle – to the Alto del Naranjo viewpoint (950 m/ 3,120 ft). With a permit (obtainable from the visitors' office north of Villa Santo Domingo), you can go on to Comandancia de la Plata, Castro's headquarters in the 1950s. Here there is a museum, a small camp hospital and the site from which Che Guevara made his radio broadcasts. Comandancia de la Plata is accessible only on foot – a 90-minute walk through lovely, though often foggy, forest. The area was made into a national park in 1980 and the dense, humid forest conceals many species of orchid and various kinds of local fauna. The Sierra Maestra mountains are excellent hiking territory, and also attract mountain climbers. The scenery is spectacular but be prepared for spartan

facilities. A limited number of treks can be organized from the visitors' office, where guides must be hired and overnight accommodation in the mountains is available either at campsites or in simple refuges. Note, however, that since much of this area is a military zone, lone trekking is not permitted.

At present, it is possible to do a three-day guided trek across the park, beginning at Alto del Naranjo and ending at Las Cuevas, a small town on the Caribbean Sea. Hikers do not need to be expert mountaineers in order to take part in this walking tour, because the path is equipped with ladders, handrails and rock-cut steps. However, it is still advisable to do a certain amount of training beforehand. The final descent from Pico Turquino onwards is fairly strenuous and walkers need to be reasonably fit.

It is important to take proper mountain gear with you: walking boots, thick socks, a sun hat, a sweater, a windproof jacket, and perhaps even a waterproof groundsheet and a good tent. Humidity in the often misty Sierra is very high, and showers are common.

> The dense, humid forest conceals many species of orchid and various kinds of local fauna. The Sierra Maestra mountains are excellent hiking territory.

The coast at the southern edge of the Sierra Maestra is spectacular. The coastal road runs close above the waters of the Caribbean Sea and offers excellent views. However, great care should be taken if driving after dark as the road is in need of repair in some places.

㉑

Basílica del Cobre

🅰 E7 **📍 Santiago de Cuba** **🚍 Carretera Central 21; (22) 346 118** **🕐 6:30am–6pm daily**

The village of El Cobre, set about 20 km (12 miles) west of Santiago de Cuba, was once famous for its copper (cobre) mines. A great number of slaves worked here up until 1807. Nowadays the village is best known for Cuba's most famous church, the Basílica de Nuestra Señora de la Caridad del Cobre. This fine three-aisled church, built in 1926, stands on a hill, the

→

A car passing the striking Basílica del Cobre, home to the Virgen del Cobre statue

Cerro de la Cantera, which is linked to the village by a flight of 254 steps. The structure's elegant central bell tower and two side towers crowned by brick-red domes are a striking sight above the cream-coloured façade.

Here the main attraction is a statue of the Virgen del Cobre. This black Madonna is richly dressed in yellow, and wears a crown encrusted with diamonds, emeralds and rubies, with a golden halo above. She carries a cross of diamonds and amethysts. The statue is kept in an air-conditioned glass case behind the high altar, but it is taken out on 8 September every year when a procession takes place to commemorate the Virgin's saint's day. The Virgen del Cobre was proclaimed the protectress of Cuba in 1916 and was blessed and crowned by Pope John Paul II in 1998. Pope Francis laid a silver vase with his coat of arms during a subsequent papal visit in 2015.

The basilica is the object of pilgrimages from all over the

island. In the Los Milagros chapel, thousands of curious ex votos left by pilgrims are on display, including a TV, crutches and stethoscopes. There's also an object that once belonged to Castro's mother and earth collected by Cuban soldiers who fought in Angola. A guestbook is there for visitors to peruse and sign. Ernest Hemingway donated his 1954 Nobel Prize medal to the basilica.

Did You Know?

Offerings in the Basílica del Cobre include clumps of hair from the beards of revolutionaries.

22
Guantánamo

F7 Guantánamo
Infotur, Calle
Galixto García el Crombet
y Emilio Giró; (21) 351 993

If it were not for the US naval base and the famous song *Guantanamera*, this town would probably only be known to Cubans and music experts. Its name, in fact, is linked with the *changuí*, a variation of *son* music that developed in the coffee plantations in the mountains and was made famous by the musician Elio Revé.

Guantanamera (the girl from Guantánamo) was composed by Joseíto Fernández in the 1940s almost for fun, inspired by a proud local girl who is said to have not reacted to a compliment he paid her. Later, some "literary" verses from the *Versos Sencillos* by José Martí were adapted to the music.

The town of Guantánamo was founded in 1796 to take in the French fleeing from Haiti and developed during the 19th century. The capital of a varied province, where desert areas studded with cactus alternate with green mountains, the town has few sights of note. Principal Parque Martí is dominated by the Parroquial de Santa Catalina de Riccis, dating from 1863.

Opposite the church stands a statue of General Pedro A Pérez, sculpted in 1928. On Calle Pedro A Pérez nearby is one of the town's most impressive buildings, the Palacio de Salcines. Designed by José Leticio Salcines in 1919, this building's eclectic style features a decorative façade of cornices and columns. A Neo-Classical cupola crowns the building, topped by a statue of La Fama – the messenger of Zeus in Greek mythology – designed by Italian architect Américo J Chini. The Palacio contains the **Museo de Artes Decorativas**, with antique furniture and decorative objects.

> **If it were not for the US naval base and the famous song *Guantanamera*, this town would probably only be known to Cubans.**

Facing Principal Parque Martí stands an interesting colonial building, which once served as the old Spanish prison. The structure is now home to the town's modest **Museo Provincial de Guantánamo**, which has a fascinating room dedicated to Cuba's first space flight in 1980, a joint mission with the USSR.

The kitsch 1960s Hotel Guantánamo dominates the vast, concrete Plaza Mariana Garajales, which itself is

---

🔺 GREAT VIEW
Mirador La Gobernadora

The US Naval Base, in a Cuban defence zone, is virtually impossible to see, but atop a hill 25 km (16 miles) to the east, the Mirador La Gobernadora restaurant has a viewing tower and provides binoculars for patrons.

Cacti *(inset)* growing above the pebbled Cajobabo beach in the Costa Sur, near Guantánamo

dominated by a towering Brutalist sculpture, *Monument to the Heroes*, which honours Cuba's independence fighters, including Frank País.

Around 20 km (12 miles) east of Guantánamo, on the road to the coffee-growing area of Lomas de Yateras, is an unusual open-air museum, the **Museo Zoológico de Piedra**. It was founded by Angel Iñigo (1935–2014), a farmer and self-taught sculptor. Beginning in 1978 he produced sculptures of about 40 animals in stone, all of which are on display.

Some 23 km (14 miles) south of Guantánamo city is the small port of Caimanera. North of the US naval base, it lies within a Cuban military zone and is currently off-limits to everyone except residents and those with a special pass. It is relatively straightforward to get hold of a pass, which permits a day visit or an overnight stay at Hotel Caimanera (*Loma Norte; (21) 516 900*), where there are views of the base through the hotel telescope and a small, interesting museum. You will need to get permission from the Ministry of the Interior to be granted a pass and this can be arranged, with at least 72 hours' notice, through Izlazul at Hotel Guantánamo ((*21) 381 015*).

THE AMERICAN NAVAL BASE

In 1901, the United States - the victors in the war against Spain - obliged the Cuban Republic to accept the Platt Amendment, granting the US Navy the right to a naval base in the bay of Guantánamo. For this, the American government pays $2,000 per year, increasing to $4,085 in 1934 by a treaty extending the lease indefinitely. Since 1959, the Cuban government has refused to cash the money, demanding the US to vacate the territory.

Museo de Artes Decorativas

🏛 Calle Pedro A Pérez 804
📞 (21) 324 704 🕐 8am-noon & 2-5pm Mon-Thu, 8am-noon & 5-9pm Fri, 5-9pm Sat

Museo Provincial de Guantánamo

🎫🚫 🏛 Plaza Martí, esq Prado
📞 (21) 325 872 🕐 8am-noon & 2:30-4:30pm Mon-Fri, 8am-noon Sat 🚫 1 Jan, 1 May, 26 Jul, 10 Oct, 25 Dec

Museo Zoológico de Piedra

🚫 🏛 Boquerón de Yateras
🕐 9am-6pm daily 🚫 1 Jan, 1 May, 26 Jul, 10 Oct, 25 Dec

㉓

Costa Sur

🗺 G7 🏛 Guantánamo

East of Guantánamo, the land lies within the rain shadow of the towering Sierra Maestra. Its desert-like climate, with cacti and succulents the main vegetation, makes this a unique area on the island.

Cajobabo, 45 km (28 miles) east of Guantánamo, is a coastal hamlet at the base of the mountains. It was here, on 11 April 1895, that José Martí returned from exile to launch the War of Independence.

EXPERIENCE Eastern Cuba

24

Parque Nacional Río Toa

🅰 G6 🏛 Guantánamo

The valley fed by the Río Toa, Cuba's biggest river, has been made into this nature reserve. Still lacking in roads and facilities, it is part of a wide-ranging project to create refuges and camping sites that will not interfere with the local ecosystems.

Farmers here still use an old-fashioned type of craft to travel upstream – the *cayuca*, a flat canoe of Taíno origin. Those who travel on the river can admire the majestic Pico Galán, at 974 m (3,200 ft) high, and the great waterfalls that cascade into the river from steep cliffs above. Make enquiries at the Ecotur

office in Baracoa *(p248)* if you are interested in exploring the national park area.

Northwest of Baracoa, 21 km (12 miles) past the mouth of the Río Toa, is Playa Maguana, undoubtedly the most beautiful beach in the province, with dazzling white sand. The Taíno name for the beach refers to the presence of a nearby archaeological site. A 2-km- (1-mile-) long coral reef, populated by a colourful cast of fish, lies only 500 m (1,640 ft) from the shore. Be warned, though, if you are planning to take a dip or do some snorkelling, that the sea can often be rather choppy in this area.

There is a smart, rustic hotel hidden away among the coconut palms here, where villas are available to be rented, but this lovely place still remains unspoiled.

> Farmers here still use an old-fashioned type of craft to travel upstream – the *cayuca*, a flat canoe of Taíno origin.

PICTURE PERFECT
Song and Dance

Dressed in straw hats and colourful costumes, the El Güirito Nengón y Kiribá ensemble is a delight to behold as they dance and play traditional instruments, such as the tres and gourds. Have your camera at the ready.

25

Parque Nacional Alejandro de Humboldt

🅰 G6 🏛 Holguín; Guantánamo

This mountainous rainforest 56 km (35 miles) north of Baracoa is Cuba's most richly biodiverse park and a UNESCO World Heritage Site, named after the 19th-century German naturalist and explorer Alexander von Humboldt. Here you'll find a

variety of birds, scorpions, snails, frogs and the rare Cuban solenodon (also known as the almiquí), which looks like a giant shrew with an extraordinarily long snout. At the edge of the park is the stunning Bahía Taco bay, home to a small group of manatees. Ecotur can help with arranging walks and boat trips.

26
Boca de Yumurí

G7 Guantánamo

Around 30 km (18 miles) east of Baracoa, this village of *bohíos* (traditional dwellings with palm-leaf roofs) takes its name from the Yumurí river, which flows into the sea here. Its inhabitants live by fishing, but earn a little extra by taking tourists out on river boat rides.

The Río Yumurí is home to amazing wildlife. Colourful tropical birdlife abounds, including the *zunzún*, the

A wide bridge crossing the estuary of the Boca de Yumurí river

tocororo and the *cartacuba*. Don't miss El Güirito, a hamlet where the community, who have a distinct Taíno bloodline, keep alive traditional *kiribá* and *nengón* music and dance. Catch a performance, or have lunch with the villagers, by arrangement with tour agencies in Baracoa.

27
Punta Maisí

G7 Guantánamo

In 2017, a coastal highway was completed linking Boca de Yumurí to Punta Maisí, the easternmost point of Cuba, pinned by a *faro* (lighthouse) built in 1862. This road offers dramatic scenery, with the land rising immediately inland in a series of stepped limestone platforms that emerged from the sea over the centuries. Beyond Maisí, the road continues to Cojababo via coffee-growing country and the Reserva Ecológico Maisí-Caleta, which protects this delicate desert ecosystem.

One of the idyllic beaches in Parque Nacional Alejandro de Humboldt

EAT

San Salvador de Bayamo
The best *paladar* in town serves typical *criolla* fare.

D7 Calle Maceo 107, Bayamo (23) 426 942

$⑤⑤

Restaurante Los Girasoles
Order the shrimp enchilada here.

F7 Calle Ahogados 6501, Guantánamo (21) 384 178

$⑤⑤

Sabor Melián
Remember to bring *moneda nacional* to this *paladar* specializing in seafood.

F7 Avenida Camilo Cienfuegos 407, Guantánamo (21) 324 422

$⑤⑤

A DRIVING TOUR
SIERRA MAESTRA

Length 350 km (220 miles) **Stopping-off points** Niquero Town **Difficulty** Mountainous and steep in places; sometimes roads are extremely narrow

This fascinating route by road to Santiago skirts the high slopes of the Sierra Maestra which, along the south coast, forces the road into the sea in places, especially after hurricanes. The scenery is unspoiled and at times wild, and conceals several places of historical significance. The route can be covered in a long day, but for a more relaxing drive visitors could consider staying in Marea del Portillo or Chivirico.

Locator Map
For more detail see p228

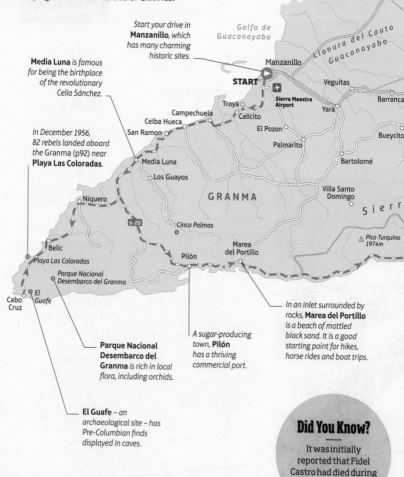

Start your drive in **Manzanillo,** *which has many charming historic sites.*

Media Luna *is famous for being the birthplace of the revolutionary Celia Sánchez.*

In December 1956, 82 rebels landed aboard the Granma (p92) *near* **Playa Las Coloradas**.

Parque Nacional Desembarco del Granma *is rich in local flora, including orchids.*

El Guafe – *an archaeological site – has Pre-Columbian finds displayed in caves.*

A sugar-producing town, **Pilón** *has a thriving commercial port.*

In an inlet surrounded by rocks, **Marea del Portillo** *is a beach of mottled black sand. It is a good starting point for hikes, horse rides and boat trips.*

Did You Know?

It was initially reported that Fidel Castro had died during the *Granma* landing.

→ Strolling through a colourful street in Santiago de Cuba

Finish your drive in Cuba's second largest city – **Santiago de Cuba** *(p232). This city is ebullient with Afro-Cuban traditions and revolutionary history.*

Bayamo

Jiguaní

Contramaestre

Guisa

Buey Arriba

Los Horneros

Cobero

SANTIAGO DE CUBA

Palma Soriano

M a e s t r a

Santiago de Cuba

FINISH

Antonio Maceo International Airport

Playa Aserradero

Uvero

Chivirico

Playa El Frances

Playa Bueycabón

Caribbean Sea

| 0 kilometres | 15 |
| 0 miles | 15 |

N ↑

The **southern coastline** *of the province of Granma is outstanding, with scenic cliffs and bays. The coastal road connecting Marea del Portillo and Santiago de Cuba is flanked by mountains covered with vegetation on one side and sparkling sea on the other.*

→ A large sweeping beach on Cuba's verdant southern coastline

NEED TO KNOW

Classic cars on Havana's Malécon

Before You Go 268

Getting Around 270

Practical Information 274

BEFORE YOU GO

Forward planning is essential for any successful trip. Be prepared for all eventualities by considering the following points before you travel.

Passports and Visas

EU nationals and citizens of the US, Canada, Australia and New Zealand need a Tourist Card for stays of up to 30 days. These are issued by airlines, travel agencies and Cuban consulates, and are extendable for an additional 30 days when you are on the island.

In addition to a Tourist Card, US citizens need a "general licence" to visit Cuba. To be eligible for one of these, your travel purpose must fall into one of 12 categories. All US citizens, however, can travel with a group tour or cruise, under the "people to people" educational category, and individually under the "Support for the Cuban people" category, as long as they adhere to specific regulations, including refraining from using any entities owned by Cuba's military. These restrictions are administered by the **Office of Foreign Assets Control** (OFAC).
Office of Foreign Assets Control
W treasury.gov/resource-center/sanctions/Programs/pages/cuba.aspxe

Travel Safety Advice

Visitors can get up-to-date travel safety information from the **UK Foreign and Commonwealth Office**, the **US State Department** and the **Australian Department of Foreign Affairs and Trade**.
AUS
W smarttraveller.gov.au
UK
W gov.uk/foreign-travel-advice
US
W travel.state.gov

Customs Information

An individual is permitted to carry the following within the EU for personal use:
Tobacco products 400 cigarettes, 50 cigars or 500 grams of smoking tobacco.
Alcohol 3 litres of alcoholic beverages.
Cash If you plan to enter Cuba with US$5,000 or more in cash, you must declare it to the customs authorities upon arrival.

Insurance

It is wise to take out an insurance policy covering theft, loss of belongings, medical problems, cancellation and delays. Medical insurance is sometimes provided by Cuba's **Asistur**, and included in the cost of airline tickets. Check with your airline. Otherwise, visitors must arrange their own private medical insurance before arriving in Cuba.

Asistur
w asistur.cu

Vaccinations

No inoculations are needed for Cuba, but it is recommended that you are inoculated against tetanus, typhoid and hepatitis A and B. Bring mosquito repellent, especially if you are travelling during summer months.

Money

Cuba has two currencies. All tourist transactions are in pesos convertible (CUC, shown as $ throughout this guide), while for most everyday purchases Cubans use the peso (also called moneda nacional). Both currencies are divided into 100 centavos. One peso convertible is worth 24 pesos. The vast majority of visitors will only use pesos convertible and will have no need for the peso, except when buying ice cream at Coppelia stores or for local *colectivo* taxis.

Many state-run establishments, plus a few private restaurants, accept major credit cards (except cards issued or processed by US banks), but an 11 per cent service charge may apply and the system often malfunctions.

Booking Accommodation

In the summer months the state-run hotels fill up fast, and prices are inflated. Local *casas particulares* (private B&Bs) offer better bargains compared to hotels, and there is a huge selection catering to every budget. Many *casas* maintain websites, or are represented by agencies such as **AirBnB** and **TrinidadRent**.

AirBnB
w airbnb.com
TrinidadRent
w trinidadrent.com

Travellers with Specific Needs

Many historic buildings do not have wheelchair access or lifts, but most modern and renovated hotels provide toilets and other amenities for wheelchair-users, and many pavements now have wheelchair ramps. José Martí International Airport is wheelchair-accessible throughout and a programme is underway to add such facilities to other airports and stations.

Language

Spanish is the official language in Cuba, but a large percentage of the population speak English, as well as many other languages. In rural areas, however, the level of English and other foreign languages spoken can be limited. Locals appreciate visitors' efforts to speak Spanish, even if only a few words.

Closures

Lunchtime Offices and many museums close for one hour or longer at mid-day.
Monday State-run museums, public buildings and monuments close for the day.
Sunday Most museums are open in the morning only and close in the afternoon.
Public holidays Shops, offices and many museums either close early or for the entire day.

PUBLIC HOLIDAYS

1 Jan	Liberation Day
2 Jan	Victory Day
28 Jan	José Martí's Birthday
24 Feb	Anniversary of War of Independence
Mar/Apr	Good Friday
19 Apr	Bay of Pigs Victory
1 May	International Worker's Day
25–27 Jul	Anniversary of Attack on Moncada
10 Oct	Independence Day
25 Dec	Christmas Day
31 Dec	New Year's Eve

GETTING AROUND

Whether you are visiting for a short city break or rural country retreat, discover how best to reach your destination and travel like a pro.

TRANSPORT COSTS

HAVANA TO SANTIAGO DE CUBA

Taxi $250

Víazul $51

SANTIAGO TO TRINIDAD

Taxi $200

Víazul $33

HAVANA TO TRINIDAD

Taxi $125

Víazul $25

TOP TIP
Book your Víazul coach ticket as early as possible to ensure that you get a seat.

SPEED LIMIT

AUTOPISTA (MOTORWAY)

100 km/h (62mph)

HIGHWAYS

90 km/h (56mph)

RURAL ROADS

60 km/h (37mph)

URBAN AREAS

50 km/h (31mph)

Arriving by Air

Havana's José Martí International Airport is Cuba's main airport, but international flights also arrive at Varadero, Santiago de Cuba, Cienfuegos, Santa Clara, Ciego de Ávila, Camagüey, Holguín and Cayo Largo. European and Canadian budget airlines fly to these airports and several US airlines also offer scheduled flights to most cities. **Cubana Aviación** runs internal flights within the country.

There is no public bus service between downtown Havana and the international airport; taxis are the only option. For information on getting to and from Cuba's main airports, see the table opposite.
Cubana Aviación
W cubana.cu

Train Travel

Cuba has a single rail line that runs the length of the island between Pinar del Río and Santiago de Cuba, with a few short branch lines. Service is unreliable and uncomfortable, and reservations are essential but difficult to make. Tickets can only be purchased from the station from which you're departing, up to five days in advance. Foreign visitors need to show their passports.

Long-Distance Bus Travel

The Ómnibus Nacionales operates intercity buses, but visitors are barred from using these. **Víazul** connects most cities and resorts using modern air-conditioned coaches. Fares are very reasonable, and children's fares are half-price. Reservations must be made up to six days in advance. Services depart from the town's main bus station or plaza.

Conectando runs between designated hotels. Reservations can be made at tour agencies and at tour desks in hotel lobbies. Note that bags weighing over 20 kg (44 lbs) will incur a charge.
Víazul
W viazul.com
Conectando
W viajescubanacan.com

GETTING TO AND FROM THE AIRPORT

Airport	Distance to city	Taxi fare	Journey time
Havana (José Martí)	25 km (16 miles)	$25	35 mins
Camagüey (Ignacio Agramonte)	9 km (5 miles)	$10	10 mins
Ciego de Ávila (Máximo Gómez)	22 km (14 miles)	$15	25 mins
Cienfuegos (Jaime González)	5 km (3 miles)	$8	7 mins
Holguín (Frank País)	10 km (6 miles)	$10	12 mins
Santa Clara (Abel Santamaría)	10 km (6 miles)	$10	12 mins
Santiago de Cuba (Antonio Maceo)	8 km (5 miles)	$8	10 mins
Varadero (Juan Gualberto Gómez)	16 km (10 miles)	$15	20 mins

JOURNEY PLANNER

Plotting the main driving routes according to journey time, this map is a handy reference for travelling between Cuba's main towns and cities by car. The times given reflect the fastest and most direct routes available.

••• Major road connections

Bayamo to Santiago de Cuba	2 hr	**Holguín to Bayamo**	1.5 hr
Camagüey to Las Tunas	2 hr	**Las Tunas to Holguín**	1.5 hr
Ciego de Ávila to Camagüey	2 hr	**Matanzas to Varadero**	1 hr
Ciego de Ávila to Cayo Coco	1 hr	**Pinar del Río to Viñales**	0.5 hr
Cienfuegos to Playa Larga	2 hr	**Santa Clara to Cienfuegos**	1.5 hr
Cienfuegos to Trinidad	1.5 hr	**Santa Clara to Sancti Spíritus**	1.5 hr
Havana to Matanzas	2 hr	**Sancti Spíritus to Ciego de Ávila**	1.5 hr
Havana to Pinar del Río	2.5 hrs	**Santiago de Cuba to Guantánamo**	1.5 hr
Havana to Playa Larga	3 hrs	**Trinidad to Sancti Spíritus**	1.5 hr
Havana to Santa Clara	4 hrs	**Varadero to Santa Clara**	3 hrs

Public Transport

Most cities operate multiple transport services comprising buses, taxis, rudimentary *bicitaxis* (tricycles) and *camiones* (lorries).

Buses

Travelling by bus in Cuba can be something of an adventure. It is made easier in the capital, however, by the hop-on/hop-off air-conditioned tourist bus service, HabanaBusTour, with two different routes around town. Route 1 starts in Parque Central and travels west to Plaza de la Revolución, while Route 2 heads east to the Playas del Este.

In Havana, most public buses (*guaguas* – pronounced wahg-wahs) are modern, but in provincial towns and cities the standard of buses varies wildly. They range from luxurious air-conditioned cruisers to old and weary Soviet-era vehicles. Fares, which are charged in pesos, are incredibly cheap, but vehicles are usually crowded, and waiting times can be very long. Due to these inconveniences, you'll find that very few visitors use public buses.

In provincial cities, many buses are *camellos* – huge articulated *guaguas* pulled by trucks and introduced during the "Special Period" to ease the transport crisis. Usually packed to capacity, and far from comfortable, they carry several hundred people at a time. It is not hard to see how they earned their name – "camels" – as they have an inverted hump.

Neighbouring towns and rural areas are served by *camiones*: crude conversions of pre-revolutionary lorries. Privately owned, they're usually extremely crowded and insufferably hot in summer months, with passengers often exposed to the elements.

Transtur operates hop-on/hop-off sightseeing buses in Havana and popular venues, such as Viñales, Trinidad and Cayo Coco.

Transtur
🌐 transtur.tur.cu

Taxis

Cuba has multiple types of taxis. State-run Cubataxi operates yellow "tourist taxis" nationwide. Prices (in $s) are reasonable, especially outside Havana. Fares are often negotiable as drivers lease the vehicles from the state. They can be hailed outside major hotels and at taxi stands (*piqueras*) on the main squares or radio-dispatched by phone.

Cubataxi also operates *coco-taxis* in Havana and major tourist destinations. Roughly shaped like coconuts, these open-air motorized tricycles are a fun way to explore the sites.

Cubans almost exclusively use private *colectivo* taxis, which are shared with other passengers and are licensed to operate like buses along fixed routes, picking up and dropping off as many people as they can hold. Fixed fares (in pesos) are cheap; typically 50 centavos. Vehicles are invariably beaten-up pre-revolutionary classics or Soviet Ladas. In Santiago de Cuba, small motorcycles – *moto-taxis* – are the main form of taxi for single-person rides.

The default mode of transport for short journeys within La Habana Vieja, Centro Habana and provincial cities is the *bicitaxi*, a rickshaw-like tricycle with shade-covered seats. They circulate around these areas, or can be found outside hotel entrances. Visitors are typically charged in pesos convertible; be sure to negotiate the fare before departing as scamming of foreign visitors is common.

Classic pre-revolutionary American cars are available for rent as chauffeured touring vehicles and taxis in cities throughout the island. They are also called taxis and are easily recognizable because they have the Taxis Cuba sign and logo on both sides. In Havana, these quirky cars can be hired on Parque Central and outside deluxe hotels. Driving down the Malecón in one of these shiny old-school cruisers is a quintessential Cuban experience. Tourists can also legally ride in local taxi *colectivos* – old American cars, which bear the sign TAXI in the window.

In most towns and rural communities, crude horse-drawn carriages called *coches* ply the streets and charge a few pesos.

Boats and Ferries

Simple *lanchas* (ferries) link La Habana Vieja to the communities of Casablanca and Regla, charging a small fee in pesos. A similar service is offered to Cayo Granma, in Santiago de Cuba. High-speed hydrofoil catamarans offer a service to Isla de la Juventud from Surgidero de Batabanó, on the Caribbean shore south of Havana. Reservations must be made at least one day in advance at the Naviera Cubana Caribeña office in Havana's Terminal de Ómnibus.

Driving

One of the best ways to explore Cuba is by car. Traffic is extremely light, and most Cubans are safe drivers. Make sure you are familiar with the rules of the road and have all the necessary documentation, as traffic police (*tránsitos*) are ubiquitous and efficient.

Driving in Cuba

Cuba has an extensive network of paved roads. The one-lane main highway – the Carretera Central – runs through the centre of the island from Pinar del Río in the west to Guantánamo in the east. The country's main artery, it connects all the major cities. The disjointed Circuito Norte runs along the north shore and connects to the Carretera Central by feeder roads. A motorway *(autopista)* connects Havana to Pinar del Río and Santa Clara. Caution is required when driving as many highways are badly deteriorated and there are often many unpredictable obstacles.

Car Rental

To rent a car in Cuba you must be over 21 and have a valid national driver's licence or International Driver's Permit (IDP). Check with your local automobile association about obtaining an IDP.

Cuba's competing car rental agencies are all state-run and no international companies are represented. It's wise to make reservations well in advance as vehicles are in short supply, especially in high season. Prices are expensive, although discounts apply for rentals of a week or longer. A deposit is required, and you must pay in advance in cash for the first tank of fuel. The three rental agencies (Cubacar, Havanautos and Rex) operated by **Transtur** don't mind if you return the vehicle with an empty tank; **Vía** requires that the vehicle be returned with the same amount of fuel as when you depart. You may be required to take the car to a local office at a specific designated kilometre reading (noted on your contract as *aviso próximo mantanimiento*). A $50 fine usually applies for failure to honour this. Note, too, that your contract also states that it is illegal to pick up hitchhikers.

International insurance coverage is invalid in Cuba. You will be required to purchase either limited Collision Damage Waiver (CDW) or fully comprehensive insurance, but note that the "comprehensive" option has limitations, and your insurance may be invalidated if you are found guilty of causing an accident or if your blood alcohol concentraion level is found to exceed 0.05 per cent.

Transstur
W transtur.tur.cu
Vía
W gaviota-grupo.com

Rules of the Road

Drive on the right, use the left lane only for passing and yield to traffic from the right.

Seat belts are required for all front-seat passengers. A strict drink-drive policy is enforced, and it is wise to avoid all alcohol if intending to drive.

During the day, headlights are not officially permitted except during heavy rain. However, it is wise to turn on your headlights at all times and *tránsitos* usually permit visitors leeway.

Every so often on the *autopista* (motorway) you will see signs telling you to reduce your speed to around 50 km/h (30 mph). Do not ignore these instructions, as they are often followed by road blocks. In general, the police are quite tolerant of tourists, but being caught speeding may invalidate your car insurance so always stick to the limit.

In the event of an accident or breakdown, switch on your hazard warning lights and place a warning triangle or small branches, Cuban-style, 50 m (164 ft) behind your vehicle. If you are involved in an accident, do not move your vehicle. Accidents involving injury or death are treated as crimes – you may not be allowed to leave Cuba until a trial is held, often resulting in a prison term for the guilty party. Contact your embassy immediately if you are involved in a fatal accident.

Maps

An excellent and detailed road atlas, *Guía de Carreteras*, is sold throughout Cuba in souvenir outlets and at Infotur offices. Ask your car hire company for a free *automapa*, which shows where the Servi-Cupet service stations are located across the island.

Parking

Theft of car parts (but rarely of cars) is a potential problem, especially at night. Always park your car in a *parqueo* (designated car park) wherever possible as almost all of these will have a *custodio* (guard) or park on the roadside if it is attended by a state-employed *custodio* (easily identified by their red waistcoats). Private *custodios* can also be hired to watch your car overnight for a few pesos convertible.

Hitchhiking

Hitchhiking is common among Cubans of all ages. However, it is illegal for Cubans to pick up foreigners and foreign embassies warn against the practice. Always consider your own safety before entering an unknown vehicle.

Bicycle and Motorcycle Hire

Although cycling is well established in provincial cities, few Habaneros ride bicycles. Nonetheless, several companies in Havana, such as **Bike Rentals & Tours**, rent bicycles to visitors.

Many travellers bring their own bicycles to the island. If you do this, a sturdy lock is essential and be sure to park in bicycle garages *(bici parqueos)* wherever available to avoid potential thefts. Bicycle mechanics can easily be found anywhere in the country, but it's wise to bring all the spare parts you may need.

No motorcycles are available for rent in Cuba, but scooters can be hired in most cities and tourist resorts from state tour agencies. No licence is required.

Bike Rentals & Tours
W bikerentalhavana.com

PRACTICAL
INFORMATION

A little local know-how goes a long way in Cuba. Here you will find all the essential advice and information you will need during your stay.

AT A GLANCE

EMERGENCY NUMBERS

ASISTUR	AMBULANCE
7866 8527	**104**

FIRE SERVICE	POLICE
105	**106**

TIME ZONE
ETZ
Daylight Saving Time (DST) runs second Sunday in March to first Sunday in November.

TAP WATER
Water purity is unreliable so, to be safe, drink bottled water.

TIPPING

Waiter	10 per cent of bill
Hotel Porter	$1 per bag
Housekeeping	$1 a day
Concierge	$1-5
Taxi Driver	Not expected

Personal Security

Cuba, as a rule, is incredibly safe. However, petty theft occurs, so be careful when carrying cameras and other valuables loose on your shoulder. It is best to keep all of your valuables in sight at all times.

Be wary of pickpockets on public transport and in crowded city centres. If you have anything stolen, report the crime within 24 hours to the nearest police station and take your passport with you. If you need to make an insurance claim, get a copy of the crime report *(denuncia)*. Contact your embassy if your passport is stolen, or in the event of a serious crime or accident.

Health

Be sure to bring any medicine you know you will need during your stay. It is also wise to bring a small medical kit with you. If you need additional medicinal supplies, seek out one of the country's International Pharmacies *(Farmacias Internacionales)* or, if needed, local pharmacies *(farmacias)*.

Emergency medical care for visitors is given at International Clinics *(Clínicas Internacionales)*, and at local hospitals. You will need to show your medical insurance documents. You may be charged a nominal fee for any treatment that you receive, but you may be able to claim the money back later. As such, it is important to arrange comprehensive medical insurance.

Smoking, Alcohol and Drugs

Smoking is banned in many enclosed public spaces, including restaurants, but few establishments adhere to the policy, which is rarely enforced. The possession of illegal drugs is prohibited and could result in a prison sentence as Cuba has zero tolerance.

Cuba has a strict limit of 0.05 per cent BAC (blood alcohol content) for drivers. This means that you cannot drink more than a small beer or tot of rum if you plan to drive. Drivers who cause an accident and have a BAC in excess of this limit are likely to be given a prison sentence.

ID

By law you must carry identification with you at all times in Cuba. A photocopy of your passport photo page and tourist card should suffice. If you are stopped by the police you may need to present your original passport within 24 hours.

Local Customs

Cuba is a tolerant country but attitudes are still rather conservative. Nudism and topless bathing are not allowed on most beaches.

Although Cuba is still a one-party state, Cubans today are politically engaged and you will find them happy to discuss the intricacies of their political system.

Visiting Churches and Cathedrals

Most churches and cathedrals permit visitors during Sunday Mass and entrance to churches is free. Although Cuba is officially a secular state, it retains a strong Catholic identity, and Afro-Cuban religions such as Santería are even more firmly entrenched.

When visiting religious buildings ensure that you are dressed modestly, with your knees and shoulders covered.

Mobile Phones and Wi-Fi

Wi-Fi is widely available in most hotels and parks, as well as a few cafés and restaurants. All users must purchase a scratch card issued by **Etecsa**, the state telecommunications company. The card includes a username and password for a specific number of hours' use. A few hotels offer free Wi-Fi, while others charge their own rates.

Visitors bringing mobile phones should check with their service providers to determine if they will work in Cuba and if they will be subject to roaming charges. A SIM card can be purchased from **Cubacel** offices for local calls and messages within Cuba. Note that an activation fee also applies.

Etecsa
W etecsa.cu
Cubacel
W etecsa.cu/telefonia_movil

Post

Stamps *(estampillas)* are sold at all post offices and prepaid postcards are sold at many state-run souvenir stalls. Cuban post is notorious for its unreliability, and letters and postcards often take over two weeks to be delivered, depending on the destination.

Taxes and Refunds

No taxes apply on purchases in Cuba, nor is there a departure tax. However, many paintings incur a $3 fee by Customs at the airport upon departure.

Organized Tours

Consider an organized tour with a reputable agency, such as **Captivating Cuba**, if you prefer your travel arrangements to be pre-arranged. **Cuba Unbound** tailors trips to allow you to pursue a special interest. "People-to-people educational programs" from the US, such as with **National Geographic Expeditions**, are often accompanied by a Cuba expert and offer an in-depth insight into Cuban culture.

Captivating Cuba
W captivatingcuba.com
Cuba Unbound
W cubaunbound.com
National Geographic Expeditions
W nationalgeographicexpeditions.com

WEBSITES AND APPS

MinTur
Check out Cuba's national tourist board website at www.cubatravel.cu.
OnCuba
This is an engaging monthly online magazine, with a weekly calendar, found at www.oncuba.com.
Cubanacan
With offices in most towns, this agency runs tours and offers accomodation advice, at www.cubanacan.cu.
Ecotur
Book a tour with this eco-tourism agency through www.ecoturcuba.tur.cu.

INDEX

Page numbers in **bold** refer to main entries

A

Accommodation
    booking 269
    see also Hotels
Agramonte, Ignacio
    Casa Natal de Ignacio
        Agramonte (Camagüey)
        211
Airports 271
Air travel 270
Alamar **134-5**
Alameda de Paula (Havana) **79**
Alcohol 274
Ambulances 274
Amusement parks
    Parque Baconao **246-7**
Ancient monuments
    El Chorro de Maíta **251**
Apps 275
Archipélago de los Canarreos
    map 145
Architecture **26-7**
    Museo de Arquitectura
        Colonial (Trinidad) **202**
    Trinidad **202**
Art **28-9**
    artists' studios in Las
        Terrazas **149**
    Callejón de Hamel (Havana)
        29, **108**
    Fusterlandia (Havana) **129**
    see also Museums and
        galleries
Art Deco architecture 27
Avenida Carlos III (Havana)
    102
Avenida del Bélgica (Havana)
    81
Ayuntamiento (Santiago de
    Cuba) 241

B

Balcón de Velázquez (Santiago
    de Cuba) 241
Balcony, The (Peláez) 29
Ballet 34
Banes **252**
Baracoa **248-9**
    map 249
Barcardí Moreau, Emilio
    Museo Emilio Barcardí
        Moreau (Santiago de Cuba)
        234-5, 242
Barrio Chino (Havana) **104**

Bars
    Central Cuba - East 204, 219
    Central Cuba - West 189
    Eastern Cuba 236, 249, 255
    Havana 81, 108, 121, 131
Basílica del Cobre **259**
Batista, Fulgencio 92
    attack by students 93, 131
    Ciudad Escolar Libertad
        (Havana) 128
    Isla de la Juventud 155
    and the Mafia 122
Bayamo **254-5**
Bay of Pigs invasion (1961) 54,
    157, **177**
    Playa Girón 43
Bazar de Artesanía (Holguín)
    243
Beaches 11, **40-41**
    Cayo Largo 165
    Cayo Levisa 41, 163
    Cayo Sabinal 41
    Cayos de Villa Clara 40
    Guardalavaca 41, **251**
    Maguana beach 41
    Playa Ancón 41
    Playa Girón **176**
    Playa Larga **175**
    Playa Santa Lucía **222**
    Playas del Este 41, **134**
    Playa Siboney 41
    Playa Sirena 40
    Varadero 41
Bicycles 32
    hiring 273
Birds 33
    Cayo Coco 209
    flamingos 218
    Las Terrazas 148
    Peninsula de Zapata 175
    Refugio de Fauna Bermejas
        174
    Sierra del Chorrillo **219**
Boats 272
    Museo Histórico Naval
        Nacional (Cienfuegos)
        180
Boca de Yumurí **263**
Bosque de los Héroes (Santiago
    de Cuba) **239**
Buena Fé 35
Buena Vista Social Club 38
Buses 270, 272

C

Cabarets 45
Cabildo de los Congos Reales de
    San Antonio (Trinidad) **205**

Cafés
    Havana 96
    see also Restaurants
Caibarién **193**
Callejón de Hamel (Havana) 29,
    108
Calle Mercaderes (Havana) **73**
Calle Obispo (Havana) **72-3**
Calle Oficios (Havana) **72**
Calle San Rafael (Havana) 111
Camagüey **210-13**
    map 211
Cámara Oscura (Havana) 75
Camellos (trucks) 273
Camilo Cienfuegos (Hershey)
    187
Camiones (lorries) 273
"Cañonazo" ceremony (Havana)
    130
Cao Campos, Jorge 184-5
Capitolio (Havana) **88-9**, 110
Cárdenas **188**
Cárdenas, Augustín 96
Carnival
    Museo del Carnaval (Santiago
        de Cuba) **235**
    Santiago de Cuba **235**
Cars
    Classic American cars 13, **99**
    driving in Cuba 272-3
    Museo Automóvil (Havana)
        79
    Museo de Automóviles
        (Havana) 75
    photographing 37
    rental 272-3
    speed limits 270
    see also Driving tours
Casablanca **131**
Casa de Africa (Havana) **74-5**
Casa de Diego Velázquez
    (Musée Ambiente Histórico
    Cubano, Santiago de Cuba)
    26, **233**, 241
Casa de la Condesa de la
    Reunión (Havana) 82
Casa de la Conspiradores
    (Trinidad) 201
Casa de la Cultura Julio Cuevas
    Díaz (Trinidad) **203**
Casa de la Cultura Miguel
    Matamoros (Santiago de
    Cuba) 241
Casa de la Obra Pía (Havana) **74**
Casa de las Américas (Havana)
    120
Casa del Científico (Havana) 91
Casa Museo Finca El Abra (Isla de
    la Juventud) **154**

Casa Natal de Antonio Maceo (Santiago de Cuba) **236**
Casa Natal de Ignacio Agramonte (Camagüey) **211**
Casa Natal de José María Heredia (Santiago de Cuba) **234**, 240
Casa Natal de José Martí (Havana) **77**
Castles and fortresses
    Castillo de Jagua (Cienfuegos) **181**
    Castillo de la Real Fuerza (Havana) **70**
    Castillo del Morro (Havana) **130**
    Castillo del Morro (Santiago de Cuba) **244-5**
    Castillo de San Salvador de la Punta (Havana) **100-101**
    Castillo de San Severino (Matanzas) **171**
    San Carlos de La Cabaña (Havana) **130-31**
Castro, Fidel 12, 153
    Bay of Pigs invasion **177**
    birthplace 252
    Ciudad Escolar Libertad (Havana) 128
    Cuban Revolution **53-5**
    Granma memorial (Havana) 92
    grave 43
    home 129
    Museo 26 de Julio - Cuartel Moncada (Santiago de Cuba) **238**
    Parque Coppelia (Havana) 120
    Revolution sites **42-3**
Castro, Raúl 53, 55
    birthplace 252
    Mayarí Arriba 253
Cathedrals 275
    Catedral de la Purísima Concepción (Cienfuegos) **178-9**
    Catedral de Nuestra Señora de la Asunción (Baracoa) **248**
    Catedral de Nuestra Señora de la Asunción (Santiago de Cuba) **232**, 241
    Catedral de Nuestra Señora de la Candelaria (Camagüey) **210-11**
    Catedral de San Cristóbal (Havana) **68-9**, 83
    Catedral de San Isidro (Holguín) **243**

Cathedrals (cont.)
    Catedral Ortodoxa Nuestra Señora de Kazán (Havana) **79**
    Parroquial Mayor de San Salvador (Bayamo) 254-5
    see also Churches
Caves 30
    Cavernas de Panaderos (Gibara) 250
    Cuevas de Bellamar **189**
    Cuevas de Punta del Este 155
    Gran Caverna de Santo Tomás 151
Cayo Coco **208-9**
Cayo Granma **245**
Cayo Largo **165**
Cayo Levisa 41, **163**
Cayo Sabinal 41
Cayo Saetía **253**
Cayos de Villa Clara 40
Cemeteries
    Cementerio de Santa Ifigenia (Santiago de Cuba) 43, **237**
    Cementerio Monumental Tomás de Acea (Cienfuegos) **180**
    Necrópolis de Colón (Havana) **116-17**
Central Cuba - East 19, **195-225**
    bars 204, 219
    hotels 209, 215, 223
    itinerary 199
    map 196-7
    restaurants 203, 207, 216
    shopping 201
Central Cuba - West 18, **167-93**
    bars 189
    hotels 176, 179, 193
    itinerary 24-5
    map 168-9
    restaurants 173, 183, 191
    shopping 180
Centro Asturiano (Havana) **96**, 111
Centro Cultural Felix Varela (Havana) **71**
Centro Habana and Prado (Havana) **85-111**
    hotels 98
    map 86-7
    restaurants 105
Centro Wifredo Lam (Havana) 82
Céspedes, Carlos Manuel de
    Casa Natal de Carlos Manuel de Céspedes (Bayamo) 254, 255
Che de los Niños (Santa Clara) **185**

Chinese community
    Havana **104**
Churches 275
    Basílica del Cobre **259**
    Basílica Menor y Convento de San Francisco de Asís (Havana) 78-9
    Copper Church (Havana) 108
    Ermita de Nuestra Señora de la Candelaria de la Popa (Trinidad) **205**
    Iglesia de la Merced (Camagüey) **212**
    Iglesia del Ángel Custodio (Havana) **81**
    Iglesia del Espíritu Santo (Havana) **77**
    Iglesia del Sagrado Corazón (Havana) **105**
    Iglesia del Sagrado Corazón de Jesús (Viñales) 151
    Iglesia de Nuestra Señora de la Merced (Havana) **77**
    Iglesia de San Francisco de Paula (Havana) **80**
    Iglesia Parroquial de la Santísima Trinidad **200**
    Iglesia y Convento de San Francisco (Trinidad) **205**
    Parroquial Mayor del Espíritu Santo (Sancti Spíritus) **206**
    Santa María del Rosario **135**
    see also Cathedrals
Ciego de Ávila **216-17**
Cienfuegos **178-81**
    map 179
Cienfuegos, Comandante Camilo
    Complejo Histórico Comandante Camilo Cienfuegos (Yaguajay) 216
Cigars **103**
    Cuban tobacco **158**
    Fábrica de Tabaco H Uppman (Havana) **102**
    Fábrica de Tabacos Francisco Donatién (Pinar del Rio) 159
    Finca El Pinar San Luis (Pinar del Rio) 159
    Museo del Tabaco (Havana) 73
    Real Fábrica de Tabacos Partagás (Havana) **100**, 110
Cinema *see* Film
Cine Payret (Havana) 110
Circuito Sur **190**
Ciudad Escolar Libertad (Havana) **128**
Closures 269

Index

Clotilde en los Jardines de la Granja (Sorolla) 96
Clubs 45
Coches (horse-drawn carts) 273
Cockerel of Morón **217**
Cocktails 11
   El Floridita (Havana) 73
Cocodrillo **155**
Cocotaxis (motorized tricycles) 273
Coffee
   Cafetal Buenavista 149
   The origins of coffee growing in Cuba **246**
Cojímar **133**
Collazo, Guillermo 96
Columbus, Christopher 188, **250**
   Catedral de Nuestra Señora de la Asunción (Baracoa) 248
   Catedral de San Cristóbal (Havana) 68–9
   Cienfuegos 178
   "discovers" Cuba 50, 51, 167
   Jardines de la Reina 222
   Parque Monumento Nacional Bariay 250
   statues of 67, 188, 234, 250
Columbus Cemetery **116–17**
Complejo Escultórico Comandante Ernesto Che Guevara (Santa Clara) 43, **184–5**
Copper Church (Havana) 108
Coral reefs 31
   see also Diving
Costa Sur **261**
Cristo de la Habana (Madera) 131
Cubanacán (Havana) **128–9**
Cuban Missile Crisis (1962) **157**
Cuban Revolution (1953–59) 36, **42–3**, **53–5**
   Museo 26 de Julio – Cuartel Moncada (Santiago de Cuba) **238**
   Museo de la Revolución (Havana) **92–3**
Cuevas de Bellamar **189**
Cuevas de Punta del Este **155**
Currency 268, 269
Customs, local 275
Customs information 268
Cycling 32
   bicycle hire 273

D

Dance **34–5**
   Danzón **170**
Delarra, José 184–5
Dirty Havana Trilogy (Gutiérrez) 39

Diving 31, 32
   Jardines de la Reina 222
   María La Gorda 164
   Playa Santa Lucía **222**
   Punta Francés **154**
Doctors 274
Dos Ríos **253**
Drinks **47**
   Fábrica de Guayabita Casa Garay (Pinar del Rio) 159
   see also Food and drink
Driving *see* Cars
Driving tours
   towards Santiago de Cuba **264–5**
Drugs 274

E

Eastern Cuba 19, **227–65**
   bars 236, 249, 255
   hotels 147, 241, 253
   map 228–9
   restaurants 233, 251, 263
Echevarría, José Antonio
   Museo Casa Natal de José Antonio Echevarria (Cárdenas) 188, 189
Edificio Bacardí (Havana) 27, **80**
Edificio Cuban Telephone Company **104**
El Chorro de Maíta **251**
Electricity supply 268
El Malecón (Baracoa) **249**
El Nicho **191**
El Templete (Havana) **71**
Emergency numbers 274
Ermita de Nuestra Señora de la Candelaria de la Popa (Trinidad) **205**
Escalinata Padre Pico (Santiago de Cuba) **236**
Escuela Nacional de Ballet (Havana) 91
Espín, Vilma 42, 252
   Museo Memorial Vilma Espín (Santiago de Cuba) **236**
Events *see* Festival and events

F

Fábrica de Tabaco H Uppman (Havana) **102**
Failde, Miguel 170
Farms
   Oranipónico Alamar 134–5
Ferries 272
Festivals and events **48–9**
   Carnival in Santiago de Cuba **235**
   Museo del Carnaval (Santiago de Cuba) **235**
   Parrandas de Remedios **192**

Films **38–9**
   Cine Payret (Havana) 110
Finca La Vigía **135**
Finlay, Dr Carlos 91
Fishing 32
Food and drink **46–7**
   cocktails 11
   see also Bars; Cafés; Restaurants
Form, Space and Light (Longa) 95
Fortresses *see* Castles and fortresses
Fuerte Matachín (Museo Municipal, Baracoa) **249**
Fuster, José 129
Fusterlandia (Havana) 29, **129**

G

Galleries *see* Museums and galleries
García Caturla, Alejandro
   House of Alejandro García Caturla (Remedios) 192, 193
Gardens *see* Parks and gardens
Gibara **250**
González, Leovigildo 151
Goyri de la Hoz, Amelia 116
Granma memorial (Havana) 92
Gran Parque Nacional Sierra Maestra **258–9**
Gran Teatro de La Habana Alicia Alonso (Havana) 26, **98–9**, 110
Greene, Graham 39, **90**, 242
Guama **174–5**
Guanabacoa **132–3**
Guantánamo **260–61**
Guardalavaca 41, **251**
Guayabera shirts **206**
Guayasamin, Oswaldo
   Casa de Guayasamin (Havana) 74
Guevara, Ernesto Che 12, 52–3, **185**
   billboards and murals 36
   Bosque de los Héroes (Santiago de Cuba) **239**
   Che de los Niños (Santa Clara) **185**
   Complejo Escultórico Comandante Ernesto Che Guevara (Santa Clara) 43, **184–5**
   Loma del Capiro (Santa Clara) 185
   Tren Blindado Monument (Santa Clara) 183
Gutiérrez, Pedro Juan
   Dirty Havana Trilogy 39

H

Havana 10, 16, **56–125**
  bars 81, 108, 121, 131
  Centro Habana and Prado **85–111**
  hotels 123, 133
  itinerary 61
  La Habana Vieja **63–83**
  map 58–9
  restaurants 119
  shopping 129
  Vedado and Plaza **113–25**
  walks **82–3**, 110–11
Health care 274
Hemingway, Ernest **135**
  Basílica del Cobre 259
  Cojímar 133
  Finca La Vigía **135**
  Old Man and the Sea, The 39
Heredia, José María
  Casa Natal de José María Heredia (Santiago de Cuba) **234**, 240
Hershey Train **187**
Hiking 33
Historic buildings
  Casa de Diego Velázquez (Musée Ambiente Histórico Cubano, Santiago de Cuba) 26, **233**, 241
  Casa de Don Tomás (Viñales) 162
  Casa de la Condesa de la Reunión (Havana) 82
  Casa de la Conspiradores (Trinidad) 201
  Casa de la Cultura Miguel Matamoros (Santiago de Cuba) 241
  Casa del Agua la Tinaja (Havana) 73
  Casa de la Obra Pía (Havana) **74**
  Casa del Cientifico (Havana) 91
  Casa de los Arabes (Havana) 72
  Casa de los Conde Jarucos (Havana) 75
  Casa Natal de Antonio Maceo (Santiago de Cuba) **236**
  Casa Natal de Carlos Manuel de Céspedes (Bayamo) 254, 255
  Casa Natal de Ignacio Agramonte (Camagüey) **211**
  Casa Natal de José María Heredia (Santiago de Cuba) **234**, 240
  Centro Cultural Felix Varela (Havana) **71**

Historic buildings (cont.)
  Edificio Cuban Telephone Company **104**
  El Templete (Havana) **71**
  Escuela Nacional de Ballet (Havana) 91
  Finca La Vigía **135**
  House of Alejandro García Caturla (Remedios) 192, 193
  Instituto Superior de Arte (Havana) **128**
  La Bodeguita del Medio (Havana) **70**, 82
  Palacio Brunet (Museo Romántico, Trinidad) **203**
  Palacio Cantero (Museo Histórico Municipal, Trinidad) **204**
  Palacio del Conde Lombillo (Havana) 83
  Palacio de Valle (Cienfuegos) **181**
  Palacio Ferrer (Cienfuegos) **179**
  Palacio Guasch (Pinar del Rio) 158, 159
  Quinta de los Molinos (Havana) **123**
  Restaurante Las Américas (Mansión Xanadú, Varadero) **173**
  Taquechel (Havana) 73
  Universal Benito Ortiz Galería de Arte (Trinidad) **202**
  US Embassy (Havana) **120**
  see also Castles and fortresses; Cathedrals; Churches; Palaces
History **50–55**
Hitchhiking 273
Holguín **242–3**
  map 233
Horse riding 33
Hospitals 274
Hotels
  booking 269
  Central Cuba – East 209, 215, 223
  Central Cuba – West 176, 179, 193
  Eastern Cuba 147, 241, 253
  Havana 98, 123, 133
  Hotel Ambos Mundos (Havana) 73
  Hotel Casa Granda (Santiago de Cuba) 240
  Hotel Inglaterra (Havana) **98**, 111
  Hotel Plaza (Havana) 111
  Hotel Riviera (Havana) 27
  Hotel Sevilla (Havana) 91
  Iberostar Parque Central (Havana) 111

Hotels (cont.)
  Isla de la Juventud 155
  La Habana Vieja 71
  Manzana de Gómez (Havana) 111
  Western Cuba 155, 163

I

Ice cream 13, **47**
  Parque Coppelia (Havana) **120**
Iglesia de la Merced (Camagüey) **212**
Iglesia del Ángel Custodio (Havana) **81**
Iglesia del Espíritu Santo (Havana) **77**
Iglesia del Sagrado Corazón (Havana) **105**
Iglesia de Nuestra Señora de la Merced (Havana) **77**
Iglesia de San Francisco de Paula (Havana) **80**
Iglesia Parroquial de la Santísima Trinidad **200**
Iglesia y Convento de San Francisco (Trinidad) **205**
Instituto Superior de Arte (Havana) 28, **128**
Insurance 269
Internet access 275
Isla de la Juventud **152–5**
  history **155**
  map 153
Itineraries
  2 days in Havana 61
  2 days in Santiago de Cuba 231
  2 weeks in Cuba 21–3
  3 days in Trinidad 199
  5 days in Western Cuba 147
  7 days in Central Cuba – West 24–5

J

Jardín Botánico Nacional **137**
Jardín Botánico Soledad **186–7**
Jardines de la Reina **222**
Jardines del Rey **218**

K

Kcho Estudio Romerillo (Havana) **129**

L

La Bodeguita del Medio (Havana) **70**, 82
La Farola **257**
Lago Hanabanilla **190**

La Habana Vieja (Havana) **63–83**
hotels 71
map 64–5
restaurants 69
shopping 73
La Milagrosa (Havana) 116
Lam, Wifredo 96
Language 268, 269
Lansky, Meyer 122
La Periquera (Museo Provincial de Holguín) **242**
La Piedad de Rita Longa (Havana) 117
Las Terrazas **148–9**
Las Tunas **222–3**
Lenin, Vladimir Ilyich 136
Lennon, John **123**
LGBT venues 45
Local customs 275
Loma de la Cruz (Holguín) **242**
Loma del Capiro (Santa Clara) **185**
Longa, Rita
Form, Space and Light 95
La Piedad de Rita Longa (Havana) 117

M

Maceo, Antonio **236**
Madera, Jilma 131
Mafia **122**
Maguana beach 41
Maine, USS
Monumento a las Victimas del *Maine* (Havana) **120**
Malecón (Havana) 37, **109**
Manzana de Gómez (Havana) 111
Manzanillo **256–7**
Maps
Archipélago de los Canarreos 145
Baracoa 249
Camagüey 211
Central Cuba - East 196–7
Central Cuba - West 168–9
Centro Habana and Prado (Havana) 86–7
Cienfuegos 179
Cuba 14–15
driving maps 273
Eastern Cuba 228–9
Havana 58–9
Havana: Beyond the Centre 127
Havana: La Habana Vieja 64–5
Havana: Parque Central 110–11
Havana: Plaza de la Catedral 82–3
Havana: Vedado and Plaza 114–15

Maps (cont.)
Holguín 243
Isla de la Juventud 153
journey planner 271
Matanzas 171
Peninsula de Zapata 175
Sancti Spíritus 207
Santa Clara 183
Santiago de Cuba 233
Santiago de Cuba: Parque Céspedes 240–1
Santiago de Cuba drive 264–5
Topes de Collantes 224–5
Trinidad 200–201
Varadero 173
Western Cuba 144–5
Maqueta de la Ciudad (Santiago de Cuba) **236**
María La Gorda **164**
Markets
Bazar de Artesanía (Holguín) **243**
see also Shopping
Martí, José **101**, 153
Casa Museo Finca El Abra (Isla de la Juventud) 154
Casa Natal de José Martí (Havana) **77**
Cementerio de Santa Ifigenia (Santiago de Cuba) 43, 237
Isla de la Juventud 155
Memorial José Martí (Havana) **118–19**
Monumento Martí (Dos Ríos) **253**
Museo Fragua Martiana (Havana) **101**
Parque Martí (Cienfuegos) 178
statues of 111, 171
Matanzas **170–71**
map 171
Mayarí Arriba **253**
Memling, Hans 96
Memorial José Martí (Havana) **118–19**
Mirador La Gobernadora (Guantánamo) 260
Miramar walk **138–9**
Miranda, Francisco de 100–101
Mobile phones 275
Mogotes (karst formations) 30, 150–51
Moncada Barracks 42
Money 268, 269
Monuments
Bosque de los Héroes (Santiago de Cuba) **239**
Complejo Escultórico Comandante Ernesto Che Guevara (Santa Clara) 43, **184–5**
La Piedad de Rita Longa (Havana) 117

Monuments (cont.)
Memorial José Martí (Havana) **118–19**
Monumento a las Victimas del *Maine* (Havana) **120**
Monumento Martí (Dos Ríos) **253**
Parque Lenin 136
Tren Blindado Monument (Santa Clara) **183**
Moré, Benny **181**
Morón **217**
Cockerel of Morón **217**
Motorcycle hire 273
Mountains 31
Mural Artístico-Histórico (Havana) 68
Museums and galleries
Armería 9 de Abril (Havana) 73
Casa de Africa (Havana) **74–5**
Casa de Diego Velázquez (Santiago de Cuba) 26, **233**, 241
Casa de Guayasamin (Havana) 74
Casa de la Cultura Julio Cuevas Díaz (Trinidad) **203**
Casa de las Américas (Havana) **120**
Casa de México (Havana) 74
Casa Museo Finca El Abra (Isla de la Juventud) 154
Casa Natal de Ignacio Agramonte (Camagüey) **211**
Casa Natal de José Martí (Havana) **77**
Centro Asturiano (Havana) **96**, 111
Centro Wifredo Lam (Havana) 82
Complejo Escultórico Comandante Ernesto Che Guevara (Santa Clara) 43, 184–5
Complejo Histórico Comandante Camilo Cienfuegos (Yaguajay) 216
Complejo Histórico de Museos del Segundo Frente (Mayarí Arriba) 253
ExpoCuba 136
Finca La Vigía **135**
Fototeca de Cuba (Havana) 75
Fuerte Matachín (Museo Municipal, Baracoa) **249**
Fusterlandia 29, **129**
Iglesia y Convento de San Francisco (Trinidad) **205**
Kcho Estudio Romerillo (Havana) **129**
La Periquera (Museo Provincial de Holguín) **242**

Museums and galleries (cont.)

Maqueta de Centro Histórico (Havana) 73

Museo 26 de Julio - Cuartel Moncada (Santiago de Cuba) **238**

Museo Abel Santamaría Cuadrado (Santiago de Cuba) **238**

Museo a la Batalla de Ideas (Cárdenas) 188, 189

Musée Ambiente Histórico Cubano (Santiago de Cuba) 26, **233**, 241

Museo Antropológico Montané (Havana) 121

Museo Arqueológico de las Cuevas del Paraíso (Baracoa) **249**

Museo Automóvil (Havana) 79

Museo Casa Natal de José Antonio Echevarria (Cárdenas) 188, 189

Museo Conjunto Histórico Birán **252**

Museo de Agroindustria Azucarera (Caibarién) 193

Museo de Arqueología Guamuhaya (Trinidad) **202**

Museo de Arquitectura Colonial (Trinidad) **202**

Museo de Arte Colonial (Havana) **69**, 83

Museo de Arte Colonial (Sancti Spíritus) **206**

Museo de Artes Decorativas (Gibara) 250

Museo de Artes Decorativas (Guantánamo) 260, 261

Museo de Artes Decorativas (Havana) **122**

Museo de Artes Decorativas (Santa Clara) **183**

Museo de Automóviles (Havana) 75

Museo de Historia Natural Antonio Núñez Jiménez (Nueva Gerona) 152-3

Museo de Historia Natural Antonio Núñez Jiménez (Pinar del Rio) 158-9

Museo de Historia Natural Carlos de la Torre (Holguín) **243**

Museo de la Industria Azúcarera Avileña (Morón) 217

Museo de la Lucha Clandestina (Santiago de Cuba) **235**

Museo de la Revolucíon (Havana) 42, **92-3**

Museums and galleries (cont.)

Museo de las Parrandas Remedianas (Remedios) 192-3

Museo del Carnaval (Santiago de Cuba) **235**

Museo del Ron (Havana) **79**

Museo del Tabaco (Havana) 73

Museo Emilio Barcardí Moreau (Santiago de Cuba) **234-5**, 240

Museo Farmacéutico de Matanzas **171**

Museo Fragua Martiana (Havana) **101**

Museo Girón (Playa Girón) 43, 176

Museo Hermanos País (Santiago de Cuba) **237**

Museo Histórico Naval Nacional (Cienfuegos) **180**

Museo Indocubana Bani (Banes) 252

Museo Memorial Vilma Espín (Santiago de Cuba) **236**

Museo Municipal (Morón) 217

Museo Municipal (Varadero) **172**

Museo Municipal de Guanabacoa 132-3

Museo Municipal de Nueva Gerona 152, 153

Museo Municipal Oscar María de Rojas (Cárdenas) 188, 189

Museo Nacional de Bellas Artes (Havana) **94-7**

Museo Napoleónico (Havana) **122-3**

Museo Provincial (Cienfuegos) **179**

Museo Provincial (Matanzas) 170

Museo Provincial de Guantánamo 260, 261

Museo Provincial de Historia (Pinar del Rio) 159

Museo Provincial Ignacio Agramonte (Camagüey) **213**

Museo Zoológico de Piedra (Guantánamo) 261

Palacio Brunet (Museo Romántico, Trinidad) **203**

Palacio de Bellas Artes (Havana) 29, **97**

Palacio del Conde Lombillo (Havana) 83

Palacio de los Marqueses de Arcos (Havana) 83

Parque Histórico Abel Santamaría (Santiago de Cuba) **238**

Museums and galleries (cont.)

Parque Museo Ñico López (Bayamo) 255

Planetario (Havana) 75

San Alejandro Fine Arts Academy 29

San Carlos de La Cabaña (Havana) **130-31**

Taller Experimental de Gráfica (Havana) 82

Music 12, **34-5**, 44

N

Napoleon I, Emperor **122-3**

National parks

Gran Parque Nacional Sierra Maestra **258-9**

Parque Nacional Alejandro de Humboldt **262-3**

Parque Nacional Ciénaga de Zapata 30, **176**

Parque Nacional Duaba y El Yunque **257**

Parque Nacional La Güira **157**

Parque Nacional Península de Guanahacabibes **164-5**

Parque Nacional Río Toa **262**

Natural wonders **30-31**

Necrópolis de Colón (Havana) **116-17**

Nightlife **44-5**

Nueva Gerona 152-3

O

Old Man and the Sea, The (Hemingway) 39

Our Man in Havana (Greene) 38-9, 90, 242

Outdoor activities see Sports and outdoor activities

P

País, Hermanos **237**

Palaces

Palacio del Marqués de Arcos (Havana) **68**, 83

Palacio de los Capitanes Generales (Havana) 27, **66-7**

Palacio de los Marqueses de Aguas Claras (Havana) 83

see also Historic buildings

Palacio Brunet (Museo Romántico, Trinidad) **203**

Palacio Cantero (Museo Histórico Municipal, Trinidad) **204**

Palacio de Bellas Artes (Havana) 29, **97**

Palaces (cont.)
Palacio del Conde Lombillo
(Havana) 83
Palacio del Marqués de Arcos
(Havana) **68**, 83
Palacio de los Capitanes
Generales (Havana) 27,
66-7
Palacio de los Marqueses de
Aguas Claras (Havana) 83
Parking 273
Parks and gardens
Jardín Botánico Nacional **137**
Jardín Botánico Soledad **186-7**
Orquideario de Soroa 156-7
Orquideario La Mensura
(Pinares de Mayarí) 252
Parque Casino Campestre
(Camagüey) **213**
Parque Central (Havana)
110-11
Parque de la Fraternidad
(Havana) **99**, 110
Parque de la Punta 100
Parque John Lennon (Havana)
123
Parque Lenin **136**
Parque Leoncio Vidal (Santa
Clara) **182**
Parque Retiro Josone
(Varadero) **172**
Parque Serafín Sánchez
(Sancti Spíritus) **207**
Parque Tudury (Santa Clara)
184
Paseo del Prado (Havana)
90-91
Parliament
Capitolio (Havana) **88-9**, 110
Parque Baconao **246-7**
Parque Casino Campestre
(Camagüey) **213**
Parque Central (Havana) **110-11**
Parque Céspedes (Santiago de
Cuba) **240-1**
Parque Coppelia (Havana) **120**
Parque de la Fraternidad
(Havana) **99**, 110
Parque de la Libertad
(Matanzas) **171**
Parque de la Punta 100
Parque Ignacio Agramonte
(Camagüey) **210**
Parque Indepencia (Baracoa)
248
Parque John Lennon (Havana)
123
Parque Lenin **136**
Parque Leoncio Vidal (Santa
Clara) **182**
Parque Martí (Cienfuegos) **178**
Parque Monumento Nacional
Bariay **250**

Parque Nacional Alejandro de
Humboldt **262-3**
Parque Nacional Ciénaga de
Zapata 30, **176**
Parque Nacional Duaba y El
Yunque **257**
Parque Nacional La Güira **157**
Parque Nacional Península de
Guanahacabibes **164-5**
Parque Nacional Río Toa **262**
Parque Retiro Josone (Varadero)
172
Parque Serafín Sánchez (Sancti
Spíritus) **207**
Parque Tudury (Santa Clara) **184**
Parque Zoológico Nacional 136
Parrandas de Remedios **192**
Parroquial Mayor del Espíritu
Santo (Sancti Spíritus) **206**
Paseo del Prado (Cienfuegos)
180
Paseo del Prado (Havana)
90-91, 111
Passports 268, 275
Peláez, Amelia
Balcony, The 29
Península de Ancón **214**
Peninsula de Zapata **174-7**
map 175
Personal security 274
Pharmacies 274
Museo Farmacéutico de
Matanzas **171**
Phones 275
Photography **36-7**
Pico Turquino 256, 258
Pinar del Rio **158-9**
Pinares de Mayarí **252**
Playa Ancón 41
Playa Girón 43, **176**
Playa Larga **175**
Playa Santa Lucía **222**
Playas del Este 41, **134**
Playa Siboney 41
Playa Sirena 40
Plaza de la Catedral (Havana)
82-3
Plaza de la Revolución (Havana)
119
Plaza de la Revolución (Holguín)
243
Plaza de la Revolución (Santiago
de Cuba) **238**
Plaza del Cristo (Havana) 80
Plaza de los Tres Cruces
(Trinidad) **205**
Plaza de Marte (Santiago de
Cuba) **238-39**
Plaza de San Francisco (Havana)
78-9
Plaza San Juan de Dios
(Camagüey) **212-13**
Plaza Santa Ana (Trinidad) **205**

Plaza Vieja (Havana) **75**
Plazuela del Jigüe (Trinidad) **204**
Police 274
Postal services 275
Prado (Havana) *see* Centro
Habana and Prado (Havana)
Prehistoric sites *see* Ancient
monuments
Presidio Modelo **153**
Prisons
Isla de la Juventud 155
Presidio Modelo **153**
Public holidays 269
Public transport 272
Puerto Padre **223**
Punta Francés **154**
Punta Gorda (Cienfuegos)
180-81
Punta Hicacos (Varadero) **173**
Punta Maisí **263**

Q

Quinta de los Molinos (Havana)
123

R

Railways *see* Train travel
Rancho La Guabina **163**
Real Fábrica de Tabacos
Partagás (Havana) **100**, 110
Refugio de Fauna Bermejas **174**
Regla **132**
Religion
Santéria **76**
see also Cathedrals; Churches
Remedios **192-3**
Restaurants
Central Cuba – East 203, 207,
216
Central Cuba – West 173, 183,
191
Eastern Cuba 233, 251, 263
Havana 69, 105, 119, 137
Santiago de Cuba 237
Western Cuba 156, 165
see also Cafés; Food and drink
Revolution *see* Cuban
Revolution
Rules of the road 273

S

Safety
personal security 274
travel safety advice 268
Salaya, Camilo 182
Salsa 35
San Alejandro Fine Arts
Academy 29
San Carlos de La Cabaña
(Havana) **130-31**

Sánchez, Celía 42, 256
Sancti Spíritus **206-7**
  map 207
San Diego de los Baños **157**
San Miguel de los Baños **189**
Santa Clara **182-5**
  map 183
Santamaría, Abel **238**
Santa María del Rosario **135**
Santéria **76**
  Iglesia de Nuestra Señora de
    la Merced (Havana) **77**
Santiago de Cuba 13, **232-41**
  Carnival **235**
  itinerary 230
  map 233
  restaurants 237
  shopping 233
  tours **264-5**
  walk **240-1**
Santiago de las Vegas **137**
Santuario Nacional de San
  Lázaro (El Rincón) **136-7**
Scuba diving 31
Seminario de San Carlos y San
  Ambrosio (Havana) 82
Shirts, *guayabera* **206**
Shopping
  Central Cuba - East 201
  Central Cuba - West 180
  Havana 73, 129
  Santiago de Cuba 233
  taxes and refunds 275
  see also Markets
Sierra de Cubitas **218-19**
Sierra del Chorrillo **219**
Sierra Maestra 31
Smoking 274
Snorkeling 10
Son 34
Soroa **156-7**
Sorolla, Joaquín 96
Specific needs, travellers with
  269
Speed limits 270
Sports and outdoor activities
  32-3
Stevenson, Robert Louis 155
Strawberry and Chocolate 39
Sugar 51, **214**
  Museo de Agroindustria
    Azucarera (Caibarién) 193
  Museo de la Industria
    Azúcarera Avileña (Morón)
    217
  Valle de los Ingenios **214-15**

T

Taller Experimental de Gráfica
  (Havana) 82
Tap water 274
Taxes 275

Taxis 270, 272
Theatre
  Gran Teatro de La Habana
    Alicia Alonso (Havana) 26,
    98-9, 110
  Teatro Fausto (Havana) 91
  Teatro La Caridad (Santa
    Clara) **182**
  Teatro Milanés (Pinar del Rio)
    159
  Teatro Principal (Camagüey)
    212
  Teatro Sauto (Matanzas)
    170-71
  Teatro Tomás Terry
    (Cienfuegos) **178**
Time zone 274
Tinajones **211**
Tipping 274
Tobacco **158**
  Vuelta Abajo 162-3
  see also Cigars
Topes de Collantes **224-5**
Tours
  organized tours 275
  see also Driving tours; Walks
Train travel 270
  Coche Mambí (Havana) 72
  Hershey Train **187**
Travel 270-71
Travel safety advice 268
Tren Blindado Monument (Santa
  Clara) **183**
Trinidad 11, **200-205**
  architecture **202**
  itinerary 199
  map 200-201

U

United States of America
  Bay of Pigs invasion (1961)
    43, 54, 157, **177**
  Classic American cars 13, **99**
  Cuban Missile Crisis (1962)
    157
  embargo 54
  Guantánamo 260, **261**
  US Embassy (Havana) **120**
Universal Benito Ortiz Galería de
  Arte (Trinidad) **202**
Universidad de La Habana
  (Havana) **121**

V

Vaccinations 269
Váldez, Chucho 35
Valle de los Ingenios **214-15**
Valle de Viñales 12, 36, **150-51**
Vanguardia Movement 29
Varadero 41, **172-3**
  map 173

Varela, Padre Félix 71
Vedado and Plaza (Havana)
  113-25
  map 114-15
Velázquez, Diego 50
  Casa de Diego Velázquez
    (Musée Ambiente Histórico
    Cubano, Santiago de Cuba)
    26, **233**, 243
Villa Pinares de Mayarí 252
Viñales **162**
Virgen del Cobre **259**
Visas 268
Vista Alegre (Santiago de Cuba)
  239
Vuelta Abajo **162-3**

W

Walks 33
  Around the Parque Central
    (Havana) **110-11**
  Miramar **138-9**
  Plaza de la Catedral (Havana)
    82-3
  Santiago de Cuba: Parque
    Céspedes **240-1**
  Topes de Collantes **224-5**
Water, drinking 274
Waterfalls 31
  El Nicho **191**
Watersports
  Varadero 172
Websites 275
Western Cuba 17, **143-65**
  hotels 155, 163
  itinerary 147
  map 144-5
  restaurants 156, 165
Wetlands 30
Wi-Fi 275
Wildlife
  Peninsula de Zapata **174**
  see also Birds; National parks;
    Zoos
Writers **38-9**

X

X-Alfonso 35

Y

Yaguajay **216**
Yayabo Bridge (Sancti Spíritus)
  207

Z

Zoos
  Parque Zoológico Nacional
    136
  see also Wildlife

PHRASE BOOK

The Spanish spoken in Cuba is basically the same as the Castilian used in Spain with certain deviations. As in the Spanish-speaking countries in Central and Southern America, the "z" is pronounced like the "s", as is the "c" when it comes before "e" or "i". Among the grammatical variations, visitors should be aware that Cubans use *Ustedes* in place of *Vosotros*, to say "you" when referring to more than one person. Some Indian, African and English words are also commonly used in present-day Cuban Spanish. This basic phrase book includes useful common phrases and words, and particular attention has been paid to typically Cuban idioms in a list of Cuban Terms.

CUBAN TERMS

apagón	apagon	black-out, power cut
babalawo	babala-wo	a priest of Afro-Cuban religion
bohío	bo-ee-o	traditional rural house, with a roof made from palm leaves
carro	karro	car
casa de la trova	kasa deh la troba	club where traditional music is played
batey	batay	village around sugar factory
cayo	ka-yo	small island
chama	chama	child
criollo	kr-yo-yo	Creole (born in Cuba of Spanish descent)
divisa	deebeesa	convertible peso (slang)
guagua	gwagwa	bus
guajiro	gwaheero	farmer
guarapo	gwarapo	sugar cane juice
ingenio	eenhen-yo	sugar factory complex
jama	hama	food, meal
eva	eba	woman
jinetera	heenetaira	prostitute, or female hustler
jinetero	heenetairo	male person hustling tourists
libreta	leebreta	rations book
moneda	moneda nas-yonal	pesos ("national nacional currency")
moros y cristianos	moros ee krist-yanos	rice and black beans (Moors and Christians)
paladar	paladar	privately-owned restaurant
puro	pooro	authentic Cuban cigar
Santero	Santairo	Santería priest
tabaco	tabako	low-quality cigar
tambor	tambor	Afro-Cuban religious musical feast
tienda	t-yenda	shop that only accepts convertible pesos
trago	trago	alcoholic drink
tunas	toonas	prickly pears
zafra	safra	sugar cane harvest

EMERGENCIES

Help!	¡socorro!	sokorro!
Stop!	¡pare!	pareh!
Call a doctor	Llamen a un médico	yamen a oon medeeko
Call an ambulance	Llamen a una ambulancia	yamen a oona amboolans-ya
Police!	¡policía!	poleesee-al
I've been robbed	Me robaron	meh rrobaron

COMMUNICATION ESSENTIALS

Yes	sí	see
No	no	no
Please	por favor	por fabor
Pardon me	perdone	pairdoneh
Excuse me	disculpe	deeskoolpeh
I'm sorry	lo siento	lo s-yento
Thanks	gracias	gras-yas
Hello!	¡hola!	ohlah!
Good day	buenos días	bwenos dee-as
Good afternoon	buenas tardes	bwenas tardes
Good evening	buenas noches	bwenas noches
Night	noche	nocheh
Morning	mañana	man-yana
Tomorrow	mañana	man-yana
Yesterday	ayer	a-yair
Here	acá	aka
How?	¿cómo?	komo?
When?	¿cuándo?	kwando?
Where?	¿dónde?	dondeh?
Why?	¿por qué?	por keh?
How are you?	¿qué tal?	keh tal?
It's a pleasure!	¡mucho gusto!	moocho goosto!
Goodbye, so long	hasta luego	asta lwego

USEFUL PHRASES

That's fine	está bien/ocá	esta b-yen/oka
Fine	¡qué bien!	keh b-yen!
How long?	¿Cuánto falta?	kwanto falta?
Do you speak a little English?	¿Habla un poco de inglés?	abla oon poko deh eengles?
I don't understand	No entiendo	no ent-yendo
Could you speak more slowly?	¿Puede hablar más despacio?	pwedeh ablas mas despas-yo?
I agree/OK	de acuerdo/ocá	deh akwairdo/oka
Certainly!	¡Claro que sí!	klaro keh see!
Let's go!	¡Vámonos!	bamonos!

USEFUL WORDS

Large	grande	grandeh
Small	pequeño	peken-yo
Hot	caliente	kal-yenteh
Cold	frío	free-o
Good	bueno	bweno

Bad	malo	malo
So-so	más o menos	mas o menos
Well/fine	bien	b-yen
Open	abierto	ab-yairto
Closed	cerrado	serrado
Full	lleno	yeno
Empty	vacío	basee-o
Right	derecha	dairecha
Left	izquierda	isk-yairda
Straight	recto	rrekto
Under	debajo	debaho
Over	arriba	arreeba
Quickly/early	pronto /temprano	pronto/ temprano
Late	tarde	tardeh
Now	ahora	a-ora
Soon	ahorita	a-oreeta
More	más	mas
Less	menos	menos
Little	poco	poko
Sufficient	suficiente	soofees-yenteh
Much	mucho/muy	moocho/mwee
Too much	demasiado	demas-yado
In front of	delante	delanteh
Behind	detrás	detras
First floor	primer piso	preemair peeso
Ground floor	planta baja	planta baha
Lift/elevator	elevador	elebador
Bathroom/toilet	servicios	sairbees-yos
Women	mujeres	moohaires
Men	hombres	ombres
Toilet paper	papel sanitario	papel saneetar-yo
Camera	cámara	kamara
Batteries	baterías	batairee-as
Passport	pasaporte	pasaporteh
Visa; tourist card	visa; tarjeta turistica	beesa; tarheta tooreesteeka

HEALTH

I don't feel well	Me siento mal	meh s-yento mal
I have a	Me duele	meh dweleh
stomach ache	el estómago	el estomago
headache	la cabeza	la kabesa
He/she is ill	Está enfermo/a	esta enfairmo
I need to rest	Necesito decansar	neseseeto dekansar
Drug store	farmacia	farmasee-ya

POST OFFICE AND BANK

Bank	banco	banko
I want to send a letter	Quiero enviar una carta	k-yairo emb-yar oona karta
Postcard	postal tarjeta	postal tarheta
Stamp	sello	se-yo
Draw out money	sacar dinero	sakar deenairo

SHOPPING

How much is it?	¿Cuánto cuesta?	kwanto kwesta?
What time do you open/close?	¿A qué hora abre/ cierra?	a ke ora abreh/s-yairra?
May I pay with a credit card?	¿Puedo pagar con tarjeta de crédito?	pwedo pagar kon tarheta deh kredeeto?

SIGHTSEEING

Beach	playa	pla-ya
Castle, fortress	castillo	kastee-yo
Cathedral	catedral	katedral
Church	iglesia	eegles-ya
District	barrio	barr-yo
Garden	jardín	hardeen
Guide	guía	gee-a
House	casa	kasa
Motorway	autopista	owtopeesta
Museum	museo	mooseh-o
Park	parque	parkeh
Road	carretera	karretaira
Square, plaza	plaza, parque	plasa, parkeh
Street	calle, callejón	ka-ye, ka-yehon
Town hall	ayuntamiento	a-yoontam-yento
Tourist bureau	buró de turismo	booro deh tooreesmo

TRANSPORT

Could you call a taxi for me?	¿Me puede llamar a un taxi?	meh pwedeh yamar a oon taksee?
Airport	aeropuerto	a-airopwairto
Train station	estación de ferrocarriles	estas-yon deh fairrokarreeles
Bus station	terminal de guagas	tairmeenal deh gwagwas
When does it leave?	¿A qué hora sale?	a keh ora saleh?
Customs	aduana	adwana
Boarding pass	tarjeta de embarque	tarheta deh embarkeh
Car hire	alquiler de carros	alkeelair deh karros
Bicycle	bicicleta	beeseekleta
Insurance	seguro	segooro
Petrol/gas station	estación de gasolina	estas-yon deh gasoleena

STAYING IN A HOTEL

Single room/ double	habitación sencilla/ doble doble	abeetas-yon sensee-ya /dobleh dobleh
Shower	ducha	doocha
Bathtub	bañera	ban-yaira
Balcony	balcón, terraza	balkon, tairrasa
Air conditioning	aire acondicionado	eye-reh akondisionado
I want to be woken at...	Necesito que me despierten a las...	neseseeto keh meh desp-yairten a las...
Warm water/ cold	agua caliente/ fría	agwa kal-yenteh/ free-a
Soap	jabón	habon
Towel	toalla	to-a-ya
Key	llave	yabeh

EATING OUT

What is there to eat?	¿Qué hay para comer?	keh I para komair?
The bill, please	la cuenta, por favor	la kwenta por fabor
Glass	vaso	baso

Cutlery	**cubiertos**	koob-yairtos
I would	**Quisiera**	kees-yaira
like some	**un poco**	oon poko
water	**de agua**	deh agwa
Have you	**¿Tienen**	t-yenen
got wine?	**vino?**	beeno?
The beer is	**La cerveza**	la sairbesa no
not cold	**no está**	no esta
enough	**bien fría**	b-yen free-a
Breakfast	**desayuno**	desa-yoono
Lunch	**almuerzo**	almwairso
Dinner	**comida/cena**	komeeda/sane-sane-er
Raw/cooked	**crudo/cocido**	kroodo/koseedo

MENU DECODER

aceite	asayteh	oil
agua mineral	agwa meenairal	mineral water
ajo	aho	garlic
arroz	arros	rice
asado	asado	roasted
atún	atoon	tuna
azúcar	asookar	sugar
bacalao	bakala-o	cod
café	kafeh	coffee
camarones	kamarones	prawns
carne	karneh	meat
congrí	kongree	rice with beans and onions
cerveza	sairbesa	beer
dulce	doolseh	sweet, dessert
ensalada	ensalada	salad
fruta	froota	fruit
fruta bomba	froota bomba	papaya
helado	elado	ice cream
huevo	webo	egg
jugo	hoogo	fruit juice
langosta	langosta	lobster
leche	lecheh	milk
marisco	mareesko	seafood
mantequilla	mantekee-ya	butter
pan	pan	bread
papas	papas	potatoes
postre	postreh	dessert
pescado	peskado	fish
plátano	platano	banana
pollo	po-yo	chicken
potaje/sopa	potaheh/sopa	soup
puerco	pwairko	pork
queso	keso	cheese
refresco	refresko	drink
sal	sal	salt
salsa	salsa	sauce
té	teh	tea
vinagre	beenagreh	vinegar

TIME

Minute	**minuto**	meenooto
Hour	**hora**	ora
Half-hour	**media hora**	med-ya ora
Monday	**lunes**	loones
Tuesday	**martes**	martes
Wednesday	**miércoles**	m-yairkoles
Thursday	**jueves**	hwebes
Friday	**viernes**	b-yairnes
Saturday	**sábado**	sabado
Sunday	**domingo**	domeengo

January	**enero**	enairo
February	**febrero**	febrairo
March	**marzo**	marso
April	**abril**	abreel
May	**mayo**	ma-yo
June	**junio**	hoon-yo
July	**julio**	hool-yo
August	**agosto**	agosto
September	**setiembre**	set-yembreh
October	**octubre**	oktoobreh
November	**noviembre**	nob-yembreh
December	**diciembre**	dees-yembreh

NUMBERS

0	**cero**	sairo
1	**uno**	oono
2	**dos**	dos
3	**tres**	tres
4	**cuatro**	kuatro
5	**cinco**	seenko
6	**seis**	says
7	**siete**	s-yeteh
8	**ocho**	ocho
9	**nueve**	nwebeh
10	**diez**	d-yes
11	**once**	onseh
12	**doce**	doseh
13	**trece**	treseh
14	**catorce**	katorseh
15	**quince**	keenseh
16	**dieciséis**	d-yeseesays
17	**diecisiete**	d-yesees-yeteh
18	**dieciocho**	d-yes-yocho
19	**diecinueve**	d-yeseenwebeh
20	**veinte**	baynteh
30	**treinta**	traynta
40	**cuarenta**	kwarenta
50	**cincuenta**	seenkwenta
60	**sesenta**	sesenta
70	**setenta**	setenta
80	**ochenta**	ochenta
90	**noventa**	nobenta
100	**cien**	s-yen
500	**quinientos**	keen-yentos
1000	**mil**	meel